Retrofitting Leninism

Retrofitting Leninism

Participation Without Democracy in China

DIMITAR D. GUEORGUIEV

OXFORD
UNIVERSITY PRESS

OXFORD
UNIVERSITY PRESS

Oxford University Press is a department of the University of Oxford. It furthers
the University's objective of excellence in research, scholarship, and education
by publishing worldwide. Oxford is a registered trade mark of Oxford University
Press in the UK and in certain other countries.

Published in the United States of America by Oxford University Press
198 Madison Avenue, New York, NY 10016, United States of America.

© Oxford University Press 2021

Library of Congress Cataloging-in-Publication Data
Names: Gueorguiev, Dimitar D., author.
Title: Retrofitting Leninism : participation without democracy in China / Dimitar D. Gueorguiev.
Description: New York : Oxford University Press, [2021] |
Includes bibliographical references and index.
Identifiers: LCCN 2021016579 (print) | LCCN 2021016580 (ebook) | ISBN 9780197555675
(paperback) | ISBN 9780197555668 (hardback) | ISBN 9780197555699 (epub)
Subjects: LCSH: Political participation—China. | Lenin, Vladimir Ilyich, 1870-1924—Political and
social views. | Political culture—China. | Democracy–China. | China–Politics and government.
Classification: LCC JQ1516 .G84 2021 (print) | LCC JQ1516 (ebook) | DDC 323/.0420951—dc23
LC record available at https://lccn.loc.gov/2021016579
LC ebook record available at https://lccn.loc.gov/2021016580

DOI: 10.1093/oso/9780197555668.001.0001

Contents

Online Appendix accessible on Oxford Scholarship Online

List of Figures

List of Tables

Preface

When I first visited China as a student in 2004, the economy was on a growth spurt in the middle of an already long-lasting period of economic expansion. Naturally, I was captivated by what I saw and the people I met, but I also had trouble reconciling how a vibrant, diverse, and increasingly open country was controlled by what seemed an antiquated and moribund communist regime. My own family had fled a similar regime in Bulgaria less than two decades earlier, and so I had strong priors about the fragility of authoritarianism.

The association I had drawn was admittedly problematic. Bulgaria's entire population could fit inside one of China's mid-tier cities, and while Bulgaria's economy in the 1980s was stagnating, China's, in 2004, was clearly booming. But there were notable parallels. Like the Chinese Communist Party (CCP), the Bulgarian Communist Party (BCP) followed Leninist tenets for political, economic, and social control. As early as the 1960s and 70s, Bulgaria's communists employed technology for mass surveillance and planning, well before similar investments in China. By the mid-1980s, however, there were signs that control in Bulgaria was slipping. Crime, shortages, and industrial accidents were increasing while promised reforms were stalling. For most Bulgarian's, the BCP's presence came mainly in the form of access to consumer goods, promotions, and housing. State security remained ubiquitous but, as was the case in my own housing block, most knew who the informants were and how to avoid them.

With this history in mind, I interpreted the dynamism I saw in China's streets and among its people as an economy and society also moving away from authoritarian control. The more I understood about the Chinese political and administrative system, however, the closer I came to the opposite conclusion. Authoritarian control in China, despite facing far graver challenges than those in Bulgaria, was not simply stable, it appeared to be evolving. Coming to terms with the idea that China's current rulers were administering what Bulgaria's former leaders, and other failed Leninists, had only dreamed of, led me to re-evaluate the meaning of authoritarian control, why it is short-lived, and how the CCP has managed to cultivate it for so long. This book is the product of that reflection and inquiry.

This book would not have been possible, however, had it not been for been for the time, trust, and investment of so many. First, I must give thanks to friends, colleagues, and mentors in China, who invited me into their networks, vouched for my research, and shared experiences with me. On this count, there are too many debts to enumerate, but I do want to highlight a number of individuals who were critical in driving my curiosity and facilitating the research. Lang Youxing's support was instrumental for my work in Zhejiang and his straightforward approach to research convinced me that rigorous and unbiased scholarship was not only possible in China but rewarded. Lai Hairong's wisdom and chivalry impressed upon me the immense intellect China's leaders possess in their think tanks and academic institutions. At the same time, conversations with censored academics helped me appreciate the boundaries scholars face in promoting a more progressive China. Finally, there are those in government and at state-owned enterprises who will go unnamed, but whose hospitality was vital for the fieldwork that facilitated this research.

I owe an equally heavy debt of gratitude to my former advisors at UC San Diego. Susan Shirk, Eddy Malesky, Philip Roeder, Barry Naughton, and Clair Adida, provided critical advice during my early dissertation research. Portions of that work went into my 2017 book, coauthored with Eddy and Jonathan Stromseth; others form key empirical components of this book. From the very start of my academic journey, Susan and Eddy have been my closest and most honest guides. I could not ask for better mentors. Their example serves as the ultimate benchmark for my own teaching and advising. I must also thank my colleagues at Syracuse University, who have been unwavering mentors, supporters, and friends throughout the last six years. In particular, I would like to acknowledge Brian Taylor for his always humorous and insightful feedback; Colin Elman and Matt Clearly for helping me cut through the fog; Mary Lovely and Daniel McDowell for always inquiring about my perspective on matters related to China and for sharing theirs in return; and Chen Xueyi, Terry Lautz, Devashish Mitra and Adbul Shifa for the community that kept me sane through more than a few Syracuse winters.

I must also extend deep appreciation to members of the scholarly community. Bruce Dickson, Jennifer Gandhi, Mikhail Filipov, and Olga Shvetsova were kind enough to read early versions of the manuscript and to give it the benefit of the doubt. Numerous others, including He Baogang, Chen Xuelian, Martin Dimitrov, Iza Ding, Christian Goebel, William Hurst, Melanie Manion, Meng Tianguang, Meg Rithmire, Shi Weiyi, Tang Wenfang, Jessica Teets, Rory Truex, Wu Jiannan, Yu Junbo, and Zhong Yang have helped me work through sections of the book during conferences, workshops, and invited lectures. A special thanks goes out to two anonymous reviewers for Oxford University Press, both of whom greatly influenced and improved the final form of the book, as well as to Mary Child for her invaluable editorial help and guidance.

My ability to write a book on China and enjoy the process is in many ways thanks to my students, who were patient enough with me to listen and ask questions. This includes my many undergraduates, but especially my stellar graduate students: Chu Sinan, Liu Dongshu, and Shao Li, who assisted me in running the China Policy Barometer survey that informs the empirical sections of this book, and helped me think through difficult questions that arose in the process of writing. This project would also not have been possible without the camaraderie and enduring support of members of my graduate school cohort. These include Cesi Cruz, Chris Fariss, Jonathan Mark, Daniel Smith, and Neil Vasilvanich. I want to give very special thanks to my two former graduate school officemates, Paul Schuler and Kai Ostwald. It was a blessing to struggle through the PhD program together and I know I would not have survived without you at my side. I must also add Steven Oliver on this count. Though we did not share an office, Steve's friendship and his untiring enthusiasm for research have always been a welcome home for me.

I am also deeply grateful for the research support provided by institutions and organizations including the Center on Emerging and Pacific Economies, the Appleby-Mosher Fund at Syracuse University, and the Chiang Ching-kuo Foundation. This support has facilitated fieldwork, survey sampling, and travel expenses for producing this book. I would also like to thank China's Ministry of Education and Zhejiang University for supporting and hosting me during 2011–2012. This was a critical period in my study of Chinese participatory institutions, and it would not have been possible without the extended period of time I spent as resident researcher at Zhejiang University. Similarly, I would like to thank Jonathan Stromseth, Ji Hongbo, and Nancy Kim for adopting me into The Asia Foundation family in Beijing. My time as a consultant with the Foundation opened doors that expanded my study beyond its initial ambitions.

Finally, I must thank my family for encouraging and tolerating me throughout this process. My parents, Annie and Mitko, risked it all, giving up friends and career, to get me and my siblings out of Bulgaria during the tumultuous and dangerous period just before the fall of communism in 1990. I would never be in a position to pen my name on a book were it not for your sacrifice. To my sister Iva and my brother Gueorgui, your little brother loves you and will always be thankful for the trust and support you vested in him. Most of all, I need to express my boundless love and gratitude to the family that puts up with me on a daily basis. To Lily, thank you for all the sacrifices you made to give me time and space to work through this project. Your love is only matched by your patience. To Anta and Remi, you two are so much fun. You make me smile, you give me energy, and you remind me to be forever thankful for the present and optimistic about the future. I dedicate this book to you.

Introduction

> At all times the Party gives top priority to the interests of the people, shares weal and woe with them and keeps in closest contact with them, and it does not allow any member to become divorced from the masses or place himself above them. The Party follows the mass line in its work, doing everything for the masses, relying on them in every task, carrying out the principle "from the masses, to the masses," and translating its correct views into conscious action of the masses. The biggest political advantage of our Party lies in its close ties with the masses while the biggest potential danger for it as a ruling party comes from its divorce from them.
>
> — CCP Constitution, Preamble

On the morning of January 23, 2020, three days after publicly acknowledging the breakout of a novel coronavirus, China's leaders announced a lockdown for over 35 million people in Wuhan and thirteen surrounding urban centers. By the end of January, this figure had increased to over 50 million, and by mid-February nearly every part of the country was under some form of travel restriction. In more hard-hit areas, people were not allowed to leave their residences for about two months, except to collect food and water.[1] In less affected regions, pharmacies were barred from selling analgesics (pain and fever reducers) so as to induce people with symptoms to seek medical attention and supervision.[2] Throughout the country, those presumed to have been exposed to the virus, often on dubious grounds, were systematically extricated and isolated from the rest of society.[3] At the time, observers described China's response as an "overreaction," "draconian," even "medieval."[4] Yet, for seasoned observers the reaction was not

---

[1] "Sealed In: Chinese Trapped at Home by Coronavirus Feel the Strain," Huizhong Wu, Reuters, Feb. 22, 2020, available at: https://reut.rs/3kmwmTN.

[2] See, for example, an emergency health notice published by Hangzhou municipal health and market supervision authorities on February 7, 2020, entitled 'Urgent Notice on the Suspension of Retail Sale of all Fever and Cough Medicines' (关于暂停全市所有零售药店销售发烧咳嗽药品的紧急通知), screenshot available at: http://society.people.com.cn/n1/2020/0208/c1008-31576772.html.

[3] "To Tame Coronavirus, Mao-Style Social Control Blankets China," Raymond Zhong and Paul Mozur, New York Times, February 20, 2020, available at: https://nyti.ms/3mc1Yvz.

[4] "'Like Europe in Medieval Times': Virus Slows China's Economy," Keith Bradsher, New York Times, Feb. 10, 2020, available at: https://nyti.ms/3okghQT.

Retrofitting Leninism. Dimitar D. Gueorguiev. Oxford University Press. © Oxford University Press 2021. DOI: 10.1093/oso/9780197555668.003.0001

surprising in the least. As China watcher Bill Bishop put it, "They [the Chinese Communist Party (CCP)] will stop at nothing to try to control and then eradicate it [the virus]."[5]

To be sure, the coronavirus response was an extraordinary event, but it was in no way out of character with how the ruling Chinese Communist Party (CCP) typically responds to governance challenges, whether social, economic, political, or otherwise. Indeed, a predilection for control represents what I see as the defining feature of the Chinese political system, and arguably of authoritarian institutions more broadly. For instance, political organizations and movements described varyingly as authoritarian, totalitarian, autocratic, hegemonic, and so on, differ in composition of leaders, parties, and ideologies, but they all share one thing in common: an overarching desire to control political, social, and economic activity within their polities. Yet there is tremendous diversity in how control is pursued and the degree to which it is exercised.

My goal throughout the following chapters is to explore a distinct approach to authoritarian control that relies, perhaps counterintuitively, on bottom-up participation. The case of China will take center stage in this study and the Chinese response to the coronavirus pandemic provides an illustrative preface. Consider, for instance, that China's dramatic lockdown, though emblematic of top-down authoritarianism, was ultimately facilitated and enforced by millions of average Chinese citizens who acted as informal agents of the state. In Zhejiang, for example, provincial authorities mobilized over 330,000 so-called grid workers to walk the streets, visit households, and check in on popular destinations and gathering spots in order to monitor compliance with the new orders.[6] Similarly, while many have taken note of China's tech-heavy approach to tracking and tracing the spread of the virus, it is often overlooked just how decentralized and dependent these technologies are on public inputs, such as the whereabouts and health of neighbors and friends.[7] Similarly, China's coronavirus mobility apps, which require all users to get clearance before moving around and using public spaces, also require users to provide detailed personal health information on a daily basis.[8] Finally, while we might anticipate intrusive controls to be unpopular, recent surveys suggest that China's public is generally positive when it comes to public monitoring.[9]

[5] Quoted in "A Historic Quarantine," James Hamblin, *The Atlantic*, January 24, 2020, available at: https://bit.ly/3jqKpGh.
[6] "330,000 Grid Workers Participate in Epidemic Prevention and Control," *Hangzhou News*, January 27, 2020, available at: https://bit.ly/2Hp2FmF.
[7] "China, Desperate to Stop Coronavirus, Turns Neighbor Against Neighbor," Paul, Mozur, *New York Times*, February 3, 2020, available at: https://nyti.ms/2IXFyQD.
[8] "In Coronavirus Fight, China Gives Citizens a Color Code, with Red Flags," Paul Mozur, Raymond Zhong, and Aaron Krolik, *New York Times*, March 1, 2020, available at: https://nyti.ms/3ksKzyA.
[9] Genia Kostka. "China's Social Credit Systems and Public Opinion: Explaining High Levels of Approval." *New Media & Society* (2018), pp. 1–29.

Why would Chinese citizens participate in a system that ultimately curtails their freedoms? Perhaps it is simply out of recognition that the system, unpleasant though it may be, is effective. In the case of coronavirus, for instance, China's intrusive controls appear to have averted hundreds of thousands of infections.[10] Then again, other countries were also successful in managing the spread of the virus without resorting to China's strong-arm tactics.[11] Alternatively, it may be that Chinese citizens have no choice and that participation is obligatory. This, however, is not the case for many types of voluntary participation that are common in China, such as sitting in on public hearings, filing petitions, or submitting comments during public policy debates. Perhaps such acts of participation are formalities that add to the thick veneer with which the CCP portrays itself as "democratic." But if so, is there anything to distinguish the contemporary Chinese approach from that of other authoritarian states, or even from China itself only a few decades ago?

There is also a more provocative proposition: that the Chinese public participates in the control system not simply because it works but because of *how* it works, and not because they are forced to participate but because there is perceived interest in doing so. This book will be of the more provocative type. In the pages and chapters to follow, I hope to shed light on China's distinctive brand of authoritarianism by exploring the origins of what I refer to as "controlled inclusion," the mechanisms that translate bottom-up inputs into top-down outputs, and the downstream governance implications of this strategy. To do so, this book will engage literature from several disciplines, including the obvious discussion of institutions and contentious politics under authoritarianism, as well as forays into cultural theory and information science. First, however, it is helpful to briefly situate the study in a historical and comparative context.

The Party and the People

For several thousand years, with a few brief intermissions, the Chinese people have been ruled by authoritarian governments, most recently by the CCP as citizens of the People's Republic of China (PRC). Since the PRC's inception in 1949, the people of China have suffered the worst that bad leaders and bad governance can deliver.[12] Countless numbers have suffered from state repression,

[10] Huaiyu Tian et al. "An Investigation of Transmission Control Measures During the First 50 Days of the COVID-19 Epidemic in China." *Science* 368.6491 (2020), pp. 638–642.

[11] Ilan Alon, Matthew Farrell, and Shaomin Li. "Regime Type and COVID-19 Response." *FIIB Business Review* (2020), pp. 152–160.

[12] Thomas Pepinsky. "The Institutional Turn in Comparative Authoritarianism." *British Journal of Political Science* (2014), pp. 631–653.

but many more as a result of misguided policies and ineffective governance. During the worst of times, stifling ideology and abrasive propaganda discouraged the masses from voicing their grievances, while a fragmented hierarchy and political ambitions prevented those in positions of influence from taking note or correcting.[13]

Under this same regime, however, the last four decades have seen over 500 million Chinese lift themselves out of poverty, vaulting China from the ranks of the poorest and least developed in the world to a competitor with the United States for global economic leadership. At the individual level, Chinese citizens have, on average, seen their personal fortunes rise by over 6,000 percent,[14] and there are now over 2,000 billionaires (in RMB) in the country.[15] Across China, industries and communities are modernizing at an unprecedented pace, with global investment piling in at levels that would have seemed unimaginable even twenty years ago.[16] As a result, some Chinese cities today have economies that rival many small and even some medium-sized countries. To be sure, not all have benefited, and the Chinese public has paid dearly in terms of environmental and health costs.[17] Perhaps most vividly, rapid economic development under a fragmented and decentralized administrative system has proven a wellspring for corruption.[18]

China's economic achievements and failures are well documented and have been the subject of numerous books and debates, some of which I reference here but do not engage directly.[19] What is clear, however, is that, by virtue of its own achievements, the PRC today is facing first-world governance challenges, such as making the transition out of manufacturing and erecting a national social safety net, with what seems like a third-world political architecture. These challenges

[13] James Kung and Shuo Chen. "The Tragedy of the Nomenklatura: Career Incentives and Political Radicalism during China's Great Leap Famine." *American Political Science Review* 105.01 (2011), pp. 27–45; Andrew G. Walder. *China under Mao*. Harvard University Press, 2015.

[14] Based on GDP per capita figures provided by the IMF, adjusted for purchasing power parity: 1978 = 313 USD, 2021 = 18,931 USD.

[15] Based on the 2019 Hurun Rich List and RMB, not USD.

[16] China is now the world's top destination for investments in electric vehicles and renewables.

[17] Shi Li, Terry Sicular, and Hiroshi Sato. *Rising Inequality in China: Challenges to a Harmonious Society*. Cambridge University Press, 2013, pp. 1–26; David Wheeler. "Racing to the Bottom? Foreign Investment and Air Pollution in Developing Countries." *The Journal of Environment & Development* 10.03 (2001): 225–245; Y. Chen et al. "Evidence on the Impact of Sustained Exposure to Air Pollution on Life Expectancy from China's Huai River Policy." *Proceedings of the National Academy of Sciences* 110.32 (2013), pp. 12936–12941.

[18] Xiaobo Lu. *Cadres and Corruption: The Organizational Involution of the Chinese Communist Party*. Stanford University Press, 2000; Yan Sun. *Corruption and Market in Contemporary China*. Cornell University Press, 2004, p. 248.

[19] Yuen Yuen Ang. *How China Escaped the Poverty Trap*. Cornell University Press, 2016; Susan L. Shirk. *The Political Logic of Economic Reform in China*. University of California Press, 1993; Barry Naughton. *Growing Out of the Plan: Chinese Economic Reform, 1978–1993*. Cambridge University Press, 1996, p. 379; Dali L. Yang. *Remaking the Chinese Leviathan: Market Transition and the Politics of Governance in China*. Stanford University Press, 2004, p. 414.

come at an inauspicious time. Domestically, rising wages, diminishing returns to investment, and an aging demography are starting to weigh on China's economy. Internationally, resentment and anxiety toward China's rise is brewing among its most powerful peers. The coronavirus pandemic, and Beijing's initial caginess about the spread and severity of the virus, have only further undercut goodwill toward the PRC.[20]

To stay in control, the CCP is taking on an ever-greater burden in convincing the public that it can manage China's present and future better than anyone else. Given the strain, the CCP appears surprisingly tuned-in and proactive in addressing emerging governance challenges. Though China remains the world's worst polluter, it is also the planet's biggest investor in renewable energy and environmental technology.[21] Some in China remain desperately poor, but the current administration committed to "eradicating" these remaining and hard-to-reach pockets of poverty by the end of 2021, and appears to have accomplished that goal just in time for the CCP's 100th anniversary.[22] As part of this effort, the state has enacted a wide range of redistributive policies that appear to have partially stunted and possibly even reversed rising levels of inequality that began in the 1980s.[23] Perhaps most dramatically from 2014 to 2020, the Chinese leadership investigated and punished on corruption charges nearly 1.8 million officials, an overwhelming majority of whom were CCP members.[24] Indeed, some refer to China's leaders as "hyper-responsive" to public opinion and public input.[25]

How the regime learns about public opinion and then responds remains an active area of research, and a bit of a puzzle.[26] As Amartya Sen reminds us, one

---

[20] Laura Silver, Kat Devlin, and Christine Huang. "*Unfavorable Views of China Reach Historic Highs in Many Countries.*" Pew Research Center, 2020.

[21] Tim Buckley and Simon Nicholas. *China's Global Renewable Energy Expansion.* Tech. rep. Institute for Energy Economy and Financial Analysis, 2017, p. 45.

[22] Xi Jinping, "China's Victory over Poverty" Speech at the National Poverty Alleviation Conference (习近平：在全国脱贫攻坚总结表彰大会上的讲话), Feb. 25, 2021.

[23] Shi Li, Terry Sicular, Finn Tarp, et al. *Inequality in China: Development, Transition, and Policy.* Tech. rep. World Institute for Development Economic Research (UNU-WIDER), 2018.

[24] Based on annual and mid-year reports from the Central Disciplinary Inspection Commission, from 2013 through April 2019.

[25] Bruce J. Dickson. *The Dictator's Dilemma: The Chinese Communist Party's Strategy for Survival.* Oxford University Press, 2016; Wenfang Tang. *Populist Authoritarianism: Chinese Political Culture and Regime Sustainability.* Oxford University Press, 2016; Jidong Chen, Jennifer Pan, and Yiqing Xu. "Sources of Authoritarian Responsiveness: A Field Experiment in China." *American Journal of Political Science* 60.2 (2015), pp. 383–400; Tianguang Meng, Jennifer Pan, and Ping Yang. "Conditional Receptivity to Citizen Participation: Evidence From a Survey Experiment in China." *Comparative Political Studies* 50.4 (2014), pp. 399–433; Christopher Heurlin. *Responsive Authoritarianism in China.* Cambridge University Press, 2016.

[26] Daniela Stockmann and Ting Luo. "Which Social Media Facilitate Online Public Opinion in China?" *Problems of Post-communism* 64.3-4 (2017), pp. 189–202; Rogier Creemers. "Cyber China: Upgrading Propaganda, Public Opinion Work and Social Management for the Twenty-First Century." *Journal of Contemporary China* 26.103 (2017), pp. 85–100.

of the principal limitations of authoritarian rule is an acute incapacity to sense and respond to the needs and concerns of the people it dominates, for the simple reason that authoritarian systems lack the incentive (political accountability) and the infrastructure (civil society) necessary for "enhancing the hearing that people get in expressing and supporting their claims."[27] Given this somewhat genetic affliction, scholars point to bottom-up "input institutions" that bridge the gap between leaders and citizens, thus enhancing regime resilience.[28] These include representative legislatures,[29] local elections,[30] and civil society organizations,[31] as well as a host of alternative mechanisms for public consultation and mass inclusion.[32] While these mechanisms may have been tedious and performative in the past, technology is making it easier for Chinese citizens to submit complaints and tip-offs online, e-mail their local leaders if they have questions, and upload comments on policy proposals at both the local and national levels.

Bringing the "Hard" into "Soft" Authoritarianism

The bottom-up input mechanisms outlined above represent the soft side of the CCP's control system. There are, however, limits and caveats to inclusion. Grassroots electoral experimentation has ground to a halt, and independent candidates have for the most part become extinct.[33] Representative bodies like the people's congresses and people's consultative committees provide forums for geographic and sectoral interest lobbying, but their agendas are dictated by Party

---

[27] Amartya Kumar Sen. "Democracy as a Universal Value." *Journal of Democracy* 10.3 (1999), pp. 3–17, p. 11.

[28] Andrew J. Nathan. "China's Changing of the Guard: Authoritarian Resilience." *Journal of Democracy* 14.1 (2003), pp. 6–17.

[29] Melanie Manion. *Information for Autocrats; Representation in Chinese Local Congresses.* Cambridge University Press, 2016, p. 195; Rory Truex. *Making Autocracy Work: Representation and Responsiveness in Modern China.* New York: Cambridge University Press, 2016.

[30] Lai Hairong. "Semi-Competitive Elections at Township Level in Sichuan Province." *China Perspectives* 51.51 (2004), pp. 1–21; Kevin J.O'Brien and Lianjiang Li. "Accommodating 'Democracy' in a One-Party State: Introducing Village Elections in China." *The China Quarterly* 162.162 (2000), pp. 465–489; Pierre F. Landry, Deborah Davis, and Shiru Wang. "Elections in Rural China: Competition Without Parties." *Comparative Political Studies* 43.6 (2010), pp. 763–790.

[31] Jessica C. Teets. *Civil Society under Authoritarianism: The China Model.* Cambridge University Press, 2014; Jessica C. Teets and William Hurst. *Local Governance Innovation in China: Experimentation, Diffusion, and Defiance.* Routledge, 2014, p. 204; Keping Yu. "Civil Society in China: Concepts, Classification and Institutional Environment (World Scientific)." *State and Civil Society* 1 (2010), pp. 63–96; Daniel C. Mattingly. *The Art of Political Control in China.* Cambridge University Press, 2019.

[32] Jonathan R. Stromseth, Edmund J. Malesky, and Dimitar D. Gueorguiev. *China's Governance Puzzle: Enabling Transparency and Participation in a Single-Party State.* Cambridge University Press, 2017; Baogang He and Mark E. Warren. "Authoritarian Deliberation: The Deliberative Turn in Chinese Political Development." *Perspectives on Politics* 9.02 (2011), pp. 269–289; Laura M. Luehrmann. "Facing Citizen Complaints in China, 1951–1996." *Asian Survey* 43.5 (2003), pp. 845–866.

[33] Junzhi He. "Independent Candidates in China's Local People's Congresses: A Typology." *Journal of Contemporary China* 19.64 (2010), pp. 311–333.

leaders.[34] Citizens are prompted to report on rule-breakers, petition against bad officials, and write complaints when they get bad service, but are often punished for doing so outside of approved channels.[35] And, while policymaking bodies appear genuine in their requests for input, we know that censorship and information distortion is pervasive.[36]

Even if the cruder forms of mass repression common in the past, such as public executions and mass labor camp internment, have subsided, they have not disappeared. Instead, coercion has become submerged and surgical, with dissidents carefully monitored by GPS trackers, spyware, and tactical units that intercept and preempt plans or actions that threaten to transgress the limits laid out by the regime. Internet monitors, algorithms, and trolls carefully dissect public discourse and manipulate it when necessary. All the while, surveillance cameras, cellphone location pings, and aerial drones provide constant input on where the population goes, flows, and congregates.

From the outside looking in, such developments are not easy to comprehend, in part because they both challenge and confirm long-held notions of how top-down authoritarianism is supposed to work. In response, scholars have tended to focus either on the soft or the hard elements of regime control, rarely synthesizing the two. This has been both a blessing and a bit of a curse. Studying the soft elements of inclusion has helped us understand the instrumental value that the CCP places on participatory governance.[37] However, a narrow focus on the soft has indirectly kept afloat a tenuous association between participation and potential for democratization.[38] At the other extreme, those who focus on the hard elements of CCP control are more inclined to see inclusion as "window-dressing"[39] for what remains a crass and brutal top-down system destined for eventual collapse.[40]

---

[34] Ying Sun. "Municipal People's Congress Elections in the PRC: A Process of Co-option." *Journal of Contemporary China* 23.85 (2014), pp. 183–195.

[35] Diana Fu and Greg Distelhorst. "Grassroots Participation and Repression under Hu Jintao and Xi Jinping." *The China Journal* 79 (2018), pp. 100–122; Christopher Marquis and Yanhua Bird. "The Paradox of Responsive Authoritarianism: How Civic Activism Spurs Environmental Penalties in China." *Organization Science* 29.5 (2018), pp. 948–968.

[36] Margaret E. Roberts. *Censored: Distraction and Diversion Inside China's Great Firewall*. Princeton University Press, 2018.

[37] Nathan, "China's Changing of the Guard: Authoritarian Resilience"; Martin K. Dimitrov. "Understanding Communist Collapse and Resilience." In *Why Communism Did Not Collapse: Understanding Authoritarian Regime Resilience in Asia and Europe*, Ed. by Martin K. Dimitrov. Cambridge University Press, 2013. Chap. 1; Stromseth, Malesky, and Gueorguiev, *China's Governance Puzzle: Enabling Transparency and Participation in a Single-Party State*.

[38] James S. Fishkin. *When the People Speak: Deliberative Democracy and Public Consultation*. Oxford University Press, 2009, p. 236; Bruce Gilley. *China's Democratic Future: How It Will Happen and Where It Will Lead*. Columbia University Press, 2004; Larry Diamond. "The Rule of Law as Transition to Democracy in China." *Journal of Contemporary China* 12.35 (2003), pp. 319–331; He and Warren, "Authoritarian Deliberation: The Deliberative Turn in Chinese Political Development."

[39] Michael Bristow, "China's Democratic 'Window Dressing,'" BBC News, March 5, 2010.

[40] Minxin Pei. *China's Crony Capitalism: The Dynamics of Regime Decay*. Harvard University Press, 2016.

Each of these perspectives is compelling, but they cannot all be right. Optimists have been sorely disappointed by China's apparent departure from institutional reform in favor of increased censorship and indoctrination. Even those who see China's soft inclusion through the lens of "regime resilience" remain vexed by a fundamental contradiction: authoritarian institutions are almost always hobbled in ways that directly undermine the very functions they are purported to deliver. How can inclusion reveal useful information if public discourse is censored and distorted?[41] Likewise, how can civil society play a meaningful role if it is meticulously compartmentalized and supervised by the state?[42] For their part, those who dismiss inclusion and focus on coercion do not offer an alternative explanation for how the regime has managed to address some of its core governance challenges, why it seems increasingly receptive and responsive to public opinion, or why the Chinese public seems satisfied with the results.[43]

One recent approach at reconciling this particular set of Chinese contradictions has been to depict participatory reforms in China as genuine but undermined by Xi Jinping's increasingly power-hungry and personalistic leadership.[44] If Xi's push for hard control undermines the progress made under soft authoritarianism, it is reasonable to conclude that China's governing institutions, especially those concerning public participation, are eroding and headed for potential collapse.[45] This perspective fits well with the view of China's contemporary political history as one comprised of clear structural breaks, such as the 1978 departure from revolutionary Maoism and transition into a more rational and liberal socioeconomic order. Xi Jinping's rise thus represents a challenge to that trajectory, which can be read either as a return to Maoism or a "third revolution" into a new era of hard authoritarianism.[46]

In this book, I present an alternative perspective that emphasizes neither structural breaks nor normative benchmarks but rather an evolution of control that marries the soft and the hard aspects of authoritarianism. Before I can expound on this idea, however, I must first distinguish the soft side of China's authoritarianism from the liberal democratic concepts and narratives that predominate in the literature. In order to do so, it is helpful to briefly consider the case of China from a wider, comparative vantage point.

[41] Roberts, *Censored: Distraction and Diversion Inside China's Great Firewall*.
[42] Marie-Eve Reny. *Authoritarian Containment: Public Security Bureaus and Protestant House Churches in Urban China*. Oxford University Press USA–OSO, 2018; Teets, *Civil Society under Authoritarianism: The China Model*.
[43] Tang, *Populist Authoritarianism: Chinese Political Culture and Regime Sustainability*.
[44] Carl Minzner. *End of an Era: How China's Authoritarian Revival is Undermining Its Rise*. Oxford University Press, 2018.
[45] Pei, *China's Crony Capitalism*; David Shambaugh, "The Coming Chinese Crackup." *Wall Street Journal*, March 6, 2015, p. 382.
[46] Minzner, *End of an Era: How China's Authoritarian Revival is Undermining Its Rise*; Elizabeth Economy. *The Third Revolution: Xi Jinping and the New Chinese State*. Oxford University Press, 2018.

China in Comparative Perspective

Though China is the principal focus of this book, the fusion of participatory institutions and authoritarian control is not a China-specific story. In a recent monograph, Garry Rodan points to the rise of "participation without democracy" in a host of Southeast Asian countries, where citizens are given a voice on policy, yet denied political rights.[47] In Cuba, the long-ruling communist regime has, for over a decade now, mobilized public debate on a broad set of economic and constitutional reforms, while maintaining strict controls over political and civil organization.[48] In the Middle East as well, nondemocratic leaders are promoting deliberation and open government while simultaneously engaging in brutal forms of political intolerance.[49]

Such trends are not unprecedented. Nearly thirty years ago, political scientists were pointing to a new form of "soft authoritarianism" that practiced persuasion instead of coercion, offered national development in the place of political rights, and espoused collective stability over that of individual liberties.[50] For better or worse, however, these conversations were overshadowed by the discourse on democratization[51] and the rapid spread of quasi-democratic institutions following the collapse of the Soviet Union.[52] These trends and contradictions have fueled a provocative and productive conversation concerning the regime-stabilizing features of quasi-democracy.[53] Yet there is a problem. Flirting with

[47] Garry Rodan. *Participation Without Democracy: Containing Conflict in Southeast Asia*. Cornell University Press, 2018.

[48] Larry Catá Backer, Flora Sapio, and James Korman. "Popular Participation in the Constitution of the Illiberal StateŬAn Empirical Study of Popular Engagement and Constitutional Reform in Cuba and the Contours of Cuban Socialist Democracy 2.0." Available at SSRN (2019).

[49] Ronald Deibert and Rafal Rohozinski. "Liberation vs. Control: The Future of Cyberspace." *Journal of Democracy* 21.4 (2010), pp. 43–57.

[50] Francis Fukuyama. "Asia's Soft-Authoritarian Alternative." *New Perspectives Quarterly* 9.2 (1992), pp. 60–61; Denny Roy. "Singapore, China, and the 'Soft Authoritarian' Challenge." *Asian Survey* 34.3 (1994), pp. 231–242; Edward Schatz. "The Soft Authoritarian Tool Kit: Agenda-setting Power in Kazakhstan and Kyrgyzstan." *Comparative Politics* 41.2 (2009), pp. 203–222; Gordon Paul Means. "Soft Authoritarianism in Malaysia and Singapore." *Journal of Democracy* 7.4 (1996), pp. 103–117; Edwin A Winckler. "Institutionalization and Participation on Taiwan: From Hard to Soft Authoritarianism?" *The China Quarterly* 99 (1984), pp. 481–499.

[51] Samuel P. Huntington. *The Third Wave: Democratization in the Late Twentieth Century*. University of Oklahoma Press, 1991, p. 366; Juan J. Linz and Alfred C. Stepan. "Toward Consolidated Democracies." *Journal of Democracy* 7.2 (1996), pp. 14–33.

[52] The proportion of autocracies that either lacked a legislature or packed it with just one party went from about 50% to 15% between 1990 and 2010. Un-elected dictators saw their representation fall from over 70% in the 1950s to less than 40% over the same period. Based on data from Barbara Geddes, Joseph Wright, and Erica Frantz. "Autocratic Breakdown and Regime Transitions: A New Data Set." *Perspectives on Politics* 12.2 (2014), pp. 313–331.

[53] Carles Boix and Milan W. Svolik. "The Foundations of Limited Authoritarian Government." *The Journal of Politics* 75.02 (2013), pp. 300–316; Jennifer Gandhi. *Political Institutions under Dictatorship*. Cambridge University Press, 2008; Beatriz Magaloni. "The Game of Electoral Fraud and the Ousting of Authoritarian Rule." *American Journal of Political Science* 54.3 (2010), pp. 751–765; Joseph

democratic institutions can be rewarding but also risky for the incumbent regime.[54] As Larry Diamond asserts, "it is just not possible in our world of mass participation and democratic consciousness to give people the right to think, speak, publish, demonstrate, and associate peacefully, and not have them use those freedoms to demand, as well, the right to choose and replace their leaders in free and fair elections."[55]

Participation Without Democracy

Diamond is right: it is not. As I will argue throughout the rest of this book, however, it might be possible to extend a controlled version of inclusion that advances governance and preempts democracy. This proposition underpins much of the extant literature on Chinese governance, both formal and informal.[56] This assumption, however, has not been rigorously tested. Instead, scholarship on the regime-strengthening effects of institutions has either avoided the obvious presence of control or dealt with it as a limitation to the instrumental benefits suggested by their theories. The clearest examples concern authoritarian elections and the types of information they reveal under different degrees of control.[57] Similar reference to the instrumental use of quasi-democratic institutions is found in discussions surrounding legislatures,[58] civil society,[59] law and courts,[60] and public consultation.[61]

This book departs from the literature insofar as I consider political control not simply as a constraint but as a complement to inclusive authoritarianism. My

Wright. "Do Authoritarian Institutions Constrain? How Legislatures Affect Economic Growth and Investment." *American Journal of Political Science* 52.2 (2008), pp. 322–343.

[54] Paul J. Schuler, Dimitar D. Gueorguiev, and Francisco Cantu. "Risk and Reward: The Differential Impact of Authoritarian Elections on Regime Decay and Breakdown." *SSRN Electronic Journal* (2013), pp. 1–46; Carl Henrik Knutsen, Håvard Mokleiv Nygård, and Tore Wig. "Autocratic Elections: Stabilizing Tool or Force for Change?" *World Politics* 69.1 (2017), pp. 98–143.

[55] Larry Jay Diamond. "The Illusion of Liberal Autocracy." *Journal of Democracy* 14.4 (2003), pp. 167–171, p. 169.

[56] Tony Saich. *Governance and Politics of China*. Macmillan International Higher Education, 2010; Lily L. Tsai. *Accountability Without Democracy: Solidary Groups and Public Goods Provision in Rural China*. Cambridge University Press, 2007.

[57] Edmund Malesky and Paul Schuler. "The Single-Party Dictator's Dilemma: Information in Elections Without Opposition." *Legislative Studies Quarterly* 36.4 (2011), pp. 491–530.

[58] Boix and Svolik, "The Foundations of Limited Authoritarian Government"; Truex, *Making Autocracy Work: Representation and Responsiveness in Modern China*.

[59] Teets, *Civil Society under Authoritarianism: The China Model*; Mattingly, *The Art of Political Control in China*.

[60] Mary E. Gallagher and Blake Miller. "Can the Chinese Government Really Control the Internet? We Found Cracks in the Great Firewall." *Washington Post*, February 21, 2017. William Hurst. *Ruling Before the Law*. Cambridge University Press, 2018.

[61] Stromseth, Malesky, and Gueorguiev, *China's Governance Puzzle: Enabling Transparency and Participation in a Single-Party State*.

approach here is not particularly novel. In reflecting on the case of Singapore in the early 1990s, Francis Fukuyama, for example, highlights two distinct features of soft authoritarianism: paternalism and collectivism.[62] Importantly, neither of these qualities are in fact describing the *process* of soft authoritarianism— namely, public inclusion through state-run channels—but rather the controlled *ecosystem* within which that inclusion proceeds. In other words, paternalism (control from above) and collectivism (control from one's peers) provide the substructure that makes soft authoritarianism possible.

For Fukuyama, paternalism and collectivism are consonant with Confucian values, which place a premium on order and the needs of society over those of the individual. Yet, as we now know, a number of Confucian societies have transitioned out of soft authoritarianism and into robust democracy.[63] To be precise, out of all the "soft" regimes identified by scholars in the 1990s, only two have really survived: China and Singapore. As I will argue in subsequent chapters, this is no coincidence, and the antecedents of control in both states might have something in common. Specifically, both Singapore and China are ruled by parties that were originally established under Leninist principles,[64] which emphasize popular inclusion and bottom-heavy, heterarchical organization.[65] Seen from this light, the fusion of soft and hard that we see in contemporary China should not be that surprising. Under Leninism, there is no contradiction between asking citizens to denounce the government while at the same time having the leaders repress the public. It is part of the same iterative and endogenous system of control. But can such a system work, for how long, and what are its limitations?

One cannot hope to answer such questions if they arrive with preconceived notions of what inclusion ought to involve. Such an approach would allow one to quantify what the CCP is not doing, but reveal little about the goals and tactics it is in fact pursuing. In other words, by priming theories with liberal democratic principles rather than on Leninist precursors scholars risk misunderstanding the purpose of inclusive authoritarianism in today's China. On this point, my argument echoes that of others who see the Party as retaining

---

[62] Fukuyama, "Asia's Soft-Authoritarian Alternative."

[63] Taiwan and South Korea being the clearest examples.

[64] Jerry F. Hough and Merle Fainsod. *How the Soviet Union is Governed*. Harvard University Press, 1979, p. 693; Pang Cheng Lian. "The People's Action Party, 1954–1963." *Journal of Southeast Asian History* 10.1 (1969), pp. 142–154.

[65] Heterarchy refers to a organizational structure that is neither purely hierarchical nor fully decentralized, resulting in un-ranked modes of network communication. Contained heterarchy refers to a heterarchy that has a clear apex. See Warren S. McCulloch. "A Heterarchy of Values Determined by the Topology of Nervous Nets." *The Bulletin of Mathematical Biophysics* 7.2 (1945), pp. 89–93.

much of its Leninist, revolutionary core during the post-Mao period.[66] What I add is a framework that explains how interface between the soft elements of inclusion and the hard components of control can reconcile some of the practical limitations of governing under Leninism.

Traditionally, these limitations have been informational and computational in nature, with crude and reactionary repression filling in the missing pieces. In the case of China, advances in telecommunications and big data processing have greatly augmented the regime's capacity to gather and process information. As a result, the regime is not only getting more efficient and effective at governing, it is also supplanting crude political violence, such as public executions and the struggle campaigns of the Mao era, with passive surveillance, surgical repression, and tailored propaganda. How public input informs and interacts with the authoritarian control process, however, remains uncharted territory in contemporary China studies.

The Plan of the Book

This book is organized in three parts. The next two chapters round out Part I, laying out a theoretical and historical framework for thinking about inclusive authoritarianism in a CCP-controlled China. This framework is structured on two countervailing principles. First, regimes that fail to incorporate public input into their governance strategy are bound to suffer shortcomings in their ability to make informed policy decisions and legitimize those decisions with the public. Second, regimes that facilitate public participation expose themselves to popular mobilization and, thus, political competition. For much of history, noncompetitive regimes have opted for nonparticipatory political systems. Instead, kings, sultans, generalissimos, and supreme leaders have operated under various forms of hard, top-down authoritarian rule, incorporating only those small groups and individuals deemed essential for regime survival. [67]

The Leninist regimes that emerged in the first part of the twentieth century represent an exception to this pattern. To be sure, these regimes were hardly less brutal than their peers. Yet they brought forth a unique preoccupation with grassroots inclusion. It is also true that the history of Leninist participation has

---

[66] Elizabeth J. Perry. "From Mass Campaigns to Managed Campaigns." In *Mao's Invisible Hand: The Political Foundations of Adaptive Governance in China*. Ed. by Elizabeth J. Perry and Sebastian Heilmann. Harvard University Press, 2011, Chap. 2, pp. 30–61; Daniel Koss. *Where the Party Rules: The Rank and File of China's Communist State*. Cambridge University Press, 2018; S. Heilmann. "Maximum Tinkering under Uncertainty: Unorthodox Lessons from China." *Modern China* 35.4 (2009), pp. 450–462.
[67] Bruce Bueno De Mesquita and Alastair Smith. *The Dictator's Handbook: Why Bad Behavior is Almost Always Good Politics*. PublicAffairs, 2011.

proven more effective for political mobilization than actual governance; but it has not been for a lack of trying.[68] As I discuss in Chapter 2, the desire to harness public input for bureaucratic oversight and planning was a pillar of Marxist-Leninist thought, and at the political core of Maoist political philosophy. That these ambitions broadly degenerated into brutal dictatorship reflects deficiencies in both the Soviet and Chinese capacity to acquire, process, and act on information. Modern technology offers significant advantages in this regard, and I will argue that that the CCP's renewed interest in inclusive governance reflects an attempt at updating the mechanics of Leninist control, a process I refer to as "retrofitting."

What I mean by retrofitting resembles what some have termed "Leninism 2.0" or "Digital Leninism."[69] Such phrases, however, reveal relatively little about how Chinese Leninism has evolved, if at all. As I will argue in Chapter 2, the current foundations of Leninist control in China remain relatively unchanged. Indeed, control through social media or online commentary is not unlike participatory authoritarianism via old-fashioned public hearings and legislative conferences. In each format, participation is compatible and conducive to authoritarian rule because of how Leninist organizations go about compartmentalizing themselves and the systems they govern. Chapters 1 and 2 elaborate on these underlying principles and lay the groundwork for understanding controlled inclusion in three arenas: oversight, planning, and implementation.

Part II of the book unpacks the logic and mechanisms underpinning my argument by connecting the theoretical framework to an empirical record. In Chapters 3 and 4, I examine the link between public inputs and regime outputs in oversight and planning. This is a crucial link insofar as the salutary effects of inclusion can only accrue if the regime heeds and acts on public inputs. Taking advantage of data on anticorruption activity and citizen tip-offs, I show a strong and positive relationship between bottom-up corruption reporting and top-down disciplinary investigations. As further evidence of causal linkage, I leverage geographic information on China's legacy Internet communications infrastructure to help rule out confounding factors and endogeneity threats. Specifically, I find that localities that are geographically closer to Internet exchange servers built in the early 1990s are more likely to receive citizen tip-offs in the present period, and that this higher rate in citizen reporting also predicts higher rates of disciplinary action against local officials.

Having established an empirical link between public participation and oversight, I proceed to examine the relationship between bottom-up inputs and

---

[68] Philip G. Roeder. "Modernization and Participation in the Leninist Developmental Strategy." *American Political Science Review* 83.3 (1989), pp. 859–884.
[69] For instance, see Sebastian Heilmann's concept note: https://bit.ly/2FGNFg3.

policy planning. Here I take advantage of the fact that China's policymakers selectively open some policies, but not others, to public consultation. To exploit this variation, I try to approximate the input generating process by surveying Chinese citizens on the same issues for which the regime was conducting public consultation, as well as on those for which it preferred to plan internally. Based on survey data from three annual waves (2016–2018), I provide suggestive evidence that including public consultation in policymaking produces decisions that are generally more congruent with public opinion. Moreover, the surveys offer hints as to how the consultation process might help planners market their preferred policy positions to the general public.

But what does an authoritarian control regime do with several million comments, petitions, and proposals? In Chapter 6, I deal with what happens after information is generated. I argue that authoritarian regimes have to rely on heuristics (rule-of-thumb strategies) in order to screen out low-value information (noise) from high-priority inputs (signal). These heuristics should fill gaps in the regime's existing knowledge, reduce complexity, and be robust to the threat of information distortion. One attribute I see as satisfying these conditions is the distribution of preferences attached to an informational input parcel. In the case of grievances, for instance, petitions arriving from disparate segments of society help distinguish general grievances from isolated ones. In policy consultation, polarized public opinion helps leaders adopt moderating positions. When it comes to legislative representation, the diversity of sponsorship coalitions helps leaders discriminate encompassing from parochial demands. Using data from Chinese local people's congresses, I show this latter logic in action by mapping out the cosponsorship patterns around delegate-initiated proposals.

In Part III, I explore the downstream implications of controlled inclusion. For instance, if consultation is contributing policy-relevant information, it is reasonable to expect that those policies that are discussed in public prior to implementation are less likely to fail or attract mass opposition. Consistent with this logic, in Chapter 7 I show that no policies adopted with consultation between 2004 and 2012 were repealed during that same period, and that their amendment rates are significantly lower than for policies adopted without consultation. If the primary mechanisms driving such effects are indeed informational, I anticipate that effect size should be conditioned by capacity for information acquisition. Accordingly, I find that Internet connectivity acts as an amplifier in my estimates.

In Chapter 8, I turn to the legitimizing effects of controlled inclusion. Specifically, if public engagement is indeed helping endear governments to their citizens, one should be able to observe such effects in public opinion. Based on an original survey from a budget participation experiment in coastal China, I show that public engagement significantly raises public confidence in government, but that these gains are directed toward the *local* governments that invited them to participate. Importantly, however, the field experiment also shows that participation impacts the way citizens evaluate their local government, shifting their priorities away from economic performance and toward accountability.

Chapter 9 serves as a reflection on the opportunities and the limits to controlled inclusion in an increasingly technology-driven environment. In particular, I focus on two recent developments in the CCP's approach to social engagement. First, surveillance technology is indirectly reducing the need for the Party to invest in grassroots control, opting instead for algorithms and data scientists. Second, an evolving social crediting system is likely to undermine group-based management principles by turning every citizen into both a collaborator and target for control. In either case, it stands to reason that the trust link between the Party and the people would be undermined. Consistent with this expectation, I show that respondents who receive information about how social crediting works are less likely to feel that they, as citizens, are trusted by the state.

The Conclusion wraps up by tracing the arc China has made over the last forty years, one characterized by adaption but ultimately a return to Leninist roots. This trajectory has implications for at least two ongoing conversations. First, by showing how technology has opened opportunities for administrative inclusion at the expense of political inclusion, the book further undercuts any remaining optimism that China could be headed in a democratic direction. Second, the emergent scholarship on how regimes stay in power can at times give the impression that there is a "how to" manual for fully rational and strategic authoritarian resilience.[70] As this book chronicles, however, China's leaders have muddled their way through, trying out various strategies and keeping those compatible with control. Even so, the CCP's recent relapse toward personalism will likely undermine the gains and potential that inclusive forms of control have provided the Party thus far. With these thoughts in mind, I also consider the implications of my findings for other countries where authoritarian-minded incumbents seek to harness technology in advancing more sophisticated ways for staying in power.

---

[70] De Mesquita and Smith, *The Dictator's Handbook: Why Bad Behavior is Almost Always Good Politics*; Barbara Geddes et al., *How Dictatorships Work: Power, Personalization, and Collapse.* Cambridge University Press, 2018; Erica Frantz. *Authoritarianism: What Everyone Needs to Know.* Oxford University Press, 2018.

PART I

THEORY AND ORIGINS OF INCLUSIVE CONTROL IN CHINA

1

Blending Control and Inclusion

The principal direction in the development of the political system of
Soviet society is the extension of socialist democracy, namely ever
broader participation of citizens in managing the affairs of society
and the state, heightening of the activity of public organizations,
strengthening of the system of people's control, consolidation of the
legal foundations of the functioning of the state and of the public
life, greater openness and publicity, and constant responsiveness to
public opinion.

— Article 9 of the Soviet Constitution

It may seem bizarre that patently authoritarian regimes insert terms like "democratic" or "people" directly into their titles. The Democratic People's Republic
of Korea, for instance, has far less claim to such language than its southern
sister, the Republic of Korea.[1] The same could be said for the now defunct
German Democratic Republic, as well as the subject of this book, the People's
Republic of China. In each instance, the perfunctory invocation of democratic
vocabulary is clearly misleading, but it also raises basic questions as to why
and how authoritarian regimes stress their inclusive "public" credentials, and
whether such claims carry any meaning whatsoever?

As noted in the Introduction, the notion of authoritarian inclusion is often
dismissed as a form of "window dressing." This is arguably no longer the case;
new forms of inclusive politics are emerging, and in some instances displacing
democratic traditions.[2] China's case is particularly vexing to scholars insofar as
its technology-driven modes of public inclusion seem effective in generating
the soft governance improvements that citizens crave while at same time augmenting the hard social controls that leaders covet. But are these new forms of
authoritarian inclusion any more meaningful than the "bric-a-brac decorations"
of the not-so-distant past?[3]

---

[1] For an excellent introduction to public life and North Korean politics, see Andrei Lankov. *The Real North Korea: Life and Politics in the Failed Stalinist Utopia*. Oxford University Press, 2013.

[2] Rodan, *Participation Without Democracy: Containing Conflict in Southeast Asia*.

[3] Gayle Durham Hannah. *Soviet Information Networks*. Center for Strategic and International Studies, Georgetown University, 1977, p. 80; Howard R. Swearer. "Popular Participation: Myths and Realities." *Problems of Communism* September (1960), pp. 42–51.

Retrofitting Leninism. Dimitar D. Gueorguiev. Oxford University Press. © Oxford University Press 2021.
DOI: 10.1093/oso/9780197555668.003.0002

In this chapter, I outline a theoretical framework that links inclusive government with authoritarian control. In broad terms, I explain why regimes that fail to incorporate public participation into their governance strategy are likely to suffer dual deficiencies in information and legitimacy. I also explain why regimes that flirt with participation expose themselves to popular competition. For incumbent autocrats, reconciling these discordant features requires fusing methods of inclusion within the structure of control—a strategy I refer to as "controlled inclusion." In the past, attempts to achieve such synergies have been fleeting and unsustainable. Today, however, technology is making controlled forms of participation more subtle, more viable, and more socially acceptable. By focusing on the underlying logic of controlled inclusion and its technology-driven renaissance, I hope to spur a conversation about the prospects and pitfalls of participatory governance in the absence of democratic institutions, principles, or aspirations. This chapter serves as a preamble to that conversation.

Governing Under Autocracy

A commonly held view of governance under autocracy is that of a repressive and monolithic conveyor belt that translates orders from the dictator and turns them into actions on the ground. This caricature is misleading in at least two ways. First, all regimes rely to some degree on popular consent to govern.[4] In the absence of consent, opposition and noncompliance become a routine obstacle to administration and an implacable drain on resources.[5] Second, leaders, whether committed democrats or brutish tyrants, are never certain how their actions translate into outcomes,[6] either because they cannot envision all options and anticipate all contingencies[7] or because their intentions are compromised by errant agents during implementation.[8] When government efforts backfire, investments are wasted, weaknesses are exposed, and political capital is lost. Such losses

---

[4] John S. Dryzek. "Legitimacy and Economy in Deliberative Democracy." *Political Theory* 29.5 (2001), pp. 651–669; Tom R. Tyler. *Why People Obey the Law.* Princeton University Press, 2006.

[5] Max Weber. *Economy and Society: An Outline of Interpretive Sociology.* Vol. 1. University of California Press, 1978, p. 213.

[6] David Austen-Smith and William H. Riker. "Asymmetric Information and the Coherence of Legislation." *American Political Science Review* 81.3 (1987), pp. 897–918; James C. Scott. *Seeing Like a State: How Certain Schemes to Improve the Human Condition Have Failed.* Yale University Press, 1998; John Stuart Mill. *Considerations on Representative Government.* Henry Holt and Co., 1861.

[7] Herbert A. Simon. *Administrative Behavior. A Study of Decison-Making Processes in Administrative Organizations.* Macmillan, 1946; Charles E. Lindblom. "The Science of 'Muddling Through'." *Public Administration Review* 19.2 (1959), pp. 79–88.

[8] Susan Rose-Ackerman. *Corruption: A Study in Political Economy.* Academic Press, 1978; Robert Klitgaard. *Controlling Corruption.* Berkeley: University of California Press, 1988; Gary Becker and George Stigler. "Law Enforcement, Malfeasance, and Compensation of Enforcers." *The Journal of Legal Studies* 3.1 (1974), pp. 1–18.

only compound the governor's problem by further undercutting its legitimacy and discouraging economic activity. As such, cultivating consent and reducing uncertainty are first-order challenges facing any governing organization.

Public inclusion in the governing process can mitigate some of these basic challenges. Opportunities for public deliberation, for instance, allow critics to make their cases during policy formulation rather than implementation, giving planners an opportunity to preempt those concerns.[9] Even when citizens disagree with the final decisions, inclusion in the process that formed them can influence perceptions about their legitimacy.[10] Relatedly, inputs revealed through the deliberative process can help policymakers overcome their own bounded rationality and reveal more fruitful alternatives than were otherwise apparent.[11] Even with effective plans and marketing, implementation and enforcement are typically delegated to agents, resulting in opportunities for discretion, obstruction, and corruption.[12] As primary beneficiaries of government services and policy, members of the public are thus in a unique position to provide information that leaders and policymakers can use to constrain and sanction errant agents.[13]

The instrumental benefits of public inclusion, however, come with substantial risks. In addition to helping leaders map out policy options, representative legislatures can also serve as forums for opponents to coordinate against the incumbent.[14] Similarly, while elections can increase political accountability, electoral events can also generate focal points for organized opposition.[15] As noted in the Introduction a good number of authoritarian regimes have succumbed to the

[9] James S. Fishkin *Democracy and Deliberation: New Directions for Democratic Reform.* Yale University Press, 1991.
[10] Kenneth P. Ruscio. "Trust, Democracy, and Public Management: A Theoretical Argument." *Journal of Public Administration Research and Theory* 6.3 (1996), pp. 461–477; Cheryl Simrell King, Kathryn M. Feltey, and Bridget O'Neill Susel. "The Question of Participation: Toward Authentic Public Participation in Public Administration." *Public Administration Review* 58.4 (1998), pp. 317–326; Craig W. Thomas. "Maintaining and Restoring Public Trust in Government Agencies and their Employees." *Administration & Society* 30.2 (1998), pp. 166–193; Mark Warren. "Democratic Theory and Self-transformation." *American Political Science Review* 86.1 (1992), pp. 8–23.
[11] James D. Fearon. "Deliberation as Discussion." In *Deliberative Democracy.* Ed. by Jon Elster. Cambridge University Press, 1998, Chap. 3, pp. 44–68.
[12] Becker and Stigler, "Law Enforcement, Malfeasance, and Compensation of Enforcers"; Klitgaard, *Controlling Corruption*; Rose-Ackerman, *Corruption: A Study in Political Economy.*
[13] Mathew D. McCubbins and Thomas Schwartz. "Congressional Oversight Overlooked: Police Patrols versus Fire Alarms." *American Journal of Political Science* 28.1 (1984), pp. 165–179.
[14] Scott W. Desposato. "Legislative Politics in Authoritarian Brazil." *Legislative Studies Quarterly* 26.2 (2001), pp. 287–317.
[15] Schuler, Gueorguiev, and Cantu, "Risk and Reward: The Differential Impact of Authoritarian Elections on Regime Decay and Breakdown"; Joshua A. Tucker. "Enough! Electoral Fraud, Collective Action Problems, and Post-Communist Colored Revolutions." *Perspectives on Politics* 5.03 (2007), p. 535.

forces of democratization, often in the aftermath of quasi-democratic reforms.[16] It is precisely for this reason that quasi-democratic institutions, as suggested previously, are often hobbled in ways that directly undercut their theorized contributions. Put simply, what legitimacy is there in voting if the outcome is predetermined? What is the value of legislative debate if the chamber lacks a viable opposition? As Robert Dahl explains, "in the absence of the right to oppose the right to 'participate' is stripped of a very large part of the significance it has," thus rendering theoretical implications "anomalous."[17]

One approach is to accept such limitations as a defined political constraint and explore the residual benefits that remain. Malesky and Schuler, for instance, outline the various but limited types of information benefits associated with noncompetitive elections.[18] Similarly, others explore the indirect benefits of nondemocratic legislatures in terms of investor confidence and intra-elite power-sharing.[19] A related line of thinking motivates scholarship on input institutions in China.[20] In his work on China's national legislature, for instance, Truex explains that delegates are conditioned into "bounded" forms of representation, whereby they reflect public preferences but only in sanctioned topic areas.[21] In her work on civil society organizations, Teets describes nongovernment organizations as important social actors, despite being confined to specific services and localities deemed conducive to the regime's governance objectives.[22] In short, though compromised, inclusive authoritarianism can still contribute to more stable and effective government.

While intuitive, instrumentalist explanations carry some theoretical shortcomings. In particular, by interpreting instrumental benefits as hindered or bounded by authoritarian constraints, we are implicitly adopting a linear interpretation of the problem. With regard to information, for instance, the linear implication is that the more controlled an input mechanism is, the less informative. One obvious implication thus is that fewer constraints would lead to greater benefits. In their study of open governance in China, for example, Stromseth,

[16] Raymond Hinnebusch. "Syria: From 'Authoritarian Upgrading' to Revolution?" *International Affairs* 88.1 (2012), pp. 95–113; Adrian Karatnycky. "Ukraine's Orange Revolution." *Foreign Affairs*, March/April (2005), pp. 35–52; Knutsen, Nygård, and Wig, "Autocratic Elections: Stabilizing Tool or Force for Change?"

[17] Robert Alan Dahl. *Polyarchy: Participation and Opposition.* Yale University Press, 1973, p. 5.

[18] Malesky and Schuler, "The Single-Party Dictator's Dilemma: Information in Elections Without Opposition."

[19] Wright, "Do Authoritarian Institutions Constrain? How Legislatures Affect Economic Growth and Investment"; Boix and Svolik, "The Foundations of Limited Authoritarian Government."

[20] Nathan, "China's Changing of the Guard: Authoritarian Resilience."

[21] Truex, *Making Autocracy Work: Representation and Responsiveness in Modern China.*

[22] Teets, *Civil Society under Authoritarianism: The China Model*; Mattingly, *The Art of Political Control in China.*

Malesky, and Gueorguiev lament the fact that requirements for transparency and opportunities for participation, though seemingly conducive to better governance, remain highly circumscribed. Taken to one extreme, such constraints ought to dilute instrumentalism down to "window-dressing," whereby the inclusion becomes merely decorative and functionally inconsequential.[23] Yet, taken to the other extreme, it is hard to see how unfettered inclusion does not lead, as democracy proponents would hope, to further liberalization.[24]

Part of the tension, I believe, arises from an overemphasis on the instrumental functions of inclusive institutions and a reluctance to incorporate the control structure within which they the operate. Dahl's concern, for instance, does not imply that authoritarian regimes are void of competitive forces, only that struggle between actors and interests within them is thoroughly controlled by the regime. Likewise, the reason many dismiss participatory governance in China today is not because they doubt that public opinion matters or that the Chinese government is interested in good governance, but rather that participation seems heavily restricted and choreographed by the state. Indeed, control is the common denominator across all forms of authoritarianism, and it this preoccupation with control that stands in sharpest contrast to liberal democracy.

What is gained by focusing on control? For one, holding authoritarian institutions up to democratic standards reveals a great deal about what autocracies fail to include or institutionalize, but relatively little about the strategies and tactics they in fact pursue. By contrast, unpacking authoritarian control allows us to be more precise about why authoritarianism and inclusion seem so incompatible, in what respects they might be complementary, and under what conditions. In short, coming to terms with the structure of control that pervades authoritarianism offers a clearer view of how public participation fits into the broader authoritarian landscape.

In the case of China, I argue that the structure in question is one of Leninist control. Acknowledging this point helps move the conversation forward in at least two ways. Rather than dwelling on why the CCP invites public input, for example, we can ask the harder question of what they do with the millions of comments, petitions, and proposals provided by the public. Rather than debating whether or not China's inclusive reforms are democratic, acknowledging that they can be effective raises the potential that these same strategies undercut demand for real democracy. Put simply, when citizens can report petty corruption or dereliction of duty directly to oversight bodies, the utility of sanctioning through elections diminishes. To be sure, such feedback is unlikely to constrain corruption within the disciplinary bodies or the top leadership, but corruption

[23] Bristow. "China's Democratic 'Window Dressing.'" BBC News.
[24] Diamond, "The Rule of Law as Transition to Democracy in China."

in these realms is harder for members of the public to observe or perceive in the first place. Likewise, when citizens can directly express support for specific items of policy, the need for coordinating institutions and advocacy groups also diminishes. Most importantly, coming to terms with the control structure helps make sense of the parallel increase in responsiveness and repression taking place in contemporary China. Before delving into the relationship between responsiveness and repression, I address the more fundamental dilemmas of authoritarian control.

The Control Dilemma

For most authoritarian regimes, options for inclusion are precluded by what Svolik refers to as the "twin problems of dictatorship," namely the perpetual threat of revolution from the bottom and leadership struggle at the top.[25] In dealing with these threats, autocrats can turn to the tried and tested tactics of "divide and rule." European colonizers, for instance, exploited ethnic, religious, and class cleavages to segregate the societies they sought to control, while arming minority groups to exercise exclusive control over majority populations.[26] Contemporary authoritarian regimes built around identity, race, or sect follow a similar logic.[27] When demographics do not offer obvious lines of division, authoritarian leaders can still frustrate potential challengers by creating multiple, parallel, and competing security agencies[28] or even by importing mercenaries from abroad.[29]

Such control tactics, though often effective in the short run, have built-in, long-term pathologies. A regime that relies solely on repression and exclusion will suffer greater uncertainty over how much support or enmity it commands among the general population.[30] Likewise, fragmenting the security apparatus undermines organizational capacity and institutional coordination,[31] while

---

[25] Milan W Svolik. *The Politics of Authoritarian Rule*. Cambridge University Press, 2012, p. 2.

[26] Mahmood Mamdani. *Citizen and Subject: Contemporary Africa and the Legacy of Late Colonialism*. Princeton University Press, 1996.

[27] Philip Roessler. "The Enemy Within: Personal Rule, Coups, and Civil War in Africa." *World Politics* 63.2 (2011), pp. 300–346.

[28] James T. Quinlivan. "Coup-proofing: Its Practice and Consequences in the Middle East." *International Security* 24.2 (1999), pp. 131–165.

[29] Hin-Yan Liu. "Mercenaries in Libya: Ramifications of the Treatment of 'Armed Mercenary Personnel' under the Arms Embargo for Private Military Company Contractors." *Journal of Conflict & Security Law* 16.2 (2011), pp. 293–319.

[30] Timur Kuran. "Now Out of Never: The Element of Surprise in the East European Revolution of 1989." *World Politics* 44.01 (1991), pp. 7–48; Ronald Wintrobe. "The Tinpot and the Totalitarian: An Economic Theory of Dictatorship." *American Political Science Review* 84.3 (1990), pp. 849–872; Ronald Wintrobe. *The Political Economy of Dictatorship*. Vol. 94. Penguin 2006. Cambridge University Press, 1998, p. 981.

[31] Sheena Chestnut Greitens. *Dictators and Their Secret Police: Coercive Institutions and State Violence*. Cambridge University Press, 2016.

excluding large proportions of the population undercuts the grassroots linkage that might otherwise be conducive to public administration.[32] In both instances, exclusion and fragmentation commit the regime to crude and costly forms of repression, thus diverting scarce resources from other objectives like industrial upgrading and national defense, not to mention buying off other elites.[33] Such pathologies may be manageable in a small, rentier state, where economic activity is narrow and spoils are readily divisible. However, the more complex a political economy becomes, the greater the challenge of social and organizational control.[34] Cognizant of such threats, authoritarian leaders may find it rational to throttle their economies, neglect public services, and systematically inhibit the potential of their citizens.[35]

Even within the category of authoritarian regimes, however, there is still considerable variation. Consider Cuba and North Korea which, despite sharing historical and institutional legacies (not to mention the burden of US-imposed sanctions), provide two vastly different worlds for their citizens. For its part, Cuba edges out the United States on life expectancy (79 vs. 78 years on average) and has less corruption than Italy according to Transparency International. North Koreans die about ten years earlier, and the North Korean government vies with South Sudan and Somalia for the most corrupt on the planet.[36] Without going into the details of either case, it would not be an overstatement to suggest that Cuba's government is better connected *to* and enjoys more voluntary compliance *from* its citizens than does that of North Korea. Whereas citizens in North Korea are mobilized in leadership worship and public executions, those in Cuba are regularly encouraged to comment on policy proposals and voice complaints through officially sanctioned channels.[37] Even elections, which are tightly controlled in both states, appear to be more meaningful in Cuba, where voters can at least abstain from supporting the regime nominee.[38]

---

[32] David Garland. *The Culture of Control: Crime and Social Order in Contemporary Society.* University of Chicago Press, 2012; Jock Young. *The Exclusive Society: Social Exclusion, Crime and Difference in Late Modernity.* Sage, 1999.

[33] Greitens, *Dictators and Their Secret Police.*

[34] Samuel Huntington. *Political Order in Changing Societies.* Vol. 76. 5. Yale University Press, 1968, pp. 215–216.

[35] DeMesquita and Smith, *The Dictator's Handbook: Why Bad Behavior is Almost Always Good Politics.*

[36] Corruption ranking based on Transparency International's Corruption Perception Index, 2016.

[37] Philip Peters. "A Viewer's Guide to Cuba's Economic Reform." *Lexington Institute* May (2012); Martin K. Dimitrov. "The Functions of Letters to the Editor in Reform-Era Cuba." *Latin American Research Review* 54.1 (2019).

[38] According to statistics published in the Cuban Communist Party mouthpiece *Granma*, nearly 365,000 voters turned in blank ballots in the 2013 Cuban National Assembly elections. In North Korea, voting operates more as a mandatory census; abstentions are not tolerated. For background, see: https://bit.ly/2MDPzlP.

More generally, the literature has shown that inclusive institutions contribute to more stable leadership,[39] more efficient coercion[40] as well as improved oversight and implementation.[41] In each case, incorporating society within the institutions of government is believed to contribute vital bottom-up information and legitimacy to the political process. By coopting members of the private sector into a representative parliament, the regime not only benefits from their economic advice, it also insures that the fortunes of these representatives are now tied to its own.[42] Likewise, by embedding itself within the community, a regime will be more attuned to grievances and dissidents and thus better equipped to address them preemptively and with discretion.[43] Finally, by inviting the public to participate in government oversight and planning, the regime gains unique insight into the actions of its agents and the potential challenges facing its policy plans.[44] In short, inclusion operates in the service of control.

The theoretical challenge thus is explaining how a regime profits from political inclusion while avoiding pressure for liberalization.[45] This is only possible if the regime installs controls that prevent groups and prominent individuals from coordinating with one another. If inclusion is controlled, however, what can it contribute in terms of information or legitimacy? In addressing this question, it is helpful to distinguish between the two different modes of inclusion; namely, electoral participation for deciding *who* governs the polity and non-electoral participation in determining *how* it is governed.[46] This distinction is an overlooked nuance in Dahl's own definition of inclusion which, though most easily interpreted in terms of electoral contest, also references "control" over the "conduct of government."[47]

Critically, control over these two modes of inclusion involves different types of coercion. Controlling an electoral outcome, for instance, might mean holding single-party contests, voter intimidation, candidate suppression, or outright

---

[39] Boix and Svolik, "The Foundations of Limited Authoritarian Government"; Gandhi, *Political Institutions under Dictatorship*.

[40] Greitens, *Dictators and Their Secret Police*.

[41] Stromseth, Malesky, and Gueorguiev, *China's Governance Puzzle: Enabling Transparency and Participation in a Single-Party State*.

[42] Jennifer Gandhi and Adam Przeworski. "Authoritarian Institutions and the Survival of Autocrats." *Comparative Political Studies* 40.11 (2007), pp. 1279–1301.

[43] Greitens, *Dictators and Their Secret Police*.

[44] McCubbins and Schwartz, "Congressional Oversight Overlooked."

[45] Diamond, "The Illusion of Liberal Autocracy."

[46] Ruth Berins Collier and Stephen Handlin. "Popular Representation in the Interest Arena." In *Reorganizing Popular Politics: Participation and the New Interest Regime in Latin America*. Penn State Press, 2009, pp. 3–31.

[47] The full definition reads: "the proportion of the population entitled to participate on a more or less equal plane in controlling and contesting the conduct of the government." See Dahl, *Polyarchy: Participation and Opposition*, p. 4.

fraud.[48] Each of these controls invariably undermines the information or legitimacy potential of the election.[49] By contrast, controlling the range of issues and tenor of public discourse on matters of policy and governance is often less invasive or conspicuous. For instance, the regime can leverage its control over the political agenda to selectively open some topics to debate, while keeping others off limits.[50] Similarly, regimes can use censorship to control discourse and cordon off collection action, while allowing other forms of critical input.[51] In other words, non-electoral modes of inclusion are more easily controlled because the topics and issues they touch on are not yet coordinated by opposition parties or politicians.

My argument here draws some inspiration from Hirschman's classic *exit, voice, loyalty* framework. In particular, as Hirschman points out, the "feedback" that keeps organizations viable is not simply a function of voice, but rather a feature of both voice and exit. In the absence of exit options, voice is cheap talk. If we consider public participation as a *voice*, and repressive political controls as limits on *exit*, for example, it is easy to see how an overly restrictive environment would reduce public participation to a form of window-dressing. Yet, if the costs to exit are too low, voice suffers as well. Free exit, say to alternative forms of political or economic organizations, would bleed the Chinese party-state of its most valued members and resources. Hirschman illustrates this point with the example of private competition emerging for a previously public service. Applied to the case of contemporary China, controlled forms of public inclusion offer limited voice within an environment characterized by few exit options and a noncompetitive political market.

Theoretical Illustration

The premise of my argument is that a preoccupation with control at the expense of inclusion leads to brutish and crude dictatorship, riddled with policy failures and constrained by low levels of political legitimacy. Attempts at increasing inclusion without requisite control, however, can lead to authoritarian instability,

---

[48] Andreas Schedler. "The Logic of Electoral Authoritarianism." In *Electoral Authoritarianism: The Dynamics of Unfree Competition.* Ed. by Andreas Schedler. Lynne Rienner, 2006, Chap. 1, pp. 1–23.

[49] Edmund Malesky and Paul Schuler. "Nodding or Needling: Analyzing Delegate Responsiveness in an Authoritarian Parliament." *American Political Science Review* 104.03 (2010), pp. 482–502.

[50] Dimitar D. Gueorguiev and Edmund J. Malesky. "Consultation and Selective Censorship in China." *Journal of Politics* (2019), pp. 1539–1545.

[51] Gary King, Jennifer Pan, and Margaret E. Roberts "How Censorship in China Allows Government Criticism but Silences Collective Expression." *American Political Science Review* 107.02 (2013), pp. 326–343.

possibly even democratization. By contrast, a balance in coercive control and inclusion is conducive to further efficiencies in both. My logic is summarized in Figure 1.1, which offers an outline of how opportunities for political inclusion interact with priorities for authoritarian control. Panel A represents an abstract version of the argument. Panel B includes illustrative cases in place of the abstract categories.

The bottom left quadrant of Panel A depicts regimes that are weak on both dimensions, a category that I designate as "fragile" authoritarian states. These are regimes that rely on crude, indiscriminate forms of repression with little or no opportunities for inclusion. These regimes are vulnerable to coups or revolution and, if they collapse, are typically replaced by new authoritarian regimes, such as in the case of Libya in 1969 or Liberia in 1990. By contrast, the top left of Panel A represents the typical police state, in which control over society and state is pervasive, while opportunities for popular participation are limited or nonexistent. These regimes can prove quite stable but are nevertheless plagued by the information and legitimacy constraints highlighted in the previous section. Moving to the bottom right of Panel A are authoritarian regimes that have attempted to increase popular inclusion, without the requisite level of control. In these regimes, the incumbent enjoys a hegemonic position within the polity but is nevertheless susceptible to bottom-up opposition from society, usually in coordination with breakaway elements from within the regime. Like police

Figure 1.1. Intersection of Control and Inclusion

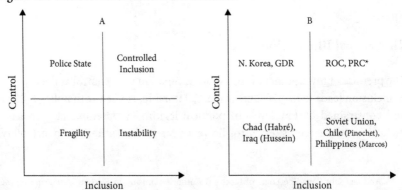

Notes: Placement along the *Control* axis in Panel B is based on Greitens 2016, who reports internal security to population ratios for prominent authoritarian regimes of the past and present. Upper quadrants are those with a ratio lower than 1:1000, which represents the sharpest discontinuity across cases in Greitens's sample. *Ratio for China is calculated by the author as between 1:500 to 1:15 using reported statistics on police officers, People's Armed Police officers, and figures concerning security personnel in Beijing. ROC refers to Taiwan (1949–1987). Placement along the *Inclusion* axis is based on a subjective assessment, with right-hand quadrants composed of regimes with either participatory or electoral methods of inclusion.

states, hegemonic regimes can prove relatively stable but are nevertheless vulnerable to collapse and primed to move in a liberalizing direction. The recent collapse of the once-dominant United Malaysia National Organization at the hands of its one-time leaders serves as a dramatic case in point. Finally, we come to the top right-hand quadrant, which I refer to as controlled inclusion. These are authoritarian regimes that, like the police states, engage in pervasive control over society, as well as over their own agents and organizations. However, these regimes also offer a wide range of mechanisms for including citizens in the governing process. Importantly, high levels of control make public participation less risky in these settings, while public inclusion facilitates more efficient forms of control.

In Panel B, I attempt to illustrate the categories with actual cases, based on a rough operationalization of control and inclusion. To approximate control, I borrow from Greitens's estimates of internal security to population ratios, along with my own approximations for the PRC.[52] Placement along the *Inclusion* axis is based on a subjective accounting of institutions and mechanisms for popular participation. Cases on the right-hand side are those with either participatory or electoral inclusion.[53] This operationalization of inclusion will require further exposition (which I provide in the subsequent section), but it is important to note that inclusion concerns the general population. For instance, Iraq held irregular elections throughout Saddam Hussein's tenure, but many in the Shia-majority country were not included in the process, leaving Iraq in the low *Inclusion* end of the spectrum.[54]

Readers may take issue with my placements along either axis, but the framework easily incorporates more cases or alternative specification. Cuba, for which we lack reliable internal security statistics, arguably has a fairly extensive control apparatus, and it also invests considerable resources to inclusion. As such, Cuba would be a strong candidate for the *Controlled Inclusion* quadrant. The same could be said for the cases of Vietnam and Singapore. Likewise, one could point to any number of tin-pot dictatorships that fit the lower left quadrant, and a smaller subset of totalitarian regimes to occupy the upper left.[55] Even within China itself, we see tremendous variation in the level of investments in control versus inclusion. Expenditures for public security in Tibet and Xinjiang, for

[52] Greitens does not provide estimates for the PRC; calculations are my own. I do not include measures for Nazi Germany, which are based only on Gestapo figures. See Greitens, *Dictators and Their Secret Police*, p. 9.

[53] By participatory, I mean inclusion in determining *how* the polity is governed. By electoral inclusion, I mean voice in deciding *who* governs.

[54] For an authoritative background on social control and inclusion in Iraq under Hussein, refer to Lisa Blaydes, *State of Repression: Iraq under Saddam Hussein*. Princeton University Press, 2018.

[55] Wintrobe, "The Tinpot and the Totalitarian: An Economic Theory of Dictatorship."

instance, are greater than in any other provincial-level unit,[56] but both provinces are at the bottom when it comes public participation.[57] By contrast, localities like Beijing, Shanghai, Zhejiang, and Guangdong spend heavily on security while also investing in various modes of public inclusion (see Figure 1.2).

Instead, I call attention to two, less obvious observations from the diagram in Figure 1.1. Specifically, each of the examples identified as *Controlled Inclusion* cases happen to be Leninist regimes. As discussed in the previous chapter, this is no coincidence. Leninist theory on government expressly notes the importance of inclusive control—what Marx referred to as a "dictatorship of the proletariat" and what Lenin described more aptly as a dictatorship by a "vanguard party." While I postpone getting into the nuances of Leninism until the next chapter, it is worth noting that Leninist regimes also appear in the top-left and bottom right-hand quadrants, namely with the cases of North Korea and the Soviet Union. The Soviet Union's position is particularly puzzling, given the emphasis on Leninism. Objectively speaking, the placement of the former Soviet Union in Figure 1.1 reflects Greitens's estimate that the Soviets had an internal security ratio of 1:5,830. Conceptually, however, a deeper understanding of why the Soviet Union failed to achieve a balance between control and inclusion will require a closer examination of the countervailing and complementary properties of these two dimensions—a topic I will touch on again in Chapters 1 and 2.

Controlled Inclusion

The discourse and agenda controls I describe under controlled inclusion are not easily mastered by an authoritarian regime. Selective censorship, for instance, requires that a regime be able to monitor vast quantities of information and to discriminate between information that is compatible with its interests and that which is not. In the case of China, this task is outsourced to armies of public and private agents.[58] Likewise, agenda control demands a compartmentalized yet coherent policymaking organization that can oversee inclusion in a piecemeal way. In other words, controlled inclusion presupposes a level of control that is most likely out of reach for low-capacity or narrowly constituted authoritarian regimes. For those regimes that have either inherited or invested in broader public support bases and more sophisticated methods of control, greater inclusion becomes an option as well as an opportunity.

---

[56] Based on 2017 figures, Xinjiang spends about 24,400 RMB per capita on public security, while Tibet spends a whopping 31,700. By comparison, Anhui spends a mere 4,200 RMB.

[57] Most public opinion surveys do not even include Tibet and Xinjiang due to restrictions on population research. However, based on what is available from a few unique studies conducted by the Unirule think tank, and a Netizen survey collected by Prof. Ma Deyong of Renmin University, citizens in both provinces exhibit markedly lower levels of efficacy and participatory opportunity than anywhere else in China.

[58] Blake Miller. "The Limits of Commercialized Censorship in China." SocArXiv, 2019. Web.

Figure 1.2. Control and Inclusion, Across Provinces

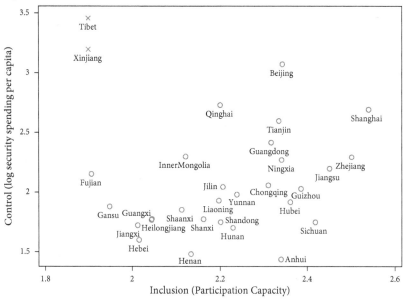

Notes: Security spending is based on local public security expenditures published by China's National Statistics Bureau. Measures of participation are derived from four questions (Section F2) in the 2015 China General Social Survey (中国综合社会调查 [CGSS]) related to a respondent's perceived capacity to participate in policymaking. Because Xinjiang and Tibet are not included in the CGSS, I impute their measures based on similar questions (Q33_R7, and Q29_R8) in the 2014 and 2015 waves of a Netizen survey (网民态度调查), as well an independently published Unirule survey. I consider the CGSS data to be more reliable because it is conducted with national probability sampling.

For instance, if a regime is able to rely on public informants to supervise agents, it might be more inclined toward economic growth-promoting decentralization.[59] Likewise, if a regime can rely on public involvement in the policymaking process, it might be more open to policy experimentation.[60] Each incremental step in development, however, must be attended to by ever more complex means of control, and thus greater demands for information. The implication here is that controlled inclusion is hard to sustain, precisely because it is effective at facilitating more complex organizations and economies. The insight here is consistent with Dickson's version of the "dictator's dilemma," whereby effective government in the present raises the bar of public expectation for good

[59] Barry R. Weingast. "The Political Foundations of Democracy and the Rule of Law." *American Political Science Review* 91.2 (1997), pp. 245–263.

[60] Sebastian Heilmann. "Policy Experimentation in China's Economic Rise." *Studies in Comparative International Development* 43.1 (2008), pp. 1–26.

government in the future.[61] Liberalized regimes resolve some of these challenges by relegating a substantial portion of control to markets.[62] Authoritarian regimes can also take advantage of liberalization to reduce complexity, but their concern for political and social control precludes optimal liberalization, favoring partial openings instead.[63] Such halfway attempts naturally result in new challenges, including corruption and obstruction from those within the regime who can exploit gray areas.[64] Note, however, that such agency problems only further augment the instrumental benefit of inclusive organizational controls that can bypass corruption in the bureaucratic and regulatory structure.

Yet even if a regime is able to embed itself in society and impose the level of social control necessary to let the public participate, there is still no guarantee that citizens will in fact do so. For instance, why would citizens complain if they don't expect anyone to come to their aid? Why would they offer incriminating information if the targets of their scorn are not punished? Why would they offer comment if they do not believe policymakers are listening? In other words, public participation depends to some degree on responsiveness, or least a broadly held public perception that the regime is responsive. Again, responsiveness entails a level of professionalization and organizational capacity that should not be taken for granted. For instance, leadership might find it hard to demonstrate responsiveness on anticorruption if the agent in question is a family member or an asset of a critical clique or faction within the establishment. Alternatively, leaders may simply become overwhelmed by the number or range of issues raised by the public. As I argue in the next chapter, what ultimately overwhelmed the Soviet Union's inclusive control system were its failures in input processing and responsiveness.

Feedback Control

Input processing and responsiveness represent a critical intersection between control and inclusion, which is an area where my argument further departs from existing work. In particular, I argue that controls not only make inclusion less risky—efficient controls also help the regime render inputs generated by inclusion into useful information. That is, whereas the conventional information

---

[61] Dickson, *The Dictator's Dilemma: The Chinese Communist Party's Strategy for Survival.*

[62] Adam Przeworski. *Democracy and the Market: Political and Economic Reforms in Eastern Europe and Latin America.* Cambridge University Press, 1991, pp. 51–99.

[63] Joel S. Hellman, "Winners Take All: The Politics of Partial Reform in Postcommunist Transitions." *World Politics* 50.2 (1998), pp. 203–234; Daniel Brumberg. "The Trap of Liberalized Autocracy." *Journal of Democracy* 13.4 (2002), pp. 56–68; Dali L. Yang. *Remaking the Chinese Leviathan: Market Transition and the Politics of Governance in China.* Stanford University Press, 2004, 414 p.

[64] Huntington, *The Third Wave: Democratization in the Late Twentieth Century*; Minxin Pei. *China's Trapped Transition: The Limits of Developmental Autocracy.* Harvard University Press, 2006.

dilemma pits control as a constraint on information gathering,[65] I propose that authoritarian controls on information and collective action might contribute to information processing. Like the resistors in an electrical circuit, controls serve to regulate and modulate the flow of public demands and opinions so that the authorities stand a better chance of rendering that information into priorities and of responding effectively.[66]

Controls can provide this function in a blunt manner. Consider, for instance, Lorentzen's notion of "screening," whereby an authoritarian regime represses protest but not completely, so that only those with more substantial grievances participate. In this scenario, coercion both prevents protests from getting out of control and reduces the number of protest events, thus allowing the regime to focus on the most serious of grievances.[67] A similar logic can be applied to other methods of control that do not rely on overt repression. Internet controls, for instance, prevent Chinese citizens from openly accessing sensitive information, but Netizens can pay to circumvent these controls through VPNs, effectively signaling to the authorities that the user's traffic is sensitive and thus a priority for monitoring.[68] More generally, such systematic compartmentalization of society makes horizontal coordination costly and therefore rare. Those few instances in which groups or individuals overcome the existing barriers to coordination thus stand out, making them more likely to gain attention and therefore induce correction.

In other words, institutions defined by integrated control offer built-in "noise-reduction" mechanisms that authoritarian regimes can leverage when harnessing and processing public input into priorities. In China's recent past, this involved physically reorganizing society into regime-controlled groups and units, each equipped with its own monitoring, filtering, and processing agents. Today, at least some of that physical burden of monitoring is being offloaded onto computers and algorithms. This evolution in control, however, has not left behind the basic logic of compartmentalization; it has simply moved it into a more digital domain. Today in China, for instance, it is far easier to create closed social media groups on WeChat than to broadcast openly on Weibo, two of China's most popular social media platforms. Soon, Chinese society will be even further atomized as a result of individual credit scores and as social ranking becomes more prevalent. State-backed blockchain ledgers could make it infinitely possibly

[65] Wintrobe, *The Political Economy of Dictatorship.*

[66] Norbert Wiener. *Cybernetics or Control and Communication in the Animal and the Machine.* Technology Press, 1948, p. 97.

[67] Peter Lorentzen. "Designing Contentious Politics in Post-1989 China." *Modern China* 43.5 (2017), pp. 459–493; McCubbins and Schwartz, "Congressional Oversight Overlooked."

[68] The government has made VPNs harder to acquire and use, but they remain readily available at higher prices.

to track, trace, and triangulate economic transactions and transgressions. To be sure, controlled, atomized societies present their own sets of challenges for development. Nevertheless, compartmentalization makes political inclusion less risky and its contributions more legible.

Updating Leninism in China

My argument is inspired by the seemingly paradoxical fusion of inclusion and control in the contemporary Chinese case, but the political strategy that animates this paradox did not originate in China. Instead, the theoretical seeds, as I will argue in Chapter 3, were sown during events that occurred in Russia more than a century ago. Leninism, as originally conceived during the Bolshevik revolution, was a theory of inclusive authoritarianism—one in which a vanguard party directs mass participation in the service of shared political and economic goals. Mao, and CCP leaders since Mao, have all embraced this rhetoric, and Leninism itself is enshrined in the CCP Constitution.

Rhetoric aside, including the masses was as much a governing necessity as it was a political philosophy. As discussed in the following chapter, neither Lenin nor Mao had the expertise or the capacity to govern the people they ruled over. Nevertheless, Leninist organizational theory is well suited for inclusion. In particular, Leninism promotes a high degree of separation between party and state. According to Lenin, the state is a necessary instrument (a "superstructure") for managing social and organizational control but, in playing that role, the state can become alienated from the masses.[69] Accordingly, party separation and hegemony over the state affords it a privileged position from which to conduct oversight of the bureaucracy while maintaining close links with the grassroots.

Furthermore, socialism necessitates a broad popular base for the Party, one that absorbs and amalgamates traditional boundaries of religion, ethnicity, language, and community. In practice, this meant sending party activists down to the grassroots where they were tasked with deconstructing existing lines of social and economic organization and reconstituting them into lateral cells and vertical branches managed by the vanguard party. As history has shown, the most effective strategy for this sort of social engineering is to mobilize those who were previously dominated (i.e., minorities, workers, landless peasants) in collective violence against incumbent elites. While divide and rule tactics are a constant

---

[69] Franz Schurmann. *Ideology and Organization in Communist China.* University of California Press, 1966, pp. 109–112.

of authoritarianism, the preoccupation with grassroots mobilization and group-based organization is unique to Leninism and it, too, is enshrined in the CCP constitution.

> Every Party member, irrespective of position, must be organized into a branch, cell or other specific unit of the Party to participate in the regular activities of the Party organization and accept supervision by the masses inside and outside the Party. Leading Party cadres must attend democratic meetings held by the Party committee or leading Party members' groups. There shall be no privileged Party members who do not participate in the regular activities of the Party organization and do not accept supervision by the masses inside and outside the Party. — (2017 CCP Constitution, Chapter 1, Article 8.)

Ultimately, however, Leninist theory on organization and inclusion is firmly grounded in the pursuit of control. As Lenin himself explains, "We are not utopians, we do not dream of dispensing at once with all administration, with all subordination. These anarchist dreams, based upon incomprehension of the tasks of the proletarian dictatorship, are totally alien to Marxism, and, as a matter of fact, serve only to postpone the socialist revolution until people are different. No, we want the socialist revolution with people as they are now, with people who cannot dispense with subordination, control, and foremen and accountants."[70] Under this overarching prerogative, public participation, whether through mass campaign or more subtle forms of participatory governance, cannot be fully understood without acknowledging the contribution of public input toward the self-adapting features of authoritarian control.

Yet we are faced with the fact that an ossified Leninist Party-state ultimately collapsed in the Soviet Union. Furthermore, Gorbachev's attempts at increasing inclusion through pluralization campaigns like *glasnost*, a deliberate attempt to liberalize public discourse in the Soviet Union, seem intimately tied to the regime's implosion.[71] In many ways, the Soviet Union's failed attempt at controlled inclusion seems to exemplify why many still believe that mixing inclusion with control is unsustainable. As Huntington put it, "the halfway house does not stand" and is destined for either democratization or a return to exclusive authoritarianism.[72] Without wading too far into the debate over democratization, two points are worth underscoring. First, skeptics tend to assume that inclusion is a democratic import. In the case of Leninism, that is

---

[70] See Lenin, in *The State and Revolution*, Chapter 3.
[71] Archie Brown. *The Gorbachev Factor*. Oxford University Press, 1997.
[72] Huntington, *The Third Wave: Democratization in the Late Twentieth Century*, p. 137.

most certainly not accurate, and the collapse of the Soviet Union could just as well be attributed to a failure of control as to an increase in inclusion. Second, the pluralizing reforms enacted by Gorbachev mixed electoral and non-electoral modes of inclusion.[73] With electoral openings, it would not be long before populists within the Communist Party of the Soviet Union (CPSU), such as Boris Yeltsin, broke ranks and started organizing as independents.

The CCP has had, as I detail in Chapter 3, little to no interest in importing democratic institutions. On the contrary, nearly all methods of inclusion in contemporary China have indigenous roots. Even local village elections, which are so often elevated as prime examples of imported democracy, can be traced to Leninist methods of controlled inclusion in the pre-1949 countryside.[74] More generally, CCP leaders are careful students of Soviet history, which they see as both a model and a cautionary tale.[75] Xi Jinping, when he led the Central Party School (2007–2012), oversaw an in-depth multidisciplinary study of the Soviet Union, pinpointing its demise to a retreat from Leninism. Recognizing this mindset is thus critical for making sense of contemporary attempts at controlled inclusion in China.

On this point, retrofitting builds on the work of others who describe the post-Mao period as having retained much of its revolutionary instincts.[76] The tendency to dismiss this legacy in favor of more contemporary comparisons risks understating strategies, rituals, and organizational principles that are well-rooted in China's Leninist traditions. Though we may look back on these methods today as purely ideological and socially destructive, an earlier generation of scholars was more open to their organizational effectiveness, whether that involved basic economic progress or social transformation.[77] More importantly, as Schurmann

[73] Plans for competitive elections between CPSU and independent candidates were announced in June 1988, during the 19th National Congress of the Soviet Union.
[74] Emerson Niou. *Bean Voting: The History and Politics of Secret Ballot.* Beijing: People's University Press, 2014.
[75] Consider, for instance, Li Shenming's 2011 treatise on the collapse of the Soviet Union, which would then inspire a 4-DVD box-set and a proliferation of online media preceding the 2012 leadership turnover: Shenming Li. *Preparing for Danger in Times of Safety: Recollections on the 20-Year Anniversary of the Collapse of the Russian Communist Party* (居安思危:苏共亡党二十年的思考, *Ju an siwei: Sulian wang dang ershi nian de sikao*). Chinese Academy of Social Sciences Press, 2011.
[76] Perry, "From Mass Campaigns to Managed Campaigns: Constructing a 'New Socialist Countryside'"; Daniel Koss. *Where the Party Rules: The Rank and File of China's Communist State.* Cambridge University Press, 2018.
[77] Charles P. Cell. *Revolution at Work: Mobilization Campaigns in China.* Academic Press New York, 1977; Gordon A Bennett. *Yundong: Mass Campaigns in Chinese Communist Leadership.* Center for Chinese Studies, University of California Berkeley, 1976.

observed, the CCP is capable of using public input to move beyond coercion to "more sophisticated means of control."[78]

If Leninism is the clearest vantage point from which to view contemporary China, a firmer grasp on the collapse of Leninism in the Soviet Union is all the more instructive. Examining the history of both cases suggests that, owing to the struggles of warfare and the serendipity of inheritance, social control was quantitatively and qualitatively deeper in the newly established PRC than was the case for the USSR.[79] Moreover, and rather ironically, the CCP managed to survive long enough to benefit from a telecommunications revolution that the Soviets lucidly imagined more than half a century earlier, but never got around to constructing.[80] Indeed, as I will argue repeatedly throughout this book, technology has served as a game changer for inclusion by helping leaders connect to the public more easily and thoroughly than ever before. That the regime is leveraging this capacity to simultaneously increase participation and augment control is not surprising—it represents a concerted effort the retrofitting Leninism for the twenty-first century.

This resonance between past and present also leads to the word choice of "retrofitting" featured in the title of this book. At a most basic level, retrofitting implies "the addition of new technology to older systems."[81] While this may strike the reader as overly simplistic, it is helpful to consider what retrofitting does *not* imply. In contrast to competing notions of institutional adaptation and hybridization,[82] retrofitting denotes that the underlying hardware remains unaltered. Accordingly, China's CCP-run operating system now runs stock markets, conducts scientific opinion polls, and holds public auction for procurement bids. Yet little has changed in terms of its bulky organizational structure or its steadfast commitment to one-party politics, both of which are firmly grounded in a platform for control.[83]

Contemporary Implications of the Argument

If inclusion offers autocrats a way to improve control while circumventing pressure for democratization, why have so few regimes opted for inclusion in the past, and why are we seeing an uptick in the present? We have some

---

[78] Schurmann, *Ideology and Organization in Communist China*, p. 316.

[79] These points are elaborated upon in Chapter 3.

[80] Benjamin Peters. *How Not to Network a Nation: The Uneasy History of the Soviet Internet.* MIT Press, 2016.

[81] Collins Dictionary 2019, *Harper Collins.*

[82] Steven Levitsky and Lucan Way. "The Rise of Competitive Authoritarianism." *Journal of Democracy* 13.2 (2002), pp. 51–65.

[83] This platform, by which I mean hardware plus operating system, is a critical feature of my argument. Hardware and operating systems are often mated in ways that prevent the adoption of new operating systems or certain types of hardware.

answers to the first questions. Greitens, for instance, offers a rational trade-off as explanation, arguing that authoritarian founders who perceive elite challenge as their main threat tend toward socially exclusive and fragmented authority, while only those concerned with popular unrest will prefer inclusive and better coordinated alternatives. Though this trade-off and its implications are helpful for understanding variation in coercive institutions, a broader interpretation of control that extends to governance seems less affected by it. Indeed, a regime interested in economic as well as coercive control may find it rational to embed itself within society, while at the same time fragmenting agents of authority.[84]

Moreover, we should not overlook the fact that embedding a regime within broader society is arduous, expensive, and potentially risky. It is thus no coincidence that the greatest investments in inclusive control have arguably come at hands of, as Greitens describes them, more "ambitious" and ideologically driven movements.[85] It is also not surprising that building inclusive and cohesive institutions did not occur overnight. It took time, and only within consolidated regimes. Nor can we deny that there are cultural and racial elements in play. This is perhaps why colonial-era dictatorships and more modern apartheid states, which are obvious hotbeds for popular unrest, nevertheless employed sharply exclusive, divide-and-rule tactics.

Comparatively speaking, China's brand of inclusion is a rare feature in the authoritarian landscape; only a handful of single-party, Leninist-inspired regimes employ it as a formal policymaking strategy.[86] As argued in this chapter, one explanation may be that the requisite levels of control are difficult to achieve. Another possible explanation is that consultation is only viable in certain types of authoritarian settings. In countries like North Korea, anything from bus routes to hairstyles can be linked to the central leadership.[87] In heavily personalized settings like this, allowing bottom-up input is unlikely to yield useful feedback because policy criticism is impossible to distinguish from political dissent. In most single-party regimes, by contrast, policy and politics are more easily decoupled.[88] As Geddes points out: "single-party regimes survive in part because their institutional structures make it relatively easy for them to allow greater

---

[84] This is indeed what Greitens finds when it comes to regimes inspired by "revolutionary communists."

[85] Greitens, *Dictators and Their Secret Police*, p. 304.

[86] The most prominent of these include Singapore, Vietnam, and Cuba.

[87] Adam Taylor. *Are the Men of North Korea Really Being Forced to get Kim Jong Un Haircuts?* Washington Post, March 26, 2014.

[88] Guillermo O'Donnell and Phillipe Schmitter. "Tentative Conclusions about Uncertain Democracies." In *Transitions from Authoritarian Rule: Prospects for Democracy.* Ed. by O'Donnell and Schimtter. Johns Hopkins University Press, 1986; Stathis N. Kalyvas. "The Decay and Breakdown of Communist One-Party Systems." *Annual Review of Political Science* 2.1 (1999), pp. 323–343.

participation and popular influence on policy without giving up their dominant role in the political system."[89]

This basic institutional difference may help explain why inclusive strategies for authoritarian control have been limited to a small subset of Leninist regimes. For example, prior to adopting landmark economic liberalization reforms in 2011, the Cuban regime spent over a year organizing deliberative forums for around eight million public-sector employees and has continued to do so since. Similarly, in Vietnam, major constitutional revisions in 2013 were preceded by a mass consultation campaign that yielded around 26 million comments.[90] Perhaps most adroitly, Singapore's People's Action Party (PAP) has actively leveraged participatory methods since the 1970s.[91] Though devoutly anticommunist, it should come as no surprise that the PAP was originally organized under Leninist principles.[92]

Empirical Strategy

The theoretical argument I have presented offers testable implications, but it is not a single causal narrative. As such, the empirical strategy employed throughout the rest of the book is neither structured around a specific dependent variable nor a core explanatory variable. Furthermore, the implications outlined in the hypotheses are difficult to address through a single set of cases or comparisons. Instead, the empirical approach relies on different methods and sources for triangulating particular features of the argument—as well as the mechanisms and assumptions on which it rests. Rather than addressing alternative explanations as an afterthought, they are dealt with from the outset and repeatedly as the analysis proceeds. As such, no single test or chapter embodies the complete framework as laid out in this theoretical chapter, yet each, when considered in concert, points to the core thrust of the argument: that popular inclusion in China is conducive to better governance while also complementary to control, and that these synergies are partly thanks to technology.

What is gained from this approach is a more thorough account of the final conclusions. For example, this book could have revolved around the policy stability and public opinion findings discussed in Chapters 7 and 8. Unfortunately, doing so without a critical discussion about the origins of participatory institutions that comprise the independent variables would have left a notable gap in our

---

[89] Barbara Geddes. "What Do We Know About Democratization After Twenty Years?" *Annual Review of Political Science* 2.1 (1999), pp. 115–144, p. 135.

[90] For Cuba, see Philip Peters, "A Viewer's Guide to Cuba's Economic Reform." Lexington Institute, Washington DC, 2012; for Vietnam, see Edmund Malesky, "Vietnam in 2013: Single-Party Politics in the Internet Age." Asian Survey 54.1 (2014), pp. 30–38.

[91] Rodan, *Participation Without Democracy: Containing Conflict in Southeast Asia.*

[92] Lian, "The People's Action Party, 1954–1963." *Journal of Southeast Asian History* 10.1 (1960), pp. 142–154.

interpretation of their effects. While previous attempts to study authoritarian reforms have either avoided the possibility that Chinese reforms are selectively adopted to appear successful or have tried to control for that selection problem with covariates, I deal with selection issues from a long-view historical perspective alongside dedicated research design strategies. Likewise, whereas previous efforts to measure the effect of participatory governance on outcomes have had to assume that bottom-up inputs are being translated into top-down outputs,[93] Chapters 4 and 5 are devoted to testing input mechanisms before evaluating outputs.

The data used across these chapters come from a number of primary and secondary sources. Interviews with Chinese officials and intellectuals are referenced throughout the book. Survey data on public opinion compiled under the China Policy Barometer (CPB) and an extensive field experiment provide a backdoor into the input stage of the Chinese participatory process, while I use archival data, along with legislative records, to study the mechanisms that regulate the transmission between inputs and outputs, as well as their downstream governance effects. Much of the data produced by these methods reflects recent periods, underscoring the technological upgrading taking place. When reaching further back in time, I lean heavily on existing historical studies. In all instances, data limitations and biases are discussed in detail. Where possible, I have deployed econometric solutions and adapted research design strategies. A summary of the data sources, survey instruments, and descriptive statistics are provided in the appendices. Before presenting the data and quantitative analyses that anchor my arguments however, it is necessary to understand the genesis and traditions of public participation in Chinese politics. The following chapter initiates this discussion with a historical review of public inclusion in the Chinese political system.

---

[93] Stromseth, Malesky, and Gueorguiev, *China's Governance Puzzle.*

2

Foundations of Controlled Inclusion

> It is not as though in the difficult ascent of an unexplored and
> heretofore inaccessible mountain, we were to renounce beforehand
> the idea that at times we might have to go sometimes in zig-zags,
> sometimes retracing our steps, sometimes giving up the course once
> selected and trying various others.[1]
>
> — Vladimir Ilyich Lenin, 1921

An old Chinese parable describes a young prince learning the art of leadership
from an old Taoist monk. The monk instructs the prince to enter a deep forest
and report back what he hears. It is only after countless failed attempts that the
young prince finally begins to discern the sound of the earth warming from
the sun, flowers opening and pulling water up into their roots, from the more
obvious ruckus of birds, crickets, and a blowing breeze. To hear the unheard is the
true mark of an enlightened leader, remarks the monk.[2] Such tales are common
in Chinese philosophy, and it is tempting to connect the CCP's contemporary
shift toward consultative government with traditional elements in the political
culture.[3] At the same time, a benevolent leadership frame is not at all adequate,
given the CCP's aggressive intolerance of dissident voices and ideas.

This is why most contemporary scholarship sees the rise of consultative
authoritarianism in China as a relatively recent phenomenon that borrows from
modern administrative cultures abroad, rather than from Chinese tradition at
home.[4] A contemporary focus is to some extent unavoidable. Institutionalized
participation only came into routine use during the mid-1990s and 2000s. As
a consequence, the theoretical framework underpinning recent scholarship is

---

[1] Vladimir Ilyich Lenin. *"Left-wing" Communism: An Infantile Disorder.* The Marxian Educational Society, 1921.

[2] W. Chan Kim and Renee Mauborgne. "Parables of Leadership." *Harvard Business Review* (1992), pp. 123–130.

[3] For instance, see Baogang He. "Deliberative Culture and Politics: The Persistence of Authoritarian Deliberation in China." *Political Theory* 42.1 (2014), pp. 58–81.

[4] For example, see Teets and Hurst, *Local Governance Innovation in China: Experimentation, Diffusion, and Defiance*; Steve Tsang, "Consultative Leninism: China's New Political Framework." *Journal of Contemporary China* 18.62 (2009), pp. 865–880; Stromseth, Malesky, and Gueorguiev, *China's Governance Puzzle: Enabling Transparency and Participation in a Single-Party State.*

Retrofitting Leninism. Dimitar D. Gueorguiev. Oxford University Press. © Oxford University Press 2021.
DOI: 10.1093/oso/9780197555668.003.0003

heavily influenced by Western understandings of governance and democracy. It is no coincidence that around the same time that Chinese leaders were advocating public participation and transparency, the same advice followed from Western development organizations for China's accession into the World Trade Organization (WTO).[5]

However, the instrumental fusion of popular inclusion with authoritarian control that we observe in China today seems fundamentally inconsistent with both the philosophy of benevolent leadership and the principles of liberal deliberation. Our understanding of China's contemporary methods for inclusive control will profit from further inquiry as to their origins. To that end, this chapter provides a historical perspective on the evolution of inclusive forms of control in China.

A proper accounting of culture and history would require far more length and expertise than this book or its author are able to contribute. Instead, I lean on the shoulders of more reliable sources, adapting their insights to help make sense of my own. The classic studies of Franz Schurmann and Martin Whyte stand out, as do the more recent accounts by Chinese scholars such as He Baogang and Gao Hua. What follows is my attempt at navigating participatory methods of the past as a prelude to exploring how they operate in the present. The principal conclusion of this effort is that the proper foundation for inclusion in contemporary China is situated not in tradition nor in Western models, but rather in communist revolutions that raged in the early twentieth century.

Historical Roots

Even with secondary sources as a guide, it is impossible to offer a single starting point for inclusive governance in Chinese political thought. This is partly due to China's uniquely long history. In his rendition of China's deliberative culture, for instance, He Baogang contends that consultative and deliberative traditions in China date back thousands of years.[6] By contrast, John Fairbank, in his comparative review of early Chinese political institutions, questions whether any sort of meaningful public participation existed prior to the 1911 revolution. Another challenge is that China's contemporary approach to inclusion is steeped in dialectical contradiction. As discussed in the Introduction, there is the soft

---

[5] Jamie P. Horsley. "Public Participation in the People's Republic: Developing a More Participatory Governance Model in China." *Yale China Law Center* September (2009), pp. 1–19.

[6] As an example, He Baogang cites the story of Emperor Yao (2356–2255 BCE), who allegedly relinquished his throne after consultations with his feudal lords. See: He, "Deliberative Culture and Politics: The Persistence of Authoritarian Deliberation in China" *Political Theory* 42.1 (2014), pp. 58–81.

version of consultation, which carries an unavoidable affinity to Western notions of deliberative democracy; and there is also the hard version, which bears the hallmarks of control so valued by Lenin and Stalin.[7] Likewise, there are contradictions within the cultural, organizational, and rhetorical dimensions of Chinese participatory institutions. Culturally speaking, Confucian traditions for consultation, discussed further below, clash with communist rituals for criticism. Organizationally, delegation facilitates decentralization, yet the overarching goal of the Party has always been and continues to be that of greater centralization. Rhetorically, popular will enjoys ideological primacy in China but is rarely given anything but the lowest priority in practice. It is only when we consider how these competing notions work in tandem that we can gain something of a conceptual footing.

The soft version of China's consultative model is most naturally situated within China's Confucian tradition. As He Baogang and others point out,[8] the Confucian ideal of *minben* (people-centric) demands that wise leaders are attentive and receptive to the needs and interests of the people. Likewise, the Chinese practice of *jian* (remonstration), a form of official deliberation, was present at the provincial level, as early as the Eastern Zhou period (770–256 BCE).[9] By the Tang Dynasty (618–907) official remonstrators were regularly dispatched to admonish the emperor.[10] Such institutions, however, were never intended to be democratic. That is, while traditional versions of consultation emphasized the value of constructive criticism, they did not support opposition to an unjust ruler. Instead, their function was to better equip the emperor with the insight and awareness to more effectively exercise his authority and control over society.

This is not to say that resistance and revolution are not rooted in Chinese political culture; just that such ideas were foreign to the regime-sustaining functions of consultation in imperial Chinese rule. Instead, a ruler's right to rule was a function of "mandate," chosen not by the people, but by heaven.[11] While this may seem highly dogmatic, the mandate can also be interpreted as a pragmatic function of military, administrative, and political prerogative,

[7] See Introduction, p. 6.
[8] See Tianjian Shi and Jie Lu. "The Meanings of Democracy: The Shadow of Confucianism." *Journal of Democracy* 21.4 (2010), pp. 123–130 and Viren Murthy. "The Democratic Potential of Confucian Minben Thought." *Asian Philosophy* 10.1 (2000), pp. 33–47.
[9] David Schaberg. "Playing at Critique: Indirect Remonstrance and the Formation of Shi Identity." In *Text and Ritual in Early China*. Ed. by Martin Kern. University of Washington Press, 2005, pp. 194–218.
[10] Hu Baohua. *A Study of the Supervising System under the Tang Dynasty* (唐代監察制度研究). Beijing: Shangwu Publishers, 2005, pp. 208–209.
[11] Elizabeth J. Perry. "Challenging the Mandate of Heaven: Popular Protest in Modern China." *Critical Asian Studies* 33.2 (2001), pp. 163–180.

judged plainly by the emperor's ability to maintain harmony in nature and society. Consequently, periods defined by good harvests and prosperity only confirmed that the emperor enjoyed the confidence of heaven. Likewise, periods of famine and conflict were evidence to the contrary. The place for consultation and criticism in this arrangement was thus in the service of the emperor fulfilling his mandate.

Moreover, China's consultative legacy did not extend to the general public. Instead, the traditional Chinese system, and its administrative capacity, ended at the county level, at which point local magistrates were delegated the responsibility of collecting taxes, conducting trade, and enforcing law and order.[12] In practice, each of these functions were further outsourced to local leaders at the village level, who were hierarchically accountable to county magistrates but had almost no formal links with the central leadership.[13] According to Townsend, most local leaders (baochang) under the traditional household administrative system (baojia),[14] were either clan elders or retired scholars, owing their positions to traditional or meritocratic authority, but not in any way "selected" by local citizens.

In the absence of institutional linkage between the state and society, grassroots social organization in traditional China rarely penetrated above the local village. When it did, it usually came in the form of guilds or secret societies,[15] neither of which conform to what scholars today would describe as civil society.[16] Guilds, despite clear professional motives, for the most part did not interface with the political state, operating instead as autonomous entities that were more than happy to avoid the bureaucracy.[17] For their part, secret societies, including the republican movement that eventually toppled the Qing dynasty, were by necessity informal and fragmented. The absence of such organizations means there was arguably little that the emperor needed to control beyond the loyalty and agency of the local bosses who dominated the localities. Such a system is efficient and can prove highly stable until, of course, it is on the brink of collapse as it was during various peasant rebellions that erupted in traditional China.

In short, while there is ample record to support the idea that administration in traditional China was decentralized and that central authorities consulted

[12] Denis Crispin Twitchett. "Provincial Autonomy and Central Finance in Late T'ang." *Asia Major* 11.2 (1965), pp. 211–232.

[13] L.T. Hobson. "Preface." In *Village and Town Life in China*. Ed. by Y.K. Leong and L.K. Tao. London: George Allen & Unwin, 1915, p. 14.

[14] First established under the Song (960–1279).

[15] Joseph Fewsmith. *Party, State, and Local Elites in Republican China: Merchant Organizations and Politics in Shanghai, 1890–1930.* University of Hawaii Press, 1985, p. 275.

[16] Robert Putnam. "Bowling Alone: America's Declining Social Capital." *Journal of Democracy* 6.1 (1995), pp. 65–78.

[17] John Stewart Burgess. *The Guilds of Peking.* Beijing (China): Columbia University Press, 1928.

with mid-level magistrates, the multiple layers of delegation suggest that contact with the general population, either representative or direct, was marginal at best. As such, traditional China does not provide us with an obvious legacy from which to explain the depth and breadth of social embeddedness exercised by the CCP in contemporary China. To borrow a management metaphor, the organizational basis for consultation in traditional China resembled that of a monopolistic franchise rather than an embedded corporation. The average emperor neither knew nor cared what the ordinary citizen thought or did. As Schurmann summarizes, "[D]uring most of Chinese history the state let society govern itself."[18]

Things did change with the dawn of Republican China in 1912, if for no other reason than that China's new leaders were eager to differentiate from the Qing rulers they had usurped.[19] Unfortunately, while the basis of rule had shifted from empire to republic, the system for governing China remained largely intact. According to Townsend, the Guomindang (GMD) did not invest in civil society beyond what was politically expedient.[20] Even Sun Yat-sen, father of the Chinese Republic, depicted the role of the public individual as an accessory to the pursuit of the nation: ". . . on no account must we give more liberty to the individual; let us secure liberty for the nation."[21] Indeed, there are hardly any examples of direct public participation during the GMD's rule (1928–1949). The closest opportunity came in the 1936–37 elections for a National Assembly that would eventually draft and adopt a constitution. For a variety of reasons, including Japanese military offensives, this election was never completed.

The arenas in which the GMD did invest in inclusive institutions tended to be heavily politicized and ultimately were too little too late. For instance, the GMD established the San-Min Chu Youth Corps (named for the *Sanmin zhuyi*, Sun Yat-sen's Three Principles of the People) in July of 1938, but only as a vehicle for political recruitment, not as a broader social organization.[22] For their part, the Communists had a Socialist Youth League in place as early as October of 1920, nearly a year before the CCP was officially inaugurated in July of 1921.[23] Such parallels are many, but not in the least surprising.[24] Both the

---

[18] Schurmann, *Ideology and Organization in Communist China*, p. 407.

[19] Ssu-yu Teng and John King Fairbank. *China's Response to the West: A Documentary Survey, 1839–1923.* Harvard University Press, 1954.

[20] Roger James Townsend. *Political Participation in Communist China.* University of California Press, 1969.

[21] Sun Yat-sen, *San Min Chu I/The Three Principles of the People.* Translated by Frank W. Price. Commercial Press, Shanghai, 1928, pp. 178–181.

[22] Png Poh Seng. "The Kuomintang in Malaya, 1912–1941." *Journal of Southeast Asian History* 2.1 (1961), pp. 1–32.

[23] Paul Myron Anthony Linebarger. *The China of Chiang K'ai-shek.* Boston: World Peace Foundation, 1943.

[24] C. Martin Wilbur. *The Nationalist Revolution in China, 1923–1928.* Cambridge University Press, 1984, pp. 24–26.

GMD and CCP were responding to and borrowing from examples laid out by the Bolsheviks in the Soviet Union. Indeed, it was Comintern operatives, such as Mikhail Borodin, who convinced the GMD to work with the Communists to set up a Unity Congress, and to court workers by organizing labor unions.[25] Although the GMD made some progress in forging links with civil society, as the incumbent political organization it was not under pressure to integrate these links into governance, industrial policy, or the political culture more generally.[26]

As a result, the GMD's connections with the local population were mercurial and unreliable. When Japanese forces receded toward the end of WWII, and Communists began pouring in through the countryside, the GMD was unable to muster grassroots resistance through these organizations. By contrast, disciplined PLA fighters, backed by a well-oiled Communist propaganda machine and vague promises of land reform, allowed the CCP not only to take territory but also to swell its ranks as it moved from the barren northwest back into China's heartland. As Deng Xiaoping reported in 1949,

> We had worked only in some of the guerrilla areas, yet all the people supported us, digging half the ditches, for example . . . They gave us every bit of grain they could spare, saying it did not matter if they suffered from hunger so long as they could help us. To help us solve the problem of firewood, people even pulled down their houses without hesitation and gave us the wood. The people also undertook other arduous tasks for the campaign, including repairing roads and transporting grain. Underground Party members and fighters also helped us in the battle.[27]

Even in places where the Communists were unpopular, peasants and workers simply had no real stake in defending the GMD.[28] When the PLA assembled around Shanghai, China's capitalist center at the time and the last GMD stronghold, Chiang Kai-Shek mobilized residents to defend the city, promising a bitter battle to the death. But when soldiers entered the main city a few weeks later, the PLA found little resistance.[29]

---

[25] Jonathan D. Spence. *The Search for Modern China*. W.W. Norton, 1990, pp. 337–360.

[26] Jen Ch'o-Hsüan. "The Introduction of Marxism-Leninism into China." *Studies in East European Thought* 10.2 (1970), pp. 138–166.

[27] Deng, Xiaoping, 1949, "From the Crossing of the Yangtze to the Capture of Shanghai," First part of a report delivered to delegates of the Preparatory Committee of the New Political Consultative Conference, August 4, 1949.

[28] Townsend, *Political Participation in Communist China*.

[29] Sam Tata and Ian McLachlan. *Shanghai 1949: The End of an Era*. Deneau Publishers, 1990.

Political Legacies

As with any successful revolution, military victory simply marked the beginning of an even greater obstacle: uniting a divided country and rebuilding a fractured state. So it was for Mao and his colleagues as they inaugurated the PRC in October of 1949. They were now in charge of a vast country which, though teeming with potential, had lacked a functioning administrative system for nearly half a century. For the revolutionaries, the new challenge of administration necessitated cooperation from elites and experts.[30] Likewise, limited bureaucratic capacity meant that peasants, workers, and students would need to partake in and implement some functions of the state.[31]

These necessities also presented risks for the Party. Over reliance on experts could lead to bureaucratization. Coopting elites was expedient, but it risked cultivating counterrevolutionary undercurrents. Opportunistic as it was, mobilizing the masses also threatened to relegate the Party's command to a blind *tailism* of popular passions.[32] To make matters more complicated, the Party's ranks swelled with the end of the civil war, from just over one million in 1945 to over five million by 1950, including many of questionable allegiance.[33] In combination, these risks amounted to a loss of control from both outside and from within the Party. To appreciate how the CCP approached competing demands for control alongside mass mobilization requires a brief segue to the Soviet Union, where a similar set of challenges had already run their course.

The Soviet Experience

As laid out in Chapter 2, the Chinese party-state borrows heavily from Lenin's vision for the Soviet Union. According to Lenin, the state is a "superstructure" for containing the interest groups and contests that give life to political struggle.[34] Nevertheless, in its function as a superstructure, the state could become alienated from the masses, and although the Party leads the state, such alienation could prove fatal for both. Importantly, the Party commands oversight powers and ideological primacy over the state. Moreover, delegation of responsibility to the state absolves the Party from the complexity of administration, which in

---

[30] Richard D. Baum. "'Red and Expert': The Politico-Ideological Foundations of China's Great Leap Forward." *Asian Survey* (1964), pp. 1048–1057.
[31] Marc Blecher. "Consensual Politics in Rural Chinese Communities: The Mass Line in Theory and Practice." *Modern China* 5.1 (1979), pp. 105–126; Harry Harding. "Maoist Theories of Policy-Making and Organization." In *The Cultural Revolution in China*. Ed. by Thomas Robinson. University of California Press, 1971, pp. 130–134.
[32] H. Arthur Steiner. "Current 'Mass line' Tactics in Communist China." *American Political Science Review* 45.2 (1951), pp. 422–436.
[33] Figures taken from the *People's Daily*.
[34] Schurmann, *Ideology and Organization in Communist China*, pp. 109–112.

turn offers it flexibility in issuing executive guidance and insulation from policy failures.

As would be the case in China, there was a clear tension here between the desire for centralized control and delegation. A purely top-down approach left the Party vulnerable to corruption and criticism, while too much delegation risked losing control over the bureaucracy. As argued in the previous chapter, the masses serve as an intermediary in resolving this tension by providing the Party the bottom-up feedback it needs to control a decentralized and fragmented governing apparatus. What makes Leninism unique, however, is the totality of control. That is, Leninism stipulates not only that mass participation facilitates Party control, but that the masses themselves must be controlled. The product of such demands comes in the form of multiple and overlapping control agencies, all of which are embedded within the communities and organizations they are intended to manage.

No sooner had the Bolsheviks taken Saint Petersburg in October of 1917 than Lenin inaugurated three separate control agencies. The *Cheka* (All-Russian Extraordinary Commission) was established "on the second day of the revolution," to investigate and prosecute counterrevolutionaries, saboteurs, and smugglers—particularly within the Bolshevik ranks.[35] Soon thereafter, the *Rabkrin* (Workers' and Peasants' Inspectorate), an oversight body composed mainly of workers and peasants, was created to provide "control from below" over the civil service and factory managers.[36] At the same time, a Central Control Commission (*Tsentral'naia Kontrol'naia Komissiia*) (TsKK) was established within the Communist Party but independent from the Party Central Committee.[37] Together, these institutions exercised a violent control over the Russian people and their nascent government. As documented by Kotkin, the first year of the Soviet Republic would see more political executions than Tsarist Russia had in over a century.[38]

Lenin's violent control apparatus, however, was taken to an even greater extreme under Stalin, who quickly repurposed it for political struggle. Very early on, the Rabkrin and the TsKK were coopted by Stalin as tools for going after critics within the Party; namely, Trotskyists and other leftist opposition groups.[39] Once Stalin had taken over the party leadership, representatives from

[35] Sidney Monas. "The Political Police: The Dream of a Beautiful Autocracy." In *Transformation of Russian Society: Aspects of Social Change Since 1861*. Ed. by Cyril Black. Harvard University Press, pp. 164–190.

[36] Isaac Deutscher. *Stalin: A Political Biography*. Oxford University Press, 1967, pp. 230–231.

[37] For instance, no one could hold concurrent membership in the central committee and TsKK. Moreover, TsKK was given independent authority to investigate and prosecute any party member, regardless of rank. This overarching authority is similar to the National Supervision Commission established by the PRC in 2018.

[38] Stephen Kotkin. *Stalin: Paradoxes of Power 1878–1928*. Penguin Books, 2014, p. 287.

[39] J. Arch Getty. "Pragmatists and Puritans. The Rise and Fall of the Party Control Commission." *The Carl Beck Papers in Russian and East European Studies* 1208 (1997), p. 47.

TsKK would sit in conference together with the Central Committee, laying bare any pretense that these bodies were independent.[40] In 1934, the TsKK and the Rabkrin were merged and reconstituted as the *Komitet Partiynogo Kontrolya* (KPK), a control body directly under the authority of the Central Committee, which by this time was dominated by Stalin. In effect, the Soviet's premier control organ was placed in the hands of one person, Stalin himself.[41]

While Stalin's political incentives were a key factor in the reorganization, his dominance over the Party and the central control organs had already been cemented by the early 1930s. As such, further concentration and centralization was as much an indication of Stalin's political ambition as it was a response to apparent failures in organizational control, especially in the regions where neither bottom-up participation nor top-down command appeared to be working.[42] Indeed, placing appointment power for the regional KPK within the Central Committee was seen by some observers as a last-ditch attempt at forcing compliance over regional party leaders who continued to stand in the way of central prerogatives.[43] Despite this intense centralization of control, the KPK proved ineffective at reining in the bureaucracy and errant regional leaders. Ultimately, Stalin would rely on secret police, the National Internal Affairs Commission (*Narodnyy Komissariat Vnutrennikh Del*), in prosecuting the Great Purge (1936–1938).[44]

It is hard to point to any one reason why Stalin turned away from inclusive control. Certainly, state-building in the midst of obstruction and foot-dragging from the regions played a role.[45] So did Stalin's penchant for personal control. Yet there were more practical concerns as well. In particular, the Soviet infrastructure had a hard time harvesting and processing bottom-up inputs into actionable information.[46] By the 1930s, for instance, public complaint bureaus, established as a check on the bureaucracy, were inundated with thousands of disparate letters each day.[47] In an attempt to resolve the information overflow, control units stopped detailing cases and employed a card catalog system that mostly summarized the easily accessible attributes of the sender for future follow-up.[48]

---

[40]   Leonard Schapiro. "'Putting the Lid on Leninism': Opposition and Dissent in the Communist One-party States." *Government and Opposition* 2.2 (1967), pp. 181–203.

[41]   Mark Neuweld. "The Origin of the Communist Control Commission." *American Slavic and East European Review* 18.3 (1959), pp. 315–333.

[42]   Getty, "Pragmatists and Puritans. The Rise and Fall of the Party Control Commission," p. 5.

[43]   David R. Shearer. *Policing Stalin's Socialism: Repression and Social Order in the Soviet Union, 1924–1953.* Yale University Press, 2014.

[44]   Getty, "Pragmatists and Puritans. The Rise and Fall of the Party Control Commission."

[45]   Ibid.

[46]   Shearer, *Policing Stalin's Socialism*, pp. 158–170.

[47]   Sheila Fitzpatrick, "Supplicants and Citizens: Public Letter-Writing in Soviet Russia in the 1930s." *Slavic Review* 55.01 (1996), pp. 78–105, p. 80.

[48]   Shearer, *Policing Stalin's Socialism*, pp. 158–170.

Internal reports suggest that nearly half of all the cards were never processed. Of those that were, department heads had little grasp of the statistics they generated.[49] In short, the complexity of input-driven control in the Soviet Union evaded the capacity of the humans running the system.

The Chinese Experience

When the CCP took power in 1949, it relied heavily on Soviet guidance and assistance.[50] The Chinese communists adopted work methods from their Soviet advisors that emphasized "one-man" responsibility, meaning managers and workers were individually and hierarchically accountable for specific work stations, tools, and tasks.[51] For recently empowered but still inexperienced workers, this kind of responsibility led to frustration, and further resentment as tasks naturally shifted to those who were more capable. For equally inexperienced grassroots cadres, indirect reliance on foreign experts led to similar frustrations.[52] For Party leaders, these tensions reflected a broader delegation problem, whereby the foremost representatives of the new party-state were undercutting its legitimacy. Reports of bureaucratic incompetence, misuse, and outright violence by CCP officials against "workers, peasants, soldiers, and cadres" were widespread,[53] and the need to reassert control was paramount.

Here, the parallels with the Soviet Union are clear. In addition to setting up parallel committees for state and Party control—the State People's Supervisory Commission (PSC) (*Zhengwuyuan renmin jiancha weiyuanhui*) and the Central Party Disciplinary Inspection Commission (CDIC) (*Zhongyong jilu jiancha weiyuanhui*)—the CCP established a political secretariat under the General Office to handle citizen complaints directed to Mao and other members of the Central Party Committee.[54] Moreover, both the PSC and the CDIC recruited "correspondents" from the masses and "informants" from within the bureaucracy for the express purpose of "observing the operations of the offices and the behavior of officials;" and collecting "opinions from the masses" on policy, laws, and operations; and "propagandiz[ing] the functions of control."[55] According to Schurmann's estimates, there were over 26,000 People's Control Correspondents

---

[49] Ibid., pp. 171–173.

[50] Under the *Sino-Soviet Treaty of Friendship Alliance and Mutual Aid*, Soviet experts and technicians were dispatched to China, especially Manchuria, where they would take the lead in infrastructure and industrial projects.

[51] David Granick. *The Red Executive*. MacMillan & Co., 1960.

[52] Schurmann, *Ideology and Organization in Communist China*, pp. 263–281.

[53] Control Commission Report published in *People's Daily*, June 13, 1950. Cited in ibid., p. 315.

[54] Prior to 1949, the PSC and CDIC existed under a common entity referred to as the Central Control Commission (*Zhongyang jiancha weiyuanhui*).

[55] Summary report published in the *People's Daily*, September 11, 1951. Cited in Schurmann, *Ideology and Organization in Communist China*, p. 317.

on official ledgers, with presumably many more operating on a part-time or informal basis.[56]

Alongside these formal recruitment efforts, the Government Administrative Council (*Zhengfu zhengyuan*)[57] issued a directive requiring the creation of "letters and visits" (*xinfang*) offices[58] across the administrative bureaucracy down to the county level. Like their Soviet counterparts, these offices were tasked with receiving, documenting, and processing citizen opinions, questions, accusations, and demands.[59] To facilitate this function, national newspapers carried editorials encouraging citizens to participate by publishing select examples of complaints and denouncements of corrupt officials.

As was the case in the Soviet Union, however, China's primary control bodies were not particularly effective. As early as 1950, PSC reports revealed that control capacity was limited: "There are not enough cadres; experience is lacking."[60] The PSC was ultimately abolished in 1959. Likewise, the CDIC was heavily criticized in the 1950s and then thoroughly restructured in 1955. These changes were in part a reflection of a general movement away from parallel structures and toward Party centralization. In effect, however, these changes were undermining the basic principles of controlled inclusion by placing Party committee secretaries, who held strong influence over control committees at the corresponding level, in charge of controlling themselves.[61] Some in the leadership recognized these contradictions, and although attempts were made to diversify the control hierarchy, there were not enough resources or professional staff to sustain the control system independent of the existing Party offices.[62]

With the Cultural Revolution underway, most informants and correspondents working with the security services were disbanded by 1967, with some denounced in public.[63] By 1969, even the CDIC, the last remaining control organ, was disbanded. The collapse of the control system in the PRC, as in the Soviet Union, reflected a range of technical and political challenges. Yet, the sequencing

---

[56] Ibid., p. 324.

[57] 政府政院, currently referred to as the State Council (*Guowuyuan*) (国务院).

[58] Various CCP offices collected citizen complaints and petitions prior to 1949, but the system was not institutionalized as a state capacity until 1951.

[59] *Zhengwu yuan guanyu chuli renmin laixin he jiejian renmin gongzuo de jueding.* (Decision of the General Administration Council on the Work of Handling Letters and Visits From the People), June 7, 1951.

[60] PSC report, referenced in the *People's Daily*, June 13, 1950, cited in Schurmann, *Ideology and Organization in Communist China*, p. 315.

[61] Graham Young. "Control and Style: Discipline Inspection Commissions Since the 11th Congress." *The China Quarterly* 97 (1984), pp. 24–52.

[62] Research Office of the Organization Department of the CCP Central Committee (CCOM), *Dangde zuzhi gongzuo wenda* (Questions and Answers on Party Organization Work). Beijing: Renmin chubanshe, 1965, pp. 11–12.

[63] Michael Schoenhals. *Spying for the People: Mao's Secret Agents, 1949–1967.* Cambridge University Press, 2013, p. 3.

and transition from revolution to state-building in the two cases followed distinct paths. Moreover, as I discuss below, Mao's rise to power and his interpretation of governance was notably different from that of both Lenin and Stalin. As a result, the Chinese case generated its own set of challenges and attempts at resolution. These differences offer additional insight into why Leninist control, though faltering in both cases, would ultimately make a comeback in the PRC but not in the Soviet Union.

Maoist Characteristics

After a quarter-century of civil war, the Chinese population and the CCP's rank-and-file were arguably more professional and more experienced in political control by 1949 than was the case for the Bolsheviks in 1917. Likewise, and also as a byproduct of war and struggle, the CCP was arguably better prepared to mobilize the citizenry and harness public input in the service of control. War and pressure from the GMD provided the CCP motive and opportunity for grassroots mobilization with the general population—a core element of Leninism that was comparatively under-incentivized and thus undervalued in Stalinist Russia.

Moreover, the basis for mass mobilization and its political necessity was never clarified by Lenin and was thus subject to interpretation by Mao. For Lenin, the Party, as a vanguard institution, had a paternalistic responsibility to serve the public interest. Mass participation, however, played no explicit role in determining how the public interest would ultimately be defined. For Mao, by contrast, the "raw data," from which the public interest would coalesce, had to come from the public as its source. In other words, even though both men agreed that the Party was ultimately empowered to perceive, propagate, and pursue the public interest, they disagreed on the practical dimensions of how the public interest was to be formulated.[64] Specifically, Mao's dogged commitment to mass inclusion in all aspects of governance sits at the heart of his so-called "mass line" doctrine.[65] In making this observation it is important not to overstate Mao's faith in the masses. As Young and others have pointed out, Mao, even as he elevated

---

[64] Phyllis M. Frakt. "Mao's Concept of Representation." *American Journal of Political Science* (1979), pp. 684–704.

[65] There are no formal definitions of the mass line, and I refer to the concept loosely as a theory of leadership that demands the meticulous involvement of those being led. At its best, such a system reflects the ideals of political representation and responsiveness. At its worst, the mass line amounts to forced complicity in tyranny. For further discussion, see Mitch Meisner. "Dazhai: The Mass Line in Practice." *Modern China* 4.1 (1978), pp. 27–62; Frakt, "Mao's Concept of Representation"; Graham Young. "On the Mass Line." *Modern China* 6.2 (1980), pp. 225–240.

the role of the people, nevertheless assumed that mass criticism and struggle would invariably arrive at the wisdom of Mao Zedong Thought.[66]

Rhetoric aside, Mao's preoccupation with the masses served a more practical purpose. As Martin Whyte explains, a revolutionary organization bent on social control can try to coopt indigenous cleavages and groupings that permeate a society, including family, neighborhood, clan, work unit, and interest-based groups.[67] Alternatively, it can try to bypass these primary groupings, targeting and "atomizing" individuals instead. Further still, a particularly earnest regime can try to penetrate and control society by creating new primary groups that bind individuals together.[68] According to Whyte, the most distinctive quality of Mao's political philosophy was his ardent commitment to this latter, most ambitious strategy, and its principal vehicle has been the creation of small groups (xiaozu) and mass organizations (qunzhong zuzhi) that permeate society and weave the Chinese people into the party-state features that I earlier referred to as "integrated control." In both Jiangxi and Yan'an, two of the CCP's early strongholds, party activists were expressly tasked with reconstructing the social fabric of local villages, including the creation of new groups for women, youth, farmers, intellectuals, physicians, and so on.

Infiltrating society was no simple task. It involved sending thousands of CCP cadres to live within the local communities for extended periods of time. These "public servants" thus became involved in the daily lives of the local community, organizing agricultural cooperatives, setting up schools and hospitals, and organizing political study sessions.[69] Mao was also keen on gauging the public mood and probing local conditions. In Jiangxi, Hunan, and later in Yan'an, Mao oversaw dozens of village surveys and participated in frequent "representative" investigations (dianxing diaocha).[70] Mao's stratagem for mass participation also placed a special importance on criticism.[71] As was the case with Lenin, Mao believed that the wisdom of his own views, and by extension that of the Party's, would persevere through public debates. Thus public criticism meetings were

[66] Young, "On the Mass Line"; Harry Harding. "Maoist Theories of Policy-Making and Organization." In The Cultural Revolution in China (1971), pp. 130–134.

[67] In the Jiangxi Soviet, for instance, many party branches were effectively clan-based, and party conferences thus resembled clan meetings.

[68] Martin King Whyte. Small Groups and Political Rituals in China. University of California Press, 1975, p. 10.

[69] Gao Hua. Hong taiyang shi zenyang shengqi de–Yan'an zhengfeng yundong de lailong qumai. (How the Red Sun Rose). Chinese University of Hong Kong Press, 2000.

[70] Patricia Thornton. "Retrofitting the Steel Frame: From Mobilizing the Masses to Surveying the Public." Mao's Invisible Hand: The Political Foundations of Adaptive Governance in China. Harvard University Council on Asian Studies, 2011, Chap. 8, pp. 237–268.

[71] Ilpyong J. Kim et al. The Politics of Chinese Communism: Kiangsi under the Soviets. Vol. 12. University of California Press, 1973; Mark Selden. China in Revolution: Yenan Way Revisited. Routledge, 2016.

staged throughout the countryside, mainly targeting local elites and intellectuals but also Party members and their policy preferences.

These tactics would prove quite popular and helpful in dealing with Mao's principal strategic weakness: a lack of manpower. By 1938, for instance, the CCP was severely depleted, with less than 30,000 members, most of whom were soldiers. By allowing critical discourse, Mao and his head of personnel, Chen Yun, hoped to encourage new recruits, especially among intellectuals who were otherwise dispirited by the more martial GMD.[72] By and large the strategy worked; by the early 1940s Yan'an had transformed into a "college town," replete with arts, music, and even a burgeoning sex culture.[73] Mass criticism tactics also served Mao's individual political interests. As Gao Hua explains, Mao was bitter about operating in the shadow of the Soviet Union, and resented other CCP leaders who had closer connections with Moscow. Encouraging criticism of the Party and its Soviet dogmatism would prove an effective strategy for undermining his colleagues, and was no doubt cathartic. The strategy was to draw out enemies, especially those in high places, and then organize mass criticism against them, using their own words. Yet, even when it came to political hit jobs, Mao, unlike Stalin, always managed to conduct them in broad daylight, with the masses complicit in the act through their presence. Where Stalin delivered millions to the Gulag, Mao sent them to the public square.

More importantly, Mao sought to leverage public participation in political campaigns in order to undercut existing bonds of trust and community. Land reform campaigns offer a dark illustration of this logic. First, CCP scouts would enter the villages to survey the food stocks and identify the poorest and most downtrodden members of the community. Soon thereafter Party activists would arrive and organize "speak bitterness" events, pitting the poor against the middle- and upper-class residents. Observers in the audience would be encouraged to participate and offer more accusations against the targeted members. Future targets also would be encouraged to attend the meetings, as a preview of what to expect. At the end of such sessions, the victims of abuse were often stoned or knifed to death. According to recent estimates, more than two million "landlords" and up to three million others were killed as a result of these campaigns.[74]

While the rhetoric around these campaigns was steeped in egalitarian propaganda and agrarian revolution, the truth was that Chinese land plots were already

---

[72] Hua, *How the Red Sun Rose*, p. 483.

[73] Hua, *Hong taiyang shi zenyang shengqi de–Yan'an zhengfeng yundong de lailong qumai*, p. 222.

[74] Frank Dikotter. *The Tragedy of Liberation: A History of the Chinese Revolution 1945–1957.* Bloomsbury Publishing USA, 2015.

quite small, and making them smaller would only undermine productivity.[75] Indeed, what China needed was a way to consolidate land plots, so as to profit from mechanization. The CCP, of course, envisioned consolidation in terms of collectivization, which would come soon enough. The violence of land reform arguably served a different, political purpose. As described in a 1930s CCP handbook, internecine carnage served to "make the peasant participate in mob violence so as to brand him forever as a Mao Tsetung man."[76]

The challenge for Mao and the CCP was that Chinese society at the time was not sharply variegated across classes. Radicalization under the land reform campaigns provided a pretense to uproot the people psychologically and instill a new understanding of group and standing in a socialist society. The brilliance of the strategy is that it was implemented by the peasants themselves, who were ultimately the ones to determine who qualified as a "bad class." Specifically, the formal process of assigning class through "democratic estimation" was to first have the individual self-report their appropriate class, then, after public discussion, have the village meeting make the decision.[77] This had less to do with social justice, in effect, than with fracturing communities and dividing society. Indeed, even after land reforms had concluded and class-leveling had eliminated much of the meaning behind class labels, they were retained for their instrumental use in atomizing the public and maintaining an enemy class.[78]

Though brutal and calculating, these efforts, Schurmann explains, helped the CCP achieve what no other state had accomplished: to "create an organization loyal to the state which was also solidly embedded in the natural village."[79] By 1949, the foundation for social control was thus firmly rooted in rural China, with "informants" and "correspondents" deployed in the cities and factories.[80] More than that, the CCP was handed a gift by the retreating GMD: millions of population cards (renkou kapian), remnants of the traditional baojia system but updated, curated, and catalogued by GMD public security. Using this information, the CCP quickly established a household registration system (hukou), which it used to further compartmentalize and control the urban masses.[81]

---

[75] Contemporary surveys showed almost all of China's land plots were family farms, 80 percent of which were already too small to be economically viable. See J. Lossing Buck. "Fact and Theory about China's Land." Foreign Affairs 28 (1949), p. 92.

[76] Li Shi-nung, "The Bourgeoisie and Peasantry as Reserves of the Chinese Communist Party," 1950. Cited in C.M. Chang, "Mao's Stratagem of Land Reform." Foreign Affairs 29.4 (1951), pp. 550–563.

[77] Jonathan Unger. "The Class System in Rural China: A Case Study." Class and Social Stratification in Post-revolution China (1984), pp. 121–141.

[78] Richard Curt Kraus. "Class Conflict and the Vocabulary of Social Analysis in China." The China Quarterly 69 (1977), pp. 54–74.

[79] Schurmann, Ideology and Organization in Communist China, p. 416.

[80] Schoenhals, Spying for the People: Mao's Secret Agents, 1949–1967.

[81] Fei-Ling Wang. Organizing through Division and Exclusion: China's Hukou System. Stanford University Press, 2005.

Even with the benefit of this trove of information, as well as the demands and opportunity to refine mass mobilization through war and political struggle, China's control institutions remained largely ineffective in generating the type of information officials needed for planning and administrative oversight. As in the Soviet Union, this failure was precipitated by the gradual encroachment by the Party into the control system. Yet, the inability of control organs to incorporate bottom-up inputs into governing wisdom was also a function of capacity as well. Mao's mass-line tactics had proven effective and manageable in Yan'an, but the whole of mainland China was arguably too large and too complex for the CCP to fully grasp. As a result, the CCP was forced to target its control functions within urban centers and production corps,[82] and toward specific population groups (*zhongdian renkou*),[83] with little insight into the general public, especially in rural areas.

While specialization, in conjunction with further investment, might have helped to improve capacity in key aspects of planning and oversight, Mao interpreted the setbacks in control functions as evidence of insufficient mass participation.[84] Accordingly, his push for grassroots mobilization and a new Party constitution only further decentralized the administrative system and opened it up to mass criticism.[85] Yet, by strengthening bottom-up pressure while weakening the bureaucratic capacity of the control organs, Mao's reforms only further stressed the Party and a leadership struggling to deal with rising instability.[86] The ensuing chaos that punctuated the rest of the Cultural Revolution period (1966–1976) was thus marked by intense bottom-up participation and a fundamental breakdown of top-down control.

With the end of the Cultural Revolution and then Mao's death in 1976, China and its people were exhausted and poised for a new beginning. As it would happen, Deng Xiaoping and his reform-minded supporters were able to steer the PRC in a more pragmatic, economically oriented trajectory. Accordingly, the period beginning 1978 onward is generally referred to as the "Reform and Opening Up" era and, for many, marks a fundamental departure from Maoism. This interpretation sits comfortably with the notion that China's economic liberalization led not only to growth, but also to some degree of rational-legal institutionalization and with it, small steps toward political liberalization. There is little question, for instance, that Deng was vigilant in his efforts to prevent a

---

[82] Schoenhals, *Spying for the People: Mao's Secret Agents, 1949–1967.*

[83] Fei-Ling Wang. *Organizing through Division and Exclusion: China's hukou system.* Stanford University Press, 2005.

[84] Harding, "Maoist Theories of Policy-Making and Organization."

[85] New grassroots organizations included the Red Guards and peasant/lower/middle income associations. The 1969 Constitution included provisions that allowed these organizations to attend Party branch meetings and initiate arbitration proceedings.

[86] Harding, "Maoist Theories of Policy-Making and Organization," p. 28.

return to Maoist-style mass mobilization. It is also true that Deng and his chosen successors adopted reforms and institutions that, on occasion, resembled liberal versions practiced in the West.

By contrast Xi Jinping's governance style has a distinct Maoist flare to it, including his personality cult, the blurring of institutional lines, and an affinity for mass-line rhetoric. This is why many observers express deep regret with Xi's administration, seeing it as a dangerous departure from political institutionalization and reform.[87] These concerns are well warranted. Yet we would be mistaken to assume that the primacy of control was somehow absent or muted during the post-1978 period, or really at any point prior to Xi's ascent to power in 2012. Likewise, as a number of scholars have already shown, there is little evidence that the instrumental utility of mass-line strategies was somehow forgotten or abandoned during the more technocratic reform period.[88]

Even during the chaos of the Cultural Revolution, the CCP maintained direct lines of communication to the grassroots by continuing to collect citizen letters throughout the period and later redeploying informants in 1973.[89] Ultimately, as Koss's recent study demonstrates, the CCP's embeddedness within the masses, not the intervention of the army, was central to restoring order.[90] Similarly, throughout the early reforms in the 1980s, the CCP repeatedly reached out to the masses in both oversight and planning, even when it was dabbling with legal-rational institutionalization.[91] Moreover, despite nearly four decades of market reform and mass migration, the CCP continues to divide society based on where people are from, what they do, how much they have, and how they behave. Though these divisions, and the resentment they fostered, arguably fueled the Cultural Revolution, their sustained presence, combined with more state control, would prove critical to policy implementation as the country embarked on the road toward market liberalization. The control and input dynamics of the related economic reforms are the focus of the following section.

Selective Reform

As China's leaders gathered for the famed Third Plenum of the 11th Congress in 1978, they were aware that in order to liberalize the economy and attract

[87] For example, see David Shambaugh, *The Coming Chinese Crackup*; and Minzner, *End of an Era: How China's Authoritarian Revival is Undermining Its Rise.*

[88] Tyrene White. *China's Longest Campaign: Birth Planning in the People's Republic, 1949–2005.* Cornell University Press, 2006; Elizabeth J. Perry. "From Mass Campaigns to Managed Campaigns." In *Mao's Invisible Hand: The Political Foundations of Adaptive Governance in China.* Ed. by Elizabeth J. Perry and Sebastian Heilmann. Harvard University Press, 2011. Chap. 2, pp. 30–61.

[89] Schoenhals, *Spying for the People: Mao's Secret Agents, 1949–1967.*

[90] Koss, *Where the Party Rules: The Rank and File of China's Communist State.*

[91] White, *China's Longest Campaign*; Perry, "From Mass Campaigns to Managed Campaigns."

investment they would have to implement difficult and often unpopular reforms.[92] They were also aware that such liberalization would likely magnify social divisions and lead to greater pluralization of individual and group interests.[93] Accordingly, the CCP leadership resurrected a control architecture, promptly reestablishing the CDIC in 1978, creating a Ministry of State Security in 1983, and reopening a Ministry of Supervision in 1987.[94] The motives for reasserting control were clear: "End arbitrary decision-making . . . struggle against unhealthy tendencies . . . and increase responsiveness to mass grievances against the Party."[95]

The revival of Leninist control sent a powerful signal to officials in the state, as well as individuals in society, that the CCP was not stepping aside. On the contrary, it was more embedded and invested than ever before. In practice, these controls would make it possible for the leadership to adopt experimental and pragmatic approaches to difficult challenges. In the case of price reform, for instance, market prices were introduced to incentivize competition and productivity gains for some, and subsidies for others.[96] It was only thanks to strict control over social and economic actors, however, that the state was able to sustain such arbitrage. Likewise, the practice of setting up "experimental" Special Economic Zones (SEZs) was facilitated by economic controls over resources and population controls over migration, as well as strict organizational control over personnel and promotion.[97] As Cai and Treisman forcefully argue, the fingerprints of CCP control were present on nearly every aspect of what many saw as market-oriented liberalization.[98]

Gradual opening and political expediency inevitably fueled inefficiencies and corruption. Acutely aware of the dangers associated with mass-line mobilization, however, Deng Xiaoping sought to avoid overt reference to campaigns: "Rely on the masses, but do not launch campaigns."[99] According to Perry, such statements were aimed narrowly at preventing unruly mass campaigns. In other words, they

---

[92] Naughton, *Growing Out of the Plan: Chinese Economic Reform, 1978–1993*; Yongshun Cai. "Managed Participation in China." *Political Science Quarterly* 119.3 (2004), pp. 425–451.

[93] John P. Burns. *The Chinese Communist Party's Nomenklatura System: A Documentary Study of Party Control of Leadership Selection, 1979–1984*. M.E. Sharpe, 1989, p. 166.

[94] Lawrence R. Sullivan. "The Role of the Control Organs in the Chinese Communist Party, 1977–83." *Asian Survey* 24.6 (1984), pp. 597–617.

[95] Summary report published in *Xinhua*, July 30, 1979.

[96] Lawrence J. Lau, Yingyi Qian, and Gerard Roland. "Reform Without Losers: An Interpretation of China's Dual-Track Approach to Transition." *Journal of Political Economy* 108.1 (2000), p. 120.

[97] Susan H. Whiting. "The Cadre Evaluation System at the Grass Roots: The Paradox of Party Rule." *Holding China Together: Diversity and National Integration in the Post-Deng Era* 28. September (2004), pp. 101–120.

[98] Hongbin Cai and Daniel Treisman. "Did Government Decentralization Cause China's Economic Miracle?" *World Politics* 58.04 (2006), pp. 505–535.

[99] Deng Xiaoping, *Selected Works (1982–1992)* Beijing: Foreign Languages Press, 1994, 3:44. Cited in Perry, "From Mass Campaigns to Managed Campaigns."

did not preclude attempts at leveraging mass supervision for the purpose of organizational control. As Figure 2.1 illustrates, by 1978 the reference to mass campaigns virtually disappears from usage in the *People's Daily*, the preeminent mouthpiece of the CCP. Nevertheless, the emphasis on "mass supervision" increased and has continued to do so steadily to this day.

While mass campaigns were no longer encouraged, more managed forms of mass "activities" (*huodong*) and "actions" (*xingdong*) persisted, most prominently in 1982 and again in 1986 against corruption,[100] and against inflation in 1988.[101] During such activities, propaganda outlets were directed to publish critical editorials on government excesses. Likewise, citizens were encouraged

Figure 2.1. Mass Supervision vs. Mass Campaigns

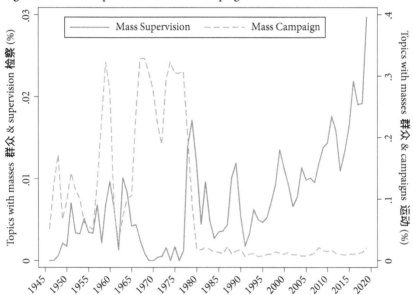

Notes: Frequencies are based on the concurrent usage of the masses (*qunzhong*, 群众) and campaigns (*yundong*, 运动) or supervision (*jiancha*, 检查) respectively. Synonyms for campaign (*huodong*, 活动, and *xingdong*, 行动), and supervision (*jiandu*, 监督) were all included into the content search algorithm. Whereas campaigns reflect the regime's reliance on the public for policy implementation, supervision emphasizes the role of public participation in the service of organizational control. Data is based on an automated content analysis of the *People's Daily* between 1945 and 2019. Because the newspaper has expanded over time, I only focus on the first section of the paper, which is reserved for the most important news and ideological messaging.

100   Elizabeth A. Quade. "The Logic of Anticorruption Enforcement Campaigns in Contemporary China." *Journal of Contemporary China* 16.50 (2007), pp. 65–77.
101   Perry, "From Mass Campaigns to Managed Campaigns."

to air their grievances and report on errant local officials.[102] As in the Maoist period, the goal of these efforts was to harness bottom-up input in the service of top-down control. As Premier Li Peng explained in 1988, the aim was to "incite the masses to file reports, strengthen oversight, pursue clues, thoroughly investigate, analyze causes, adopt correct policies, prevent loopholes, and manage prices well."[103]

Though the rhetoric and tactics had transitioned from mass campaign to more managed forms of controlled inclusion, some things did not change. For one, the basic authority of control organs remained tied to the CCP hierarchy, meaning that investigation and prosecution were easily, and indeed often, obstructed by corresponding Party committees at the same level. Moreover, the professional capacity of the control organs and public monitoring authorities was still quite low. Although the control organs included a small cohort of experienced, rehabilitated cadres, most of the staff, especially those in the local regions, were uneducated, often illiterate members from the Cultural Revolution generation. As a result, the control system remained top-heavy and unprofessional. Likewise, the internal transmission of basic inputs, such as citizen complaints, stagnated at the provincial level, and intelligence remained underutilized by central authorities.[104] While the desire for input-driven governance was present in the early reform era, the infrastructure necessary to facilitate such a system was still lacking.

In an attempt to compensate, traditional controls were complemented with some institutional reform. In adopting these reforms, China naturally borrowed from outside, primarily from Hong Kong and Singapore but also Taiwan and even the United States.[105] Some reforms, such as tenure limits and retirement rules, were introduced in high doses and across various levels of government.[106] Others, like legislative development and competitive elections, were taken with apprehension.[107] Direct elections for county-level people's congresses were held throughout the country in 1980–81, but never extended to the national level as

[102] John P. Burns, "China's Governance: Political Reform in a Turbulent Environment." *The China Quarterly* 119 (1989), pp. 481–518.

[103] Li Peng, *Shichang yu tiaokong: Li Peng jingji riji* [市场与调控: 李鹏经济 日记] (Markets and Controls: Li Peng's Economic Diary). Beijing: Xinhua chubanshe, 2007, 1: 576–578. Cited in Perry, "From Mass Campaigns to Managed Campaigns," p. 51.

[104] Martin K. Dimitrov. "Understanding Communist Collapse and Resilience."

[105] Stephan Ortmann and Mark R. Thompson. "China's Obsession with Singapore: Learning Authoritarian Modernity." *The Pacific Review* 27.3 (2014), pp. 433–455.

[106] Susan L. Shirk. "The Delayed Institutionalization of Leadership Politics." *The Nature of Chinese Politics: From Mao to Jiang*. Ed. by Jonathan Unger. Routledge, 2002, pp. 297–312.

[107] Lai, "Semi-Competitive Elections at Township Level in Sichuan Province." *China Perspectives* 51.51 (2004), pp. 1–21.; Dong Lisheng. "In Search of Direction After Two Decades of Local Democratic Experiments in China." *China Perspectives*, December 2008 (2009).

in other post-Soviet states such as Vietnam, Cuba, or even North Korea.[108] Soon thereafter, experimentation started with direct elections for local village committees, but again, direct executive elections did not extend to administrative levels above the village level.[109] In the 1990s, legislative strengthening evolved into professionalization, specialization, the lengthening of sessions, and financing of more staff to allow congress to function even when not in session.[110]

These reforms contributed to an increasingly assertive Chinese legislature. In 1992, for instance, NPC delegates challenged the government on the issue of the Three Gorges Dam, with one-third of delegates voting against or abstaining.[111] Although the project was eventually approved, the incident stoked the optimism of reformers.[112] Legislative assertiveness was even more pronounced at lower levels, where delegates increasingly criticized local governments, courts, and even Party decisions.[113] In the late 1980s, the Hunan provincial congress impeached a vice governor. In 1993 congresses in Guizhou and Zhejiang rejected Party-sponsored nominees for governor. Across the country, delegates pushed back on government work reports and even Party endorsements.[114]

Perhaps in response to this assertiveness, institutional reforms tapered off in the early 2000s. The rollback began with gradual legislative recentralization.[115] During the 2001 session of the NPC, Jiang Zemin reported that, "villagers' self-government must not be extended to higher levels." In 2002, the Party reestablished top-down control over provincial legislatures by instructing provincial party secretaries to rein in their respective delegations by taking on concurrent roles as legislative chairmen.[116] A similar clampdown on electoral reform began

---

[108] Weimin Shi. "The Development of Grassroots Democratic Elections in China." *Social Sciences in China* 25.1 (2004), pp. 113–125.

[109] Kevin J. O'Brien and Lianjiang Li. "Accommodating 'Democracy' in a One-Party State: Introducing Village Elections in China." English. *The China Quarterly* 162.162 (2000), pp. 465–489.

[110] Murray Scot Tanner. "The National People's Congress." In *The Paradox of China's post-Mao Reforms*. Ed. by Merle Goldman and Roderick MacFarquhar. Harvard University Press, 1999, pp. 100–129; Kevin J. O'Brien. "Chinese People's Congresses and Legislative Embeddedness: Understanding Early Organizational Development." *Comparative Political Studies* 27.1 (1994), pp. 80–107.

[111] Murray Scot Tanner. "The Erosion of Communist Party Control over Lawmaking in China." *The China Quarterly* 138 (1994), pp. 381–403.

[112] Ming Xia. *The People's Congresses and Governance in China: Toward a Network Mode of Governance*. Routledge, 2008.

[113] Young Nam Cho. "Public Supervisors and Reflectors: Role Fulfillment of the Chinese People's Congress Deputies in the Market Socialist Era." *Development and Society* 32.2 (2003), pp. 197–227.

[114] Melanie Manion. "When Communist Party Candidates Can Lose, Who Wins? Assessing the Role of Local People's Congresses in the Selection of Leaders in China." *The China Quarterly* 195 (2008), pp. 607–630.

[115] Kevin J. O'Brien and Laura M. Luehrmann. "Institutionalizing Chinese Legislatures: Trade-Offs Between." *Legislative Studies Quarterly* 23.1 (1998), pp. 91–108.

[116] Politburo directive on provincial leadership: 《关于认真做好2003年省级人大、政府、政协领导班子换届工作的通知》 See: Shi Weimin and Liu Zhi. "*Jianjie xuanju* (Indirect Elections)," Vol. 2. Beijing: Zhongguo shehui kexue chubanshe, 2004, pp. 60–65.

in the early 2000s, with a moratorium on electoral experimentation above the grassroots level announced in 2006.[117]

Alongside institutional reforms, the regime was also exploring changes in the administrative and policymaking process. To this end, the NPC and the State Council passed a series of pathbreaking administrative reforms, beginning with the Administrative Litigation Law in 1989.[118] On paper, each of these reforms suggested a victory for citizens. Court finances and judicial appointments, however, remained under local government control. As a result, courts tasked with enforcing administrative guidelines and defending citizen rights, had few obvious incentives to do so. Nevertheless, the new rules stipulated a process for redress that involved public hearings and, with that, the prospect of public scrutiny.[119] This was a half-measure at best, but it opened a new chapter in public oversight. The next step would be to incorporate the public input into planning.

The first major example of inclusion in the planning process occurred during the drafting of the 1996 Price Law, a touchy topic insofar as the state was the only party that clearly favored reform. Consumers, primarily in the urban centers, were accustomed to stable, subsidized prices. Likewise, state-owned manufacturers were dependent on cheap inputs, and state-owned utility providers preferred production quotas to fluctuating demand. However, each group disagreed on the new prices. Producers overstated costs in order to lobby for higher prices, while consumers (both citizens and businesses) wanted to keep prices as low as possible. By pitting private citizens and state-owned providers against one another, policymakers acquired more reliable information on how far each side would be willing to compromise, while at the same time distancing themselves from the final policy.[120]

Embracing Consultation

Recognizing the potential of consultation, Jiang Zemin offered a formal endorsement in 1997, calling on township-level governments to engage the public in decision-making: "While making major policy decisions concerning reform and development, we must . . . establish a mechanism that will help

---

[117] See Sheng Huaren. (依法做好县乡两级人大换届选举工作) *Xian xiang Renda huanjie mianlin xin wenti, xu jianchi san da yuanze* 县乡人大换届面临问题,须坚持三大原则 (The term change of the County and Township People's Congresses faces new problems and three major principles must be adhered to). *Seeking Truth*, available at the website of the National People's Congress, August 30, 2006: http://npc.people.com.cn/GB/14554/4758934.html.

[118] For a review, see Stromseth, Malesky, and Gueorguiev, *China's Governance Puzzle: Enabling Transparency and Participation in a Single-Party State*, pp. 171–181.

[119] Minxin Pei. "Citizens vs. Mandarins: Administrative Litigation in China." *The China Quarterly* 152.152 (1997), pp. 832–862.

[120] Xixin Wang. "The Public, Expert, and Government in the Public Decision-Making Process: A Study of China's Price-Setting Hearing System and Its Practice." *Peking University Journal of Legal Studies* (2008), pp. 71–117.

decision-makers to go deep among the people to see their condition, adequately reflect their will and pool their wisdom so that decision-making will be more scientific, democratic and efficient and will reach a higher level."[121] In 1999, Jiang once again came out in support of consultative decision-making, a move followed by the inclusion of a participation clause in the much-anticipated Law on Legislation.[122] Shortly thereafter, the State Council promulgated its own rule-making provisions, also including provisions on participation.[123] The timing of these adoptions was not random. Part of China's 2001 WTO commitment stipulated that the Chinese government would improve regulatory transparency and provide opportunities for member states to comment on any changes before they go into effect.[124] It would be odd for a communist regime to afford such rights to foreign interests without extending the same opportunity to the Chinese public.

Though the central leadership endorsed consultation, there was no clarity on what it would entail. According to the Law on Legislation, consultation procedures were encouraged for all decisions "with direct and significant impact" on the public. What qualified as either "direct" or "significant" was not defined.[125] Further questions remained over when in the policy formulation process consultation ought to occur, in what format, and how the government should handle the inputs it received. Ultimately, clarification would occur at the local level. In 1999, Shanxi became the first provincial government to adopt implementation guidelines for holding public hearings.[126] Soon other provinces advanced similar standards concerning hearings, notice-and-comment procedures, and online polling.[127] In 2008, the State Council adopted guidelines for consultation in its Decision on Strengthening Local Administration.[128]

[121] Report to the 15th National Congress of the Communist Party of China. Part VI, Reforming the Political Structure and Strengthening Democracy and the Legal System.
[122] Jiang Zemin's Report at 16th Party Congress: Build a Well-off Society in an All-Round Way and Create a New Situation in Building Socialism with Chinese Characteristics. Section 5. Available here: https://bit.ly/30cZSSi.
[123] In addition to the National People's Congress, the State Council is empowered to create regulatory policy. To complement the Legislation Law, the State Council in 2001 adopted the Ordinance Concerning the Procedures for the Formation of Administrative Regulations and the Provisions on the Procedures for Making Administrative Rules.
[124] Horsley, "Public Participation in the People's Republic."
[125] A Ministry of Environmental Protection decision in 2006 to mandate public hearings as part of the Environmental Impact Assessment review process (EIAs) resolved some of this ambiguity, at least in the area of industrial oversight.
[126] "Shanxi Province Hearing Procedures for Policy-Making Regulation, 1999," cited in Wang. "Public Participation and Its Limits: An Observation and Evaluation on Public Hearings as Experimented in China's Administrative Process." *Yale University China Law Center* (2003).
[127] Jeffrey S. Lubbers. "Notice-and-Comment Rulemaking Comes to China." *Administrative and Regulatory Law News* 32.1 (2006), pp. 5–6; Horsley, "Public Participation in the People's Republic."
[128] See State Council Decision on Strengthening Administration under Law in Municipal and County Governments (2008) No. 17, Article 8.

Today, Chinese citizens are consulted on a variety of topics. While some of the discussions may seem mundane, the consultative process is increasingly applied to major national debates. In 2018 the public was even asked to comment on tariffs policy in connection to an ongoing trade dispute with the United States, including a list of 128 different products on which China intended to raise import tariffs.[129] In addition to consultation, other aspects of inclusion have been formalized and digitized.[130] Most prominently, bottom-up supervision through the submission of complaints, petitions, and tip-offs has been greatly expanded and shifted almost entirely to online submission. Denouncing a policy or a politician is now a mouse click or a phone swipe away. The extent to which citizens make use of these functions, and then that the government acts on them, remains an empirical question, but there is good reason, based on some of the polling discussed below, to suspect that they are.

Survey evidence from the China Policy Barometer, an annual public opinion poll of Chinese Netizens that is further discussed in Chapter 5, suggests that by 2019 a vast majority of Chinese Netizens now provide input to the Chinese State, and most do so via digital platforms. In Figure 2.2, for instance, we see that only about 12 percent of Netizens have never contacted the government. Nearly 40 percent have contacted via hotlines, and over 35 percent have submitted complaints. Of those who have issued complaints, 90 percent have done so using online complaint platforms. By contrast, less than one percent of respondents report having filed formal *xinfang* petitions.

These indicators underscore that opportunities for Chinese citizens to contact their government are expanding, and the overall mode of participation in China has rapidly transitioned to a digital format. The ease and speed offered by digitization suggests that the Chinese people's grievances, contradictions, and preferences are more legible today than in the past. This does not in any way mean that the regime will always act on this information, or that it would do so in ways that are democratic, popular, or even humane. Yet, we should be sure that the regime is taking advantage of the information in ways that it deems instrumental. When confronting corruption or engaging in planning, for example, a regime's interests can converge with those of the public. More importantly, a legible population is also a more easily managed one.[131] In that respect, technology has greatly expanded the reach of the party-state, facilitating ever more sophisticated forms of inclusions as well as control.

---

[129] See the Ministry of Commerce Notice for Comment here: https://bit.ly/2VwpfQ1.

[130] Xuequan Mu. "China's State Council to Use Internet for Public Opinion." *China Daily*, February 22, 2008; Creemers, "Cyber China: Upgrading Propaganda, Public Opinion Work and Social Management for the Twenty-First Century."

[131] Scott, *Seeing Like a State: How Certain Schemes to Improve the Human Condition Have Failed.*

Figure 2.2. Netizen Participation

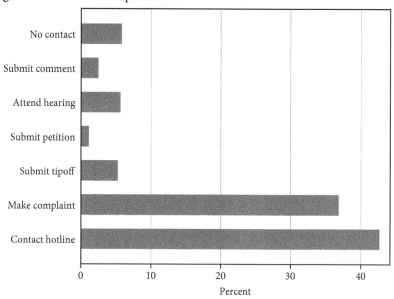

Notes: Categories are not mutually exclusive. The "No contact" category is inferred when all other categories are not selected. Participation can occur online, within the respondent's residential community, or within their work unit. Tabulations come from a sample of 3,000 Netizens surveyed as part of the 2019 wave of the China Policy Barometer, available at https://bit.ly/2YXoDQz.

From Past to Present

The goal of this chapter has been to provide historical, ideological, and structural background for thinking about participatory governance in today's China. To that end, the insights from this examination can be summarized in three broad takeaways. First, although there are precedents for participatory governance in traditional China, they were weak and there is not much evidence to suggest that the CCP sought to incorporate them. Generally speaking, inclusion of the general population in the governing process is a relatively recent phenomenon. Second, although contemporary methods for inclusion resemble Western practices, particularly with regard to transparency and consultation, there is little to suggest that the motives behind these methods is recent or borrowed from the West.

Instead, CCP administration in the PRC ultimately brought together three distinct experiences—that of traditional China; the trials and errors of the GMD; and, most influential, that of the Soviet Union and the Leninist organizational template it provided. Marxist principles concerning revolution, criticism, and class conflict were, however, rather alien to Chinese political thought.[132] Indeed,

---

[132] Ch'o-Hsüan, "The Introduction of Marxism-Leninism into China," p. 140.

these frictions likely had a role to play in preventing the GMD from fully incorporating Soviet advice.[133] That the CCP was ultimately able to incorporate Leninism and, as I argue in this book, advance it to a level beyond that which the Soviets were able to achieve, is not at all an obvious outcome.

Ironically, the Bolshevik's military success, Stalin's rapid consolidation of power, and an earlier transition to industrialization precluded the need to fundamentally restructure and compartmentalize Soviet society. By contrast, a protracted civil war gave Mao time to refine his control tactics, while insufficient resources forced him and the CCP to turn toward the masses when implementing campaigns. In combination, these factors contributed to a more socially embedded form of authoritarianism in the PRC. To quote Martin Whyte, through group-based organization and mobilization, the Chinese people became "not passive objects to be manipulated by the Party, but integral parts of a much larger and more ambitious organizational weapon."[134]

Nevertheless, the CCP under Mao was never able to fully integrate public participation into top-down control, in part because it lacked the infrastructure to fully interact with or control the masses on a national scale and because it failed to separate politics from policy. As a result, public participation in Maoist China, as in Stalinist Russia, was often limited to top-down implementation and violent political campaigns.[135] Over time, the CCP has blended mass-line tactics for inclusion with more standardized models for administrative good governance. Auspiciously for the CCP, advances in communications technology have substantially augmented the potency of this blend.[136] Ironically, China's recent embrace of participatory governance helps bring the CCP back to its Leninist roots.

The CCP's arc back to Leninist control is lamentable for Chinese society as a whole, and there is little doubt that China will become increasingly more oppressive and hostile toward those who want to participate openly and politically. This, however, does not preclude the possibility that China's unique blend of authoritarian control and popular inclusion is conducive to more effective administration. This is ultimately an empirical question, and one that occupies the rest of this book. At bare minimum, for any such hypothesized linkage to be viable we should expect that public inputs generated through inclusion are at least partially reflected in how the state governs. The following chapter probes this logic through a quantitative study of citizen complaints over corruption, as well as disciplinary investigations initiated by the state.

---

[133] Spence, *The Search for Modern China*, pp. 336–341.

[134] Whyte, *Small Groups and Political Rituals in China*, p. 35.

[135] Michel Oksenberg and James Tong. "The Evolution of Central–Provincial Fiscal Relations in China, 1971–1984: The Formal System." *The China Quarterly* 125 (1991), pp. 1–32.

[136] Creemers, "Cyber China: Upgrading Propaganda, Public Opinion Work and Social Management for the Twenty-First Century."

PART II
CONNECTING INPUTS WITH OUTPUTS

3

Participation in Oversight

The basic principle for establishing a system of consultation and dialogue is to carry on the fine tradition of "from the masses, to the masses," by engaging the public in the activities of the leading bodies, letting the people know about important events and discuss important issues . . . to give scope to the supervisory role of public opinion, to support the masses in their criticism of shortcomings and mistakes in work, to oppose bureaucratism and in general to combat all unhealthy tendencies.[1]

— Zhao Ziyang, 1987

The dream of digital control in a Leninist system began in 1952, when a Soviet military researcher by the name of Anatoly Ivanovich Kitov, at a secret library within the Special Design Bureau of the Ministry of Machine and Instrument Building, happened upon a copy of Norbert Wiener's classic *Cybernetics* (1948), an ambitious blueprint for controlled administration and planning with the help of computers.[2] For Kitov, a committed socialist who had also lived through Stalin's great purge, computers and automation offered a path forward—one that held out the prospect of rational Marxist governance without the one-man tyranny. Driven by this aspiration, Kitov would spend the next seven years translating *Cybernetics* and then spearheading a secret military computing center to study decentralized information aggregation and processing. Though the research center focused on military applications, Kitov had much broader visions concerning economic and civilian administration. In 1959, Kitov outlined these ideas in a detailed letter proposing the creation of an "Economic Automated Management System," and addressed it directly to the General Party Secretary, Nikita Khrushchev. As it happened, this letter was intercepted and destroyed

---

[1] Zhao Ziyang. "Advance along the Road of Socialism with Chinese Characteristics (*Yanzhe you zhongguo tese de Sehui Zhuyi daolu qiangjin*)." Report to the Thirteenth Part Congress of the Communist Party of China, October 5, 1987.
[2] From Kitov's personal interview with computer magazine *Computerra* No. 43, November 18, 1996.

Retrofitting Leninism. Dimitar D. Gueorguiev. Oxford University Press. © Oxford University Press 2021.
DOI: 10.1093/oso/9780197555668.003.0004

by Kitov's superiors, who were angered by the prospect of sharing military computing technology with civilian planners.[3]

Kitov's design, however, was not buried. Soon it was given a second life by one of his friends and colleagues, a computer scientist and head of the Soviet Cybernetics Institute, Viktor Glushkov, with a project that would come to be known as "The National Automated System for Computation and Information Processing," or OGAS.[4] OGAS, like Kitov's earlier conception, was aimed at integrating the socialist economy into an automated but functionally decentralized feedback and processing system. In theory, this system would involve over 200 servers and 20,000 terminals placed around the country. By 1971, when the outside world first heard about OGAS, some of this architecture was already in place.[5] If brought to full capacity, OGAS held the potential to revolutionize oversight, planning, and implementation in the Soviet economy—not to mention to lay the groundwork for a Soviet Internet, much in the way that ARPANET eventually would in the United States. Alas, and despite intermittent aspirations continuing well into the early 1980s, the Soviets never completed OGAS. According to Glushkov's own memoirs and subsequent historical analyses, OGAS was fatally crippled even before it was announced. Despite its potential, there was no political will for such an integrated system among the disparate ministries and organizational heads within the Kremlin.[6]

The dream of digital control, however, would not die in the Soviet Union. In 2014, the CCP announced a series of changes in how China would engage the "Internet of things," shorthand for harnessing the power of big data and information technology for economic and social progress. Institutionally, the Central Committee (CCOM) established a Central Cyberspace Affairs Commission (CAC) and a Cybersecurity and Informationalization Leading Small Group, with Xi Jinping as chair of both.[7] These new bodies were in fact extensions of earlier efforts to harness Internet technology and computers for administrative control, dating back to the late 1990s and early 2000s. What the establishment of the CAC signified, however, was the CCP's full-scale embrace of digital

[3] Peters, *How Not to Network a Nation: The Uneasy History of the Soviet Internet*.
[4] The first public mention of OGAS appeared within the proceedings of the 24th CPSU, in March of 1971.
[5] Boris Malinovsky, Anne Fitzpatrick, and Emmanuel Aronie. "Pioneers of Soviet Computing." Edited by Anne Fitzpatrick. Translated by Emmanuel Aronie. Np: published electronically (2010).
[6] Ibid. Slava Gerovitch. "InterNyet: Why the Soviet Union Did Not Build a Nationwide Computer Network." *History and Technology* 24.4 (2008), pp. 335–350; Peters, *How Not to Network a Nation: The Uneasy History of the Soviet Internet*.
[7] See "Establishment of the Cybersecurity and Informationalization Leading Small Group" (中央网络安全和信息化领导小组成立). *Xinhua*. February 28, 2014.

communications, not simply as an economic tool but as a means for social and organizational control through digital feedback systems.

Like OGAS, China's feedback control requires continuous information inputs. Some of this input, like the readings from an air quality monitor attached to a smokestack in a factory, can be automated. Others, however, such as information about a corrupt business transaction, an illegal building practice, or a neighbor who consistently violates a public health order require the voluntary participation of informed groups and individuals. This book is primarily concerned with this latter category of input and the means, motives, and myths that facilitate voluntary participation.

In this chapter I address a necessary condition for any form of voluntary participation: evidence of feedback. Specifically, we can assume that citizens are unlikely to participate if they do not believe their inputs are going to make any difference. The amount of difference may vary, and individuals will have different expectations of efficacy, but if any public voluntarism is to occur, we should expect at least some evidence that public inputs are transmitted into state outputs. I tap into that transmission process by examining the relationship between citizen tip-offs and anticorruption investigations. While anticorruption covers only a narrow range of the feedback spectrum, it is nevertheless a dimension in which public preferences (in this case, clean government), seem most clearly compatible with central priorities for organizational control. In other words, anticorruption activity is probably the most obvious place to begin looking for a feedback connection.

The Problem of Oversight

In his first major political speech after receiving the CCP Secretariatship in November of 2012, President Xi Jinping outlined his political priorities, including the pursuit of "socialism with Chinese characteristics" and the "rejuvenation of the Chinese nation." The most provocative parts of the speech, however, came toward the end, when Xi outlined what he saw as a life-and-death struggle by the Party against corruption. Such dramatic rhetoric is not uncommon for Chinese leaders. Hu Jintao, Jiang Zemin, and nearly every CCP leader from Mao forward has depicted corruption as a fundamental threat to the Party's survival. Xi's diagnosis of the problem, however, was slightly different. Although Xi identified the corrupt officials as the ones responsible for social grievances and "political contradictions," in true Leninist form he did not attribute the root of the problem to these individuals but rather to the organization itself. In a graphic metaphor,

Xi belittled corrupt officials as "maggots," but pointed out that "there must first be decay for maggots to set in."[8] Objective observers could hardly disagree.

What is the organizational problem? As discussed in Chapter 3, China's institutional foundations borrow heavily from the Soviet Union, whereby authority is heterarchically distributed both vertically and horizontally, yet concentrated in the Party leadership.[9] In such systems, supervision is narrow and top-heavy. At the same time, the system is highly fragmented, with multiple points of conflict and collusion between principals in core leadership positions and subordinate agents directly below them.[10] With decentralization and economic liberalization beginning in 1978, such contradictions metastasized as grand opportunities for profit, which overlapped unsurprisingly with political connections.[11] As Deng Xiaoping observed, unfettered and crosscutting executive power in a marketizing economy is bound to produce corruption.[12]

Deng envisioned two paths forward regarding anticorruption: a robust legal system or a marketized economy. Although Xi Jinping has himself repeatedly cited the need for both reforms, these are arguably not the solutions that he and the CCP leadership envisions. To the seasoned China scholar, or any student of authoritarianism for that matter, the reasons may be obvious. Establishing rule of law requires at least some independence between legal and political institutions. For a regime bent on control, and in the absence of any legal political opposition, the prospect for such independence is little more than wishful thinking. Likewise, a fully liberalized economy would not only further undermine the CCP's socialist legitimacy, it would also mean giving up control over the means of production. Moreover, the CCP's principal political currency is its control over personnel. The value of this currency is thus a function of the demand for official positions, which is itself a function of opportunities for political self-enrichment. At the same time, without controlling levels of corruption, the Party risks losing popular legitimacy, while at the same time

---

[8] See Xi Jinping Speech to the First Session of 18th Party Congress Politburo Study Session (习近平在十八届中共中央政治局第一次集体学习时的讲话); his specific phrasing was, "*Wu bi xian fu, erhou chong sheng.*"

[9] Heterarchy refers to a organizational structure that is neither purely hierarchical or fully decentralized, resulting in un-ranked modes of network communication. Contained heterarchy refers to a heterarchy that has a clear apex (McCulloch, "A Heterarchy of Values Determined by the Topology of Nervous Nets").

[10] Harry Harding. *Organizing China: The Problem of Bureaucracy, 1949–1976*. Stanford University Press, 1981, p. 432; Ting Gong. "Dangerous Collusion: Corruption as a Collective Venture in Contemporary China." *Communist and Post-Communist Studies* 35.1 (2002), pp. 85–103; Graham Smith. "Political Machinations in a Rural County." *China Journal* 31.62 (2009), pp. 29–59.

[11] Melanie Manion. *Retirement of Revolutionaries in China: Public Policies, Social Norms, Private Interests*. Princeton University Press, 1993, p. 209.

[12] Deng Xiaoping. "On the Reform of the System of Party and State Leadership." *Selected Works of Deng Xiaoping (1975–1982)*. University Press of the Pacific, 1980, pp. 302–325.

ceding some of the profits of office to intermediaries.[13] As such, anticorruption in China is better understood as an attempt to control the flow of political rents, not their eradication.

Anticorruption in China

When I met Wang Minggao, then Vice President of Hunan's University of Commerce, he, like Xi Jinping, tried to convey the nuance of anticorruption through bodily metaphor. Wang explained that corruption in the PRC is "like a cancer, and although most of the treatments can kill you, doing nothing will do the same."[14] The thing about cancer, he explained, is that the body, like the Party, has built-in systems that keep cancerous cells and other threats at bay. Cancers, like corruption get out of control when the immune system fails to identify them. Much of Wang's research has focused on ways to expose corruption so that the CCP's internal control system can do its job, including various transparency initiatives aimed at pushing private government information into the public domain, so that citizens can participate in oversight, a process he refers to vaguely as "scientific supervision."

At first, Wang's statements reminded me of the oft-cited quote of former US Supreme Court Justice Louis Brandeis: "Sunshine is the best disinfectant."[15] Indeed, Chinese propaganda outlets often parrot the same wisdom: "Only by exposing to sunlight can its power be managed; only by enabling public supervision in the broadest sense will corruption find nowhere to hide."[16] But as Wang—also a veteran of the Hunan Provincial Organization Department and a disciplinary committee advisor—continued, my impression of what he had in mind changed. For example, Wang explained the need to systematize all financial transactions. As a university representative, he explains, "I should be paying for our lunch with an electronic payment, so it's clearly documented." According to Wang, China needed a national financial database, with a unique record for each individual citizen; little did he know that modern blockchain technology provides precisely this utility. Such a database, according to Wang, would improve financial decision-making and remove the oxygen from corruption because neither citizens nor officials would be able to hide their behavior.

The total monitoring approach described by Wang, especially the public's key role in that process, was thus more reminiscent of the autonomous control ideas

---

[13] Jiangnan Zhu. "Why are Offices for Sale in China? A Case Study of the Office-Selling Chain in Heilongjiang Province." *Asian Survey* 48.4 (2008), pp. 558–579.

[14] Author's interview, Changsha, Hunan Province, June 2011.

[15] See Louis Brandeis. 1913. "What Publicity Can Do." *Harper's Weekly*, December 20, 1913.

[16] Translated from: "让权力在阳光下运行，才有可能将权力关进牢笼；让权力在最广大公众的目光中接受监督，才会让贪污腐败无所遁形。" See Jingli Bai, "Network Supervision and the Power of the Public." *Xinhua News Agency*, 2012.

developed by Kitov and Glushkov in the Soviet Union than the transparency-induced good governance of Brandeis. As discussed in Chapter 2, CCP theorists have been interested in computer-assisted supervision since at least the 1970s,[17] inspired, like their Russian counterparts, by the early work on cybernetics[18] and information theory.[19] In other words, the "scientific" part of Wang's theory on supervision was really about establishing a self-cultivating form of feedback control, what Samantha Hoffman describes as an "Autonomic Nervous System"—an integrated administrative circuit to which Leninist organizations have always aspired and which technology facilitates.[20] The public face of this integration is what I refer to as "inclusive governance," whereby various aspects of administration are partially opened and accessible to public involvement. In the next section, I explore this involvement through a case study of public participation in anticorruption.

Network Supervision

Inclusive governance in contemporary China covers many aspects of administration, from policymaking to implementation. Some of these activities amount to little more than procedural performance. Yet there are also instances in which public involvement is not only genuine but, as I will argue throughout successive chapters, consequential. Of particular interest is the role of public participation in matters of oversight. As explained in Chapter 2, oversight is one area where the CCP has a keen interest in involving members of the public.[21] For one, China's massive bureaucracy makes internal, top-down oversight impractical. It is thus not uncommon for central leaders to place troves of administrative information in the public realm, offering private citizens, legal representatives, and researchers an opportunity to review bureaucratic activities on their own. For instance, in 2013, the Supreme People's Court (SPC) released all civil, administrative, criminal, and commercial case records from the high court itself, as well as from China's three thousand plus sub-national courts.[22] Similarly and also

---

[17] For example, see Yu Guangyuan, "科学有险阻 苦战能过关 (Overcoming Scientific Challenges through Struggle)," *The People's Daily*, September 21, 1977.

[18] Wiener, *Cybernetics or Control and Communication in the Animal and the Machine*.

[19] C.E. Shannon, "Two-way Communications Channels," Fourth Berkeley Symposium on Mathematical Statistical Probability, Chicago, IL, 1961, pp. 611–644.

[20] Samantha Hoffman. "Programming China." *China Monitor* (2017).

[21] Jamie P Horsley, "China Adopts First Nationwide Open Government Information Regulations." Freedominfo.org (Online) (2007), pp. 1–13; Stromseth, Malesky, and Gueorguiev, *China's Governance Puzzle: Enabling Transparency and Participation in a Single-Party State*.

[22] See "最高法院关于在互联网公布裁判文书的规定 (Provisions of the Supreme People's Court on the Issuance of Judgments on the Internet by the People's Courts)." 法释〔2013〕26号. http://tiny.cc/quuahy.

in 2013, the Ministry of Land and Resources (MLR) published several million land transaction records—covering information on buyers, sellers, location, land quality, and even land use rights—going back into the 1990s.[23]

Data releases exemplify the "sunshine is the best disinfectant" wisdom in that they shift large amounts of information into the public realm, "shedding light" on previously hidden information and obscure transactions. By engaging the public in reviewing and scrutinizing these data points, the transparency process in effect "creates millions of auditors who have been "deputized" by central authorities."[24] In late 2012, shortly after Xi's inauguration speech highlighting the need for combating corruption, China's central disciplinary body, CDIC, announced a similar strategy for crowd-sourced oversight.[25] This oversight system relies on virtual drop boxes on government websites and on social media platforms where private citizens can submit incriminating information with ease and speed.[26]

Setting up a website for citizens to report on corruption, however, is not enough. As stressed in Chapter 2, the public inputs that feed the system are voluntary actions, and for citizen to voluntarily participate in the system, several basic assumptions have to hold. At the most basic level, there must be some general expectation that someone is listening—that inputs are in some respect incorporated and reflected in outputs. Put differently, if citizen deputies are to participate they should anticipate that their inputs will be acknowledged and acted upon by the sheriff. Furthermore, citizens are unlikely to participate if they feel vulnerable to retaliation. In 2013, for instance, Li Jianxin, a well-known anticorruption vigilante, was knifed and doused with acid in his native Huiyang, a coastal district in Guangdong province. Li lost an eye, two fingers, and suffered severe burns. While no perpetrators were identified, many suspected the attack was retribution for Li's reporting on the corruption of local officials and a prominent family in Huiyang.[27] This risk is heightened by the fact that all citizen reporting requires petitioners to register their names and identification numbers along with their report. In the absence of procedural protections, this information can be readily obtained by government officials and used to retaliate and discourage future reporting.

---

[23] See 中国土地市场网 (China Land Market Portal).

[24] Stromseth, Malesky, and Gueorguiev, *China's Governance Puzzle: Enabling Transparency and Participation in a Single-Party State*, p. 43.

[25] Hairong Wang. "New Platform for Whistleblowers." *Beijing Review* 44 (2013), pp. 22–23; Vanessa Piao. "China Lets Citizens' Fingers Do the Talking to Report Graft." *New York Times* (2015).

[26] Xuming Liu. "The Efforts 网络监督在反腐败中的作用研究 (Research on the Role of Network Supervision in Anticorruption)." PhD thesis. The Central Party School, 2012.

[27] Joanna Chiu. "Chinese Censors Silence Corruption Blogger." *Committee to Protect Journalists* (2013).

One could interpret such risks through the "screening" logic offered by Lorentzen.[28] That is, the risks involved with reporting discourage individuals from making frivolous accusations, leaving only the most serious concerns reported. Then again, such a screening process is grossly inefficient, and seems counterproductive if the most serious cases are also the ones most likely to involve retaliation. For a regime that is interested in organizational control as well as social control, such screening strategies can lead to blindspots and undermine citzens' critical trust relationship with the feedback system.

Counter to the expectations about blunt screening, disciplinary control authorities have tried to reduce fears and facilitate feedback. National and local leaders have, on a number of occasions, advanced procedural protections for citizen informants. In 1988, the Supreme Procuratorate adopted an experimental *Whistleblower Protection* provision, followed by similar guidelines in some provinces (see Table 3.1). However, this experimental provision, codified into law in 1996, had several drawbacks. First, it applied only to citizens contacting physical petition offices, without guidance for managing online reporting. Second, while the 1996 law made retaliation illegal, it did not guarantee the anonymity of citizen informants. In other words, the law raised the costs of retaliation but did little to prevent it as an option. Moreover, the fact that only a handful of provinces adopted local interpretations of the provision meant that Chinese citizens enjoyed different levels of protection not only across time but also depending on where they lived.

Recognizing the contradictions of the whistleblower provision, China's State Council and the National People's Congress moved to strengthen the law in 2009 and again in 2014, resulting in two substantive amendments to the original legislation. In particular, protections were extended to Netizens submitting corruption reports through formal channels. More importantly, under the 2014 version, releasing information about informants or the circumstances of their reports became a criminal act. Perhaps acknowledging that legal restrictions are less than robust, the central Organization Department moved to calm the concerns of local officials as well, announcing that it would no longer be counting citizen complaints as demerits for cadre promotion.[29]

There is strong indication—whether from assurances provided by the authorities, or simply a surfeit of public grievances—that public informants are actively engaging the system. According to official statistics, the CDIC

---

[28] Peter Lorentzen. "Designing Contentious Politics in Post-1989 China." *Modern China* 43.5 (2017), pp. 459–493.

[29] See "Abolish Petitions Ranking and Let Petitions Go Towards the Rule of Law." (取消信排名, 信走向法治). *Beijing News*, 2013.

Table 3.1 Provincial Whistleblower Protections

Whistleblower Protection (保护公民举报权利条例)	Early	Version 1 (1996)	Version 1.2 (2009)	Version 1.3 (2014)
Guangdong	1989	National 1996	.	2014
Anhui	1989		.	.
Hubei	1991		.	.
Shanxi	1991		.	.
Shaanxi	1991		2010	2014
Guangxi	1991		2010	.
Ningxia	1991		.	.
Hebei	1992		.	.
Jiangxi	1994		.	.
Hainan	1995		.	.

Notes: Early adopters based local statutes on an experimental *Whistleblower Protection* provision, released by the Supreme People's Procuratorate in 1988: 《人民检察院保护工作若干规定（试行）》 Early trials were later incorporated into a national regulation 《人民检察院举报工作规定》, which went into effect throughout the country in 1996. Amendments to the national regulation were passed by the National People's Congress in 2009 and 2014, resulting in Versions 1.2 and 1.3, respectively. Both amendments aimed to strengthen the 1996 regulations by broadening the definition of who could be protected, with special emphasis for online citizen informers. Provinces that have not adopted local statutes are effectively governed by the national regulations, with no local implementation guidelines. Data was collected using the Beijing University Law Center Legal Archive and corroborated using annual versions of the *Law Yearbook*.

received over 300,000 online citizen tip-offs between 2009 and 2013.[30] How these tip-offs contribute to actual anticorruption efforts is unclear. In one recent study, Stromseth, Malesky, and Gueorguiev, show a significant and negative relationship between online government transparency and the misuse of public funds,[31] most likely caused by a deterrent effect. Deterrence, however, only works under the assumption that citizen engagement is feeding back into the sanctioning process. As the authors point out, "since citizens have no means to sanction officials, the state must do so in their stead."

Evidence that citizen participation is affecting top-down disciplinary action, however, remains anecdotal and empirically untested. According to official statements, as much as 70 percent of anticorruption investigations arise from

---

[30] See "中纪委5年收网络举报30.1万件次怎样处理举报 (Top Anti-Graft Authority Received 301,000 Online Whistle-Blowing Reports)" *Xinhua News Agency*, 2013. http://tiny.cc/3ruahy.

[31] Stromseth, Malesky, and Gueorguiev, *China's Governance Puzzle: Enabling Transparency and Participation in a Single-Party State*.

citizen tip-offs![32] This is a startling figure, especially given the fact that current anticorruption investigations number into the millions.[33] Unfortunately, the aggregate numbers are vague and difficult to verify. More importantly, they don't explain why citizens would take the risk of becoming informants. In the next section, I explore more granular data on disciplinary investigations and bottom-up monitoring capacity, to estimate the transmission rate between bottom-up inputs and top-down outputs.

Whistleblower Effects

To measure the impact of bottom-up input on anticorruption activity, I constructed an original dataset of anticorruption investigations and citizen corruption reports by piecing together information from the CDIC web-based public interface, alongside statistics from official yearbooks, almanacs, and reports from the CDIC. A summary of the main variables to be deployed is provided in Figure 3.1, which displays statistics on *Citizen Reporting* alongside province-level *Disciplinary Investigations* over the last thirty years. A rough eyeball examination of trends in reporting and investigation suggests an obvious relationship, at least in recent years.

There are clear problems with drawing conclusions from trends, however. For instance, Citizen Reporting and disciplinary actions are, in theory at least, a function of the underlying degree of corruption, which, unfortunately, is unobservable (a concern I return to later in this section). Alternatively, upticks in *Citizen Reporting* and *Disciplinary Investigations* might simply coincide with regime anticorruption campaigns (*fanfu yundong*), whereby citizens and disciplinarians respectively but independently report and investigate at higher rates simply because both are aware of the ongoing political exercise. Both scenarios are paradigmatic examples of omitted variable bias, a common form of endogeneity in observational studies. Another closely related source of endogeneity is the potential feedback that investigations might have on *Citizen Reporting*. For instance, it is easy to imagine that public reports of corruption investigations might inspire more citizens to file reports without necessarily leading to a concomitant increase in investigations.

To overcome these empirical challenges, I rely on an instrumental variable strategy that takes advantage of variation in telecommunications infrastructure,

---

[32] See Chen Zhi. "Xinhua Insight: Real-Name Whistleblowing Fuels China's Online Anticorruption Efforts," *Xinhua News Agency*, May 15, 2013.

[33] According to official statistics from the CDIC in 2018, about 1.5 million officials, including 35 members of the Party Central Committee and nine members of the CDIC itself, had been disciplined. See: https://www.scmp.com/comment/insight-opinion/article/2125369/can-xi-jinpings-corruption-battle-china-place-people-above.

Figure 3.1. Reports and Disciplinary Action

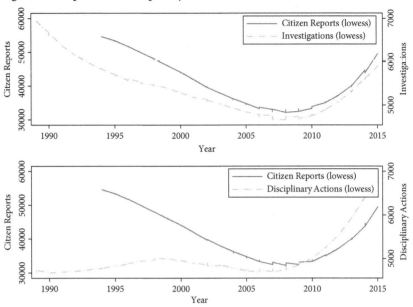

Notes: Data on *Citizen Reporting* and corruption investigations are compiled and triangulated using statistics from various years from the *Supreme Procuratorate Yearbook* 检察院年鉴, the *National Audits Yearbook* 审计年鉴, and the official reports from the Central Disciplinary Inspection Commission 中央纪委.

which is most likely to impact disciplinary action through bottom-up citizen participation. In making this argument I borrow from the insights brought forth by the Soviet cyberneticists, who recognized that feedback control necessitated a communications infrastructure for input acquisition. Specifically, I point to the fact that China's massive Internet infrastructure is hard-wired into a series of eight nodes, or bottlenecks, distributed across the country. As a consequence, Internet quality and opportunities for expansion today are partially constrained by an architecture that was largely determined nearly three decades earlier. Below, I briefly describe China's Internet choke points and illustrate their direct and indirect influence on Internet quality using measures of Internet expansion and network quality.

China's Internet Backbone

On August 25, 1986, Wu Weimin, a researcher at the Institute of High Energy Physics at the Chinese Academy of Sciences, used an IBM personal computer to send an email to Jack Steinberger, a colleague at CERN (the European Organization for Nuclear Research) in Switzerland, via satellite link.[34] The following year, a group of research institutes in Beijing, called the "China Academic Network," used a patchwork of cables connected to a gateway in Germany to send another email, stating "Across the Great Wall we can reach every corner in the world." It was these same researchers who apparently adopted ".cn" as the country's national domain name, by adding the letters to their server address. Over the next five years, Chinese universities, with the help of overseas partners, built a series of cabled networks, ultimately leading to the establishment in 1994 of China's first domestically operated transmission control protocol (TCP), the China Education and Research Network (CERNET).

By 1995, China had three core "national level" Internet exchange hubs, in Beijing, Shanghai, and Guangzhou. Prior to 2015, these would remain the only international exchange points that were connected to the outside word. These critical hubs were joined by five additional nodes in Shenyang, Xi'an, Chengdu, Wuhan, and Nanjing. Together these eight nodes formed an "incomplete reticular structure," where each node was connected to another but not all nodes were connected to each other by way of 22 main optical-fiber trunks and large earth stations.[35] In effect, this meant that internal as well as global traffic was bottle-necked at each node.[36]

According to estimates published by the Ministry of Industry and Information Technology (MIIT), every 100 miles of distance from a core node reduces Internet users by about 7 percent, domain usage by 11 percent, and the creation and maintenance of websites by 12 percent.[37] As such, the distance from a core node represents a critical determinant for Internet capacity. Indeed, this is exactly what we see in Figure 3.2, which overlays Internet speed estimates on a map of China, with each core node highlighted in light grey.[38] Core nodes should have little bearing on anticorruption behavior today, since their placement was determined nearly three decades ago and was driven mainly by the location of Chinese research universities.

Econometrically speaking, distance from an Internet exchange hub places an exogenous constraint on Internet speed and quality in ways that should affect

---

[34] See CNNIC Timeline at The Internet Timeline of China 1986–2003, available at: https://www.cnnic.com.cn/IDR/hlwfzdsj/201306/t20130628_40563.htm.

[35] The fiber trunks provide the main communications medium across hubs and nodes, while earth stations enable communications over one or more orbiting satellites.

[36] Lisa Hanson. "The Chinese Internet Gets a Stronger Backbone." *Forbes*, February 24, 2015; Zixiang Tan, William Foster, and Seymour Goodman. "China's State-coordinated Internet Infrastructure." *Communications of the ACM* 42.6 (1999), pp. 44–52.

[37] See CNNIC report, 2014.

[38] Internet speeds are calculated based on about 91,000 Internet upload speed observations conducted and documented by TestMy.net, an international broadband quality evaluation firm.

Figure 3.2. ICT Infrastructure and Network Speed

Notes: Shading is based on over 91,000 internet upload speed tests conducted by TestMy.net, an international broadband testing firm, from private users across China. Darker shades represent higher speeds. The grey dots represent China's eight-node Internet backbone, which starts with three international hubs in Beijing, Shanghai, and Guangzhou, and five domestic nodes in Shenyang, Xi'an, Chengdu, Wuhan, and Nanjing.

disciplinary action through bottom-up citizen informants, who overwhelmingly use the Internet to lodge their reports. Statistically, this means that we can observe an exogenous effect of citizen reporting S_{it} on disciplinary action y_{it}, as explained by distance from an Internet hub Z_{it}. In the two-stage model, S_{it} is estimated in the first stage (equation 1) and y_{it} is estimated in the second stage (equation 2). Additional controls and the error term are captured by the terms ζ_{it} and v_{it} respectively.

$$S_{it} = \beta_0 + \upsilon Z_{it} + \zeta_{it} \tag{3.1}$$

$$y_{it} = \beta_0 + \rho \hat{S}_{it} + v_{it} \tag{3.2}$$

Data Analysis and Modeling

It is important to remember that, in theory at least, corruption investigations are first and foremost a response to corruption. The greater the underlying rate of corruption the more investigations we should expect to observe. As such, it is worth trying to approximate the underlying conditions that either encourage or discourage political corruption. For example, the more administrative units there are, the more potential corrupt actors.[39] Administrative units, however,

---

[39] Xiaobo Lu. "Booty Socialism, Bureau-Preneurs, and the State in Transition: Organizational Corruption in China." *Comparative Politics* 32.3 (2000), pp. 273–294.

are strongly correlated (r = .7) with population size. Since the number of administrative units rarely fluctuates, while population size changes, I include a logged measure of population alongside provincial controls.

Other variables are more clearly associated with corruption propensity. In particular, the literature has identified potential links between wealth and the size of budget expenditures,[40] the size of the state-owned-enterprise (SOE) sector,[41] and human capital.[42] To capture these variables, I include measures of GDP per capita as an indicator of wealth and development, logged expenditures as a proxy for opportunity to misuse public funds, SOE share of industrial output as a proxy for the size of the state-owned sector, and the number of higher education institutions (per 10,000 residents) as an indicator of the human capital. A summary of all variables is provided in Table 3.2.

The results from the two-stage regression are reported in Table 3.3. The upper panel presents the second-stage results, while the bottom panel presents first-stage estimates. In Model 1, I calculate the bivariate relationship of exogenous *Citizen Reporting*, as estimated in the first stage regression, on logged *Disciplinary Investigations*. Model 2 replicates the bivariate estimate but with the full set of controls. Model 3 includes an additional excluded instrument, average

Table 3.2 Supervision and Control Variables

Variable	Mean	Std. Dev.	Min.	Max.	N
Citizen Reports	39462	26724	658	155793	573
CDIC Investigations	5264	4211	52	20229	722
High-Profile Arrests	9.215	9.127	0	43	93
Whistleblower Protections	0.790	0.458	0	3	837
Internet Penetration	0.183	0.189	0	0.752	558
Website Information	0.563	0.163	0.126	0.9	337
Population (log)	8.005	0.903	5.375	9.344	805
GDP Per Capita	16454	18578	750	105202	806
Expenditures (log)	5.965	1.476	2.478	9.044	794
SOE Share of Output	0.433	0.292	0.008	1.013	678
Higher Education	2.457	2.107	0.07	10.83	775

[40] G. Guo. "China's Local Political Budget Cycles." *American Journal of Political Science* 53.3 (2009), pp. 621–32.
[41] Hongbin Cai, Hanming Fang, and Lixin Colin Xu. "Eat, Drink, Firms, Government: An Investigation of Corruption from the Entertainment and Travel Costs of Chinese Firms." *Journal of Law and Economics* 54.1. (2011), pp. 55–78; Peter L. Lorentzen, Pierre Landry, and John Yasuda. "Undermining Authoritarian Innovation: The Power of China's Industrial Giants." *The Journal of Politics* 76.01 (2013), pp. 182–194.
[42] Sun, *Corruption and Market in Contemporary China*.

Table 3.3 Instrumental Variable Estimate of Citizen Reporting Impact

	Treat (DV=Investigations)			Placebo (DV–Audits)	
	(1)	(2)	(3)	(4)	(5)
	Bivariate	Controls	Add'l IV	Controls	Add'l IV
Citizen Reports (log)	1.160	1.052	0.700	0.724	0.759
	(0.043)	(0.416)	(0.303)	(0.557)	(0.512)
Provincial Controls		Y	Y	Y	Y
Constant	−3.335	−4.227	−3.909	0.414	0.414
	(0.466)	(0.708)	(0.602)	(0.883)	(0.883)
Observations	571	444	375	204	204
Wu-Hausman (p-val)	0.386	0.405	0.789	0.205	0.141
R-squared	0.814	0.867	0.871	0.764	0.764

First Stage: Citizen Reports

Distance to Node	−1.129	−0.142	−0.185	−0.161	−0.171
	(0.069)	(0.037)	(0.039)	(0.050)	(0.050)
Internet Penetration			Y		Y
Network Speed			Y		Y
Provincial Controls		Y	Y	Y	Y
R-squared	0.372	0.912	0.922	0.934	0.934
F-statistic	264.414	14.802	10.348	10.383	4.157
Sargan (p-val)	n|a	n|a	0.375	n|a	0.000

Notes: This table presents the two-stage least squares estimates of the effects of *Citizen Reports*. The upper panel presents the second-stage results, while the bottom panel presents first-stage results. The dependent variables for the *Treat* models 1-3 is the logged number of disciplinary investigations in a province for a given year. The dependent variables for the *Placebo* Models 4–5 is the logged number of audits conducted in a province for a given year. Models 2–4 include the full set of provincial controls: provincial Population, GDP per capita, Local Expenditures, SOE Share of Output, and Higher Education. The excluded instrument, average distance to Network Node measures the average geodesic distance between a province and eight different network interchanges located in Beijing, Shanghai, Guangzhou, Nanjing, Chengdu, Shenyang, and Wuhan. Models 3 and 5 include additional excluded instruments, namely *Internet Penetration* and average *Network Speed*, both of which capture different aspects of network bottlenecks in China's Internet infrastructure. All specifications include year-level fixed effects. Standard errors in parentheses.

network speed, which provides a more direct measure of network bottlenecks. Across each of the three models, the effect of *Citizen Reporting* on *Disciplinary Investigation* is positive and significant to the conventional .05 level. Extrapolating from the log–log estimate suggests that a 10 percent increase in citizen reports leads to roughly a 7 percent increase in investigations, or roughly one additional investigation for every ten reports, based on sample averages.

Model diagnostics suggest the instrument variable approach was warranted, as evinced by the null Wu-Hausman tests, and properly identified, as demonstrated by the sufficiently large F-statistics. Though the instrumental variable results seem robust, however, it is never certain that they are properly estimated. In particular, it is impossible to prove that the exclusion restriction on the instrument is fully satisfied. For instance, one could argue that distance from an exchange hub might have also constrained economic development and therefore the opportunities for corruption. In other words, distance from an exchange hub could be correlated with disciplinary investigations through processes other than bottom-up citizen reporting. Objectively speaking, this argument would make the most sense if corruption were systematically related to Internet-dependent economic activity. While this is a plausible scenario, no study of corruption has yet alluded to such a relationship. Nevertheless, concerns such as this can never be fully discounted.

Instead, I rely on indirect evaluations of the instrumental variable. First, by including an additional instrument in Model 3, I can run what is called an "over-identification test" on the second stage results, to indirectly evaluate the assumption that both instruments are valid. The logic here is that if at least one instrument is valid, it should deliver an unbiased estimate in the second stage, and that if both are valid, their respective estimates would thus both be unbiased and consistent. However, if even one instrument fails the exclusion restriction, their second stage estimates will not be consistent. The test statistic to evaluate this possibility is reported as the Sargan p-value in the bottom of Table 3.3, with any value below .05 indicating inconsistency at the second stage. As Model 3 indicates, the the inclusion of an additional instrument, a measure of government website infrastructure, delivers a strong over-identification result, suggesting that the instrumental approach is producing consistent and properly identified estimates. Taken together, the results broadly support the feedback logic, whereby higher rates of bottom-up citizen reporting induce higher rates of top-down supervision.

Second, I include a placebo test in Models 4 and 5, which essentially replicate Models 2 and 3 by estimating the two-stage effect of citizen reporting on government audits which, though a form of disciplinary investigation, are not initiated by citizen reports. Instead, government audits, much like IRS audits, are primarily implemented on a rolling basis or in response to red flags raised by accounting algorithms used by budgeting departments. If the instrumental variable is correlated with corruption through means other than bottom-up reporting, we should expect the placebo effects to also produce positive and significant coefficients in the second stage. Yet, as Models 4 and 5 clearly demonstrate, this is not the case. In both instances the coefficient on citizen reporting falls flat. Moreover, model diagnostics for the over-identification test in the placebo models suggest that the instrument in the placebo is not properly identified. That is, variation in citizen reporting predicted by broadband infrastructure has no identified or consistent relationship with internal government audits.

Integrating Supervision

Research in comparative politics posits that nondemocratic regimes can leverage bottom-up input to overcome informational challenges inherent to authoritarian governance.[43] This work has been crucial for laying the theoretical and empirical groundwork for thinking about bottom-up governance under autocracy. However, it rests on a crucial and thus untested assumption, which is that autocrats act on the information generated by citizens. In demonstrating a direct link between citizen petitions and anticorruption efforts, this chapter offers the empirical support for this important assumption. Relying on regional and longitudinal variation, I estimate that ten citizen petitions translate into roughly one additional corruption investigation. To account for unobserved heterogeneity and endogeneity, I leverage exogenous variation in ICT infrastructure to isolate the independent effect of bottom-up supervision.

The results demonstrate that technological innovations can bolster the impact of bottom-up input, even in the absence of formal institutions for accountability. Given that most authoritarian regimes struggle with corruption and implementation at lower-levels of government, we can expect that technology will continue to play a key role in how these regimes harness public input for oversight and supervision. This may lead to cleaner governments and less government waste. As discussed in Chapter 8, a number of prominent authoritarian regimes are investing in e-government technologies and corruption reporting methods.

---

[43] Nathan, "China's Changing of the Guard: Authoritarian Resilience"; Stromseth, Malesky, and Gueorguiev, *China's Governance Puzzle: Enabling Transparency and Participation in a Single-Party State*; Melanie Manion. *Information for Autocrats: Representation in Chinese Local Congresses*. Cambridge University Press, 2016, p. 195; Martin K. Dimitrov. "Vertical Accountability in Communist Regimes: The Role of Citizen Complaints in Bulgaria." In *Why Communism Did Not Collapse: Understanding Authoritarian Regime Resilience in Asia and Europe*. Ed. by Martin K. Dimitrov. Cambridge University Press, 2013, pp. 276–302.

If effective, such investments have the potential to defuse a common per-ception that authoritarian governments are corrupt. This is not to say that technology will get rid of corruption in authoritarian countries, but that it will help leaders cordon off the kinds of corruption that lead to frictions with the public. Put differently, technology that brings the public closer to oversight is also technology that keeps demands for democracy at bay. This interpretation adds to a growing list of scholarship that challenges the apocryphal notion that the digital revolution in information technology will undermine authoritarian regimes.[44] In the next chapter, I extend this same logic to control in the policy planning process.

---

[44] For an excellent review of the regime-strengthening effects of information technology, see Shanthi Kalathil and Taylor C. Boas. *Open Networks, Closed Regimes*. Carnegie Endowment, 2003.

4

Participation in Planning

When the people have no power, they do not realize that the nation belongs to all the people, and they keep distance from the emperor. When the people have some power, then they will realize the nation is their own concern, and they will be drawn close to the emperor. When the power of the empire comes from one person, it is weak. When it comes from millions of people it is strong.[1]

— Wang Kang-nien, 1954

In the depths of winter 1921, two Soviet warships, the *Petropavlovsk* and the *Sevastopol*, stood frozen in the waters of Kronstadt Bay, less than 40km from the center of Saint Petersburg (at the time renamed simply "Petrograd," without the "Saint"). The ships were part of a large and powerful armada that included the *Aurora*—the infamous battleship that fired at the Tsar's Winter Palace on October 25, 1917. So when sailors aboard the two ships, cold and hungry like most Russians at the time, decided to turn against the local soviet and to draw up a list of demands, including an end to Bolshevik monopoly on power, it scared Moscow to the bone.[2] In response, Lenin, who up until that point believed in and promoted the maxims of internal debate, moved to crush any and all dissent—starting but hardly ending with the mutineers in Kronstadt. Within months, critical voices within the Soviet congresses were labeled, silenced, and expunged—dashing any hope that the formative years of the Soviet Union would be guided by inclusive debate among different groups and interests.[3]

Lenin likely did not anticipate that this purge, existential as it may have seemed at the time, would lay the foundations for a far more brutal and thorough political culling by his successor, Joseph Stalin.[4] When, in 1956, Nikita Khrushchev appeared in front of the 20th CPSU Congress to denounce Stalin, he was in

---

[1] Wang Kang-nien 汪康年 (1860–1911) was a Chinese political philosopher, cited in Teng and Fairbank, *China's Response to the West: A Documentary Survey, 1839–1923*, p. 163.

[2] Alexander Berkman. *Die Kronstadt Rebellion*. 3. Der Syndikalist Berlin, 1922.

[3] Critical members in the Congress included Mensheviks and socialist revolutionaries, as well as many union representatives. See Schapiro, "'Putting the Lid on Leninism': Opposition and Dissent in the Communist One-party States."

[4] Robert W. Thurston. *Life and Terror in Stalin's Russia, 1934–1941*. Yale University Press, 1998.

Retrofitting Leninism. Dimitar D. Gueorguiev. Oxford University Press. © Oxford University Press 2021.
DOI: 10.1093/oso/9780197555668.003.0005

effect trying to turn back time—signaling that internal criticism was not only acceptable but also vital to the health of the Party and the Union. In particular, Khrushchev advocated loosening controls on the arts, sciences, and media; these reforms, though broadly incomplete, came to be known collectively as part of a broader "Khrushchev thaw."[5] These efforts ultimately failed, however, and Khruschev was himself bitterly criticized at the end of his tenure for sowing discontent within the Party. After a chilling period under Leonid Brezhnev, Mikhail Gorbachev would again attempt to make space for critical debate; and again these efforts would implode, this time alongside the Soviet Union itself.[6]

The CCP in China had its own fits and starts with critical discourse. As discussed in Chapter 3, criticism and debate were an integral feature of the early Maoist period, especially during the Yan'an Rectification, and again during the "Hundred Flowers Campaign."[7] As in the Soviet Union, however, these gestures for inclusion quickly imploded. Just over a month after the start of the Hundred Flowers Campaign, the CCP launched the first of several, aggressive "Anti-Rightist" counter-campaigns against those who had spoken out against the regime. The cycle would be repeated in the late 1970s and again in the 1980s.[8] In each instance, the Party signaled an invitation for greater public participation and criticism, then cracked down bitterly.

The failed cycles of loosening and tightening in the Soviet Union and the PRC illustrate a common theme among autocracies aspiring toward inclusion: strong theoretical ambition to incorporate public feedback and a general inability to do so in practice. In Chapter 1, I proposed that this inability is partially the consequence of insufficient control. The mutiny in Konstrandt, for instance, underscored the fact that the Bolsheviks, though they had won the Russian

[5] For a good history on de-Stalinization see Robert Hornsby. *Protest, Reform and Repression in Khrushchev's Soviet Union.* Cambridge University Press, 2013.

[6] William J. Tompson. "Khrushchev and Gorbachev as Reformers: A Comparison." *British Journal of Political Science* 23.1 (1993), pp. 77–105.

[7] The earliest mention of "Let a hundred flowers bloom and a thousand thoughts contend" came during a closed session of the Politburo in May of 1956, but the official rollout through the propaganda channels did not begin until April of 1957. For an authoritative description of how the campaign unfolded, see Roderick MacFarquhar. *The Hundred Flowers Campaign and the Chinese Intellectuals.* Praeger, 1966.

[8] The Democracy Wall Movement began with a "big character" poster on Beijing's historic Xidan Wall in October 1978, but the origins of the movement came in April 1976, when people gathered in Tiananmen Square to mourn the death of Zhou Enlai and began indirectly criticizing Mao and his associates. The movement was drawn to an abrupt end in 1979 by Deng Xiaoping, and the constitutional rights that allowed such kinds of expression were expunged from the PRC Constitution in September 1980. For a thorough account of origins and crackdown, see Kjeld Erik Brodsgaard. "The Democracy Movement in China, 1978–1979: Opposition Movements, Wall Poster Campaigns, and Underground Journals." *Asian Survey* 21.7 (1981), pp. 747–774. The events in Tiananmen Square 1989 were also precipitated by the death and mourning of a popular CCP politician, Hu Yaobang, and an attempt by some members of the leadership to promote dialogue with public demonstrators; see Dingxin Zhao. *The Power of Tiananmen: State-Society Relations and the 1989 Beijing Student Movement.* University of Chicago Press, 2004.

revolution, relied on soldiers who were hardly under the political control of the Party. Moreover, failed inclusion reflects underlying shortcomings in intelligence and capacity to respond. Although the CPSU had consolidated political control under Stalin, organizational control was still spotty. As a result, Khrushchev's Thaw operated on a trial-and-error basis, ultimately delivering unhelpful and socially frustrating results.[9] In China as well, Mao, and later Deng would be rudely surprised by the range and quantity of dissatisfaction brewing among elites and mass organizations, and were challenged by limited institutional capacity to make sense or respond to these critiques.[10]

Building on the framework outlined in Chapter 2, we can approach the challenge of authoritarian inclusion along two dimensions. First, in order for the public to serve a constructive role in the governing process, the regime must have the capacity to contain, compartmentalize and, if needed, cauterize any attempts at coordinated opposition. Second, a regime must have the capacity to render societal inputs into meaningful governance outputs. Without such capacities, forays into inclusive authoritarianism risk sparking opposition movements or simply laying bare the limitations of the leadership. One of the primary contentions of this book is that China has now achieved capacity in both the control and processing power that make inclusive control both feasible and productive. Some of these controls are embedded in how the Party manages society; others come in the form of recent technological innovations. Building on those insights, in Chapter 4. I explored the resultant patterns of controlled inclusion within the scope of participatory oversight. In this chapter, I extend the discussion to participatory planning and what I refer to as "structured consultation," whereby feedback is prompted and organized within a regime-controlled agenda.

Structured Consultation

Between 1995 and 2005, about 100,000 firms, comprising around two-thirds of China's state-owned fixed capital and worth over 11.4 trillion RMB in assets, were privatized. In human terms, this resulted in layoffs of about 60 million Chinese workers, who were forced either to retire or retool for new positions in an emerging labor market. The terms of this transition were ostensibly laid out in the 1994 Labor Law, which legalized the conversion of what were essentially lifetime state-worker pacts into fixed-term employment contracts. The law

---

[9] Lucy Hornby, "China Blocks $4bn Xiaonanhai Dam Development." *Financial Times*, April 8, 2015.
[10] For Mao, see MacFarquhar, *The Hundred Flowers Campaign*. For Deng, see Spence, *The Search for Modern China*, pp. 163–178.

included a number of worker protections, most of which were vaguely defined, rarely enforced, and widely ignored—arguably provoking more disputes than they averted.[11] As privatization efforts geared up by mid-decade, labor disputes across the country skyrocketed. From 1995 through 1999, Chinese provincial labor unions recorded 431,330 labor disputes, of which 81,341 were considered "collective disputes" involving three or more participants.[12]

Recognizing the shortcomings of the Labor Law, national leaders walked back their ambitions for privatization and left it up to the provinces to figure out a way through.[13] In response, local governments moved forward with local regulations and implementation guidelines. These included new rules for severance packages, more funding for re-employment services, and living allowances for the long-term unemployed. Importantly, the majority of these stopgap measures were formulated in consultation with grassroots labor unions.[14] In all, provincial statistics on policy drafting reveal that in 1999 alone, arguably the most volatile year for privatization,[15] local governments consulted with grassroots labor unions on over 14,000 occasions.[16]

The role of labor unions here was interesting insofar as the unions represented an uncomfortable intersection between two competing interest groups: SOE managers who were eager to convert their assets, and soon-to-be laid-off workers anxious about the future. To be sure, managers held nearly all the cards at the negotiating table, but union law did stipulate that transfer of ownership required approval from 70 percent of workers.[17] Moreover, workers were, by law, entitled to a stake in the company's assets and were in some instances offered shares during privatization. Most importantly, however, these terms could only be enforced through the labor unions. Granted, Chinese labor unions hardly qualify as workers' organizations. They are CCP-organized and usually dominated by factory managers. In the face of privatization, however, the unions, like the workers, faced an existential threat in that privatized firms were not required to have union representation or form independent unions.[18] For union

---

[11] William Hurst. *The Chinese Worker after Socialism*. Cambridge University Press, 2009.

[12] *Chinese Trade Union Statistical Yearbook* (中国工会统计年鉴), various years.

[13] See: "The Circular on Several Issues Regarding the Sale of Small SOEs" (known as the Circular No. 89), jointly promulgated by the State Economic and Trade Commission, the Ministry of Finance, and the People's Bank of China, in February 1999.

[14] Jianjun Zhang. "State Power, Elite Relations, and the Politics of Privatization in China's Rural Industry—Different Approaches in Two Regions". *Asian Survey* 48.2 (2008), pp. 215–238.

[15] Jin Zeng. *State-Led Privatization in China: The Politics of Economic Reform*. Taylor & Francis, 2013, p. 216; Ching Kwan Lee. *Against the Law: Labor Protests in China's Rustbelt and Sunbelt*. University of California Press, 2007, p. 340.

[16] Stromseth, Malesky, and Gueorguiev, *China's Governance Puzzle: Enabling Transparency and Participation in a Single-Party State*.

[17] Zhang, "State Power, Elite Relations," p. 222.

[18] Feng Chen. "Between the State and Labour: The Conflict of Chinese Trade Unions' Double Identity in Market Reform." *The China Quarterly* 176 (2003), pp. 1006–1028.

representatives, the clearest route to a future position was to get involved in an emerging re-employment services sector set up by the central government to help laid-off workers transition away from SOE employment.[19] Ironically, these re-employment services were funded by local governments through the sale of state-owned assets.[20]

This setup presented an opportunity. Labor unions wanted more money diverted to re-employment services and severance benefits, while SOE managers, who would in most cases turn out to be the purchasers of the SOE themselves, wanted to undervalue company assets as much as possible.[21] Managers could try to undervalue their companies via informal means, or they could deflate assets legally by inflating their employee liabilities, which would be partly offset by central grants and subsidies anyway. Though these bargains ultimately shifted the costs onto the Chinese taxpayer, they were nevertheless instrumental in help-ing reduce lengthy and, at times, violent labor disputes. In short, by leveraging the labor unions to mediate consultation with managers and workers' groups, local governments were able to chart a course through one of the most perilous periods in modern Chinese politics.

These lessons about the value of mediating consultation would come to the fore again in 2006, when the NPC began working on a new law that would further redefine labor relations in the country. This time, the drafting effort would take full and preemptive advantage of bottom-up collaboration, including direct consultation with the public. In the thirty days after a draft of Labor Contract Law (LCL) was open for public comment, 191,849 online comments flooded in alongside approximately 150,000 comments collected during meetings between workers and local labor unions—making the LCL the most prominent instance of consultative decision-making to date.[22] The LCL was also the first example of national policymaking on which online consultation was the primary medium for input communication, allowing citizens from various perspectives, including young workers and small business owners, to weigh in.[23]

Interestingly, policymakers appear to have encouraged this diversity by em-ploying a staggered consultation campaign, targeting different groups at dif-ferent stages. In addition to the first call for comment, initiated in March

---

[19] Tim Pringle. "Industrial Relations in the People's Republic of China." *Trade Unions in China: The Challenge of Labour Unrest.* Taylor & Francis, 2011, pp. 11–56.

[20] Yuanzheng Cao, Yingyi Qian, and Barry R. Weingast. "From Federalism, Chinese Style, to Privatization, Chinese Style." *The Economics of Transition* 7.1 (1999), pp. 103–131.

[21] Russell Smyth. "Asset Stripping in Chinese State-Owned Enterprises." *Journal of Contemporary Asia* 30.1 (2000), pp. 3–16.

[22] See "Labor Contract Law Open for Notice and Comment," *Xinhua News Agency*, April 21, 2006, available at http://news.xinhuanet.com/legal/2006-04/21/content_4457789.htm.

[23] Stromseth, Malesky, and Gueorguiev, *China's Governance Puzzle: Enabling Transparency and Participation in a Single-Party State*, p. 177.

2006, policymakers hosted three additional rounds of consultation and revision, each time soliciting participants from opposing sides of the policy debate. On one end, workers, NGOs, and the state-backed All-China Federation of Trade Unions (ACFTU) pushed for greater protections from wage arrears, layoffs, and fixed-term contracting. Migrant workers, in particular, demanded mobility for pension accounts. On the other side, a smaller but better organized contingent of domestic and foreign business lobbies focused efforts on weakening collective bargaining in health, safety, wages, and layoffs, as well as on curbing limits to probationary employment. Depending on which group was targeted, average citizens (in rounds one and three) or business interests (round two), the policy pendulum swung accordingly—either strengthening or watering down the draft legislation.

In stark contrast to the closed-door policymaking tactics of the past, this back and forth precipitated a heated public debate and a series of high-profile position statements.[24] Most notably, Ms. Zhang Yin, a delegate to China's People's Political Consultative Conference and China's richest woman at the time, took on the mantle of pro-business groups, arguing that the new law amounted to a "revamping of the iron-rice-bowl."[25] Domestic and foreign business associations followed suit, warning of weaker employment and preemptive layoffs.[26] Labor advocates, as represented by the ACFTU, favored a worker-friendly policy, claiming that, "the only negative impact of the Labor Contract Law would be to help reduce the employers' excessive and inappropriate profits that result from over-exploitation of workers' rights."[27]

The regime, however, did not overtly impose its own preference during the consultative period nor in the final legislation adopted in June 2007. Instead, government set the agenda from the outset and allowed competing voices to cancel each other out over a period of almost fifteen months. Had the government chosen to formulate the policy privately, many of the criticisms that emerged during the consultation period would likely have surfaced during implementation anyway, with labor claiming the policy did not go far enough and business protesting the opposite. In the end, most observers concluded that the LCL was an acceptable compromise and an important step toward regulating

[24] Parry Leung and Alvin Y. So. "The New Labor Contract Law in 2008: China's Legal Absorption of Labor Unrest." *Journal of Studies in Social Science* 4(1), pp. 131–160. 2013.

[25] See "Zhang Yin Proposes to Eliminate the Open-Ended Clause in the New Labor Contract Law," *China Review News*, 2008, http://hk.crntt.com/doc/1005/8/1/3/100581306.html.

[26] See Mary Elizabeth Gallagher. "Industrial Relations in the World's Workshop: Participatory Legislation, Bottom-Up Law Enforcement, and Firm Behavior." APSA 2010 Annual Meeting Paper, 2010; also: US-China Business Council, "Comments on the Draft Labor Contract Law of the People's Republic of China," March 20, 2006; and European Union Chamber of Commerce in China, "Re: Comments of the European Union Chamber of Commerce in China on the Draft Labour Contract Law," April 18, 2006.

[27] See: "Disputes over the new labour contract law" https://bit.ly/2IMdcpQ.

China's massive labor market.[28] More importantly, the LCL has proven effective in achieving its primary objective—getting a larger portion of China's labor force engaged in formal relations with their employers. This resulted in millions of existing and new workers signing contracts shortly after the law came into effect.[29]

This pattern of structured consultation would not have been possible if not for the CCP's embeddedness within and control over the workplace and business organizations. Nor would public debate have been as easily managed in the absence of extensive regime controls over the legislative process and public discourse in the media. Put differently, in the absence of regime controls, public debate over something as controversial and salient as labor contracting could easily have emerged as a political flash point, which is why labor reforms in authoritarian regimes are usually done behind closed doors.[30] In the Chinese case, however, investments in grassroots organization, alongside comprehensive agenda and discourse controls, made it possible for the regime to pursue such issues out in the open. But is that the case when clear interest groups are harder to define? Moreover, such modes of inclusion raise questions about the degree to which consultation impacts policy. In the case of LCL, for instance, we can see that open consultation allowed policymakers to exploit the process and better market their policy priorities.[31] Was the end product any different as a result of the consultative process? In the sections to follow, I pursue these questions via a broader study of consultation and policymaking in contemporary China.

Trial Balloons

Chinese leaders like to describe their system of rule as a "consultative democracy." Yet as we discussed in Chapter 2, despite an abundance of consultation, there is little democracy to speak of. Ostensibly, China has a multiparty system, but all parties are subordinate to and organized by the CCP. Constitutionally, the annual *Lianghui* (or "double meeting") sessions of the NPC and CPPCC are the pinnacle of democratic decision-making. Few, however, believe that in

---

[28] Mary E. Gallagher and Baohua Dong. "Legislating Harmony: Labor Law Reform in Contemporary China." *From Iron Rice Bowl to Informalization: Markets, State and Workers in a Changing China.* Ed. by Mary E. Gallagher, Sarosh Kuruvilla, and Ching Kwan Lee. Ithaca: Cornell University Press, 2011, pp. 36–60.

[29] Xiaoying Li and Richard B. Freeman. "How Does China's New Labour Contract Law Affect Floating Workers?" *British Journal of Industrial Relations* (2014), pp. 1–25.

[30] Eva Bellin. "Contingent Democrats: Industrialists, Labor, and Democratization in Late-Developing Countries." *World Politics* 52.2 (2000), pp. 175–205.

[31] For comparative examples of consultation as marketing, see Francis Edward Rourke. *Bureaucracy, Politics, and Public Policy.* Little, Brown, 1969, p. 173, p. 54.

practice either body exercises much in the way of influence or representation. Such skepticism is warranted. The *Lianghui* comes on the heels of a far more influential conclave, the CCP Plenum, which sets the political and legislative agenda roughly six months in advance. For their part, legislative representatives are not directly elected and almost never challenge positions laid out by the Party.[32] During the annual 2019 session of the *Lianghui*, not a single NPC delegate voted against the 2019 government work report.[33]

The absence of dissenting votes, however, does not mean Chinese decision-making is void of popular sentiment or discussion. Instead, scholars have increasingly come to describe the Chinese legislature as a consultation platform, whereby representatives are provided an opportunity to provide constructive feedback and lobby for their constituencies in an apolitical manner.[34] While clearly not democratic, these consultative procedures, alongside other mediums of consultation, are thought to imbue the Chinese system with the information and legitimacy necessary to govern.[35] Indeed, a growing number, of studies find that consultation in China is associated with higher public satisfaction and trust in government,[36] along with some indication that these gains translate into more compliance.[37]

Fundamental questions remain, however. First, given that consultation is heavily controlled, is there any reason to believe that public input generated through the process actually penetrates into the substance of policy plans? Second, even if consultative procedures are simply a tool for packaging authoritarian policy for public consumption, how does this tool operate? Is it simply a legitimatizing tactic or does consultation also reveal useful information? If the latter, what is nature of that information, and how can the regime leverage it during policy formulation?

---

[32] The most prominent example of opposition occurred in 1992 when, as recounted in Chapter 2, 177 members voted against and 644 abstained from supporting the Three Gorges Dam construction.

[33] In total, 2,945 delegates voted to approve the government work report. Three delegates abstained from voting, and 27 delegates were not in attendance.

[34] Manion, *Information for Autocrats: Representation in Chinese Local Congresses*; Rory Truex. "Focal Points, Dissident Calendars, and Preemptive Repression." Working Paper (2016); Tsang, "Consultative Leninism: China's New Political Framework."

[35] Nathan, "China's Changing of the Guard: Authoritarian Resilience"; Wei Pan. "Toward a Consultative Rule of Law Regime in China." *Journal of Contemporary China* 12.34 (2003), pp. 3–43; He and Warren, "Authoritarian Deliberation: The Deliberative Turn in Chinese Political Development."

[36] See James S. Fishkin et al. "Deliberative Democracy in an Unlikely Place: Deliberative Polling in China." *British Journal of Political Science* 40.02 (2010), pp. 435–448; Rory Truex. "Consultative Authoritarianism and Its Limits." *Comparative Political Studies* (2014), pp. 1–33.

[37] Stromseth, Malesky, and Gueorguiev, *China's Governance Puzzle: Enabling Transparency and Participation in a Single-Party State*; Truex, *Making Autocracy Work: Representation and Responsiveness in Modern China*; Manion, *Information for Autocrats: Representation in Chinese Local Congresses*.

Addressing such questions is particularly difficult in countries like China precisely because the ruling party so thoroughly controls the consultative agenda and process. China's notice-and-comment process offers a clear illustration, insofar as it allows the regime to carefully stipulate the topic of discussion, as well as the parameters of debate within that topic. It does this first by outlining a draft proposal and then issuing an invitation for comment over a defined period of time (typically 30 calendar days), along with guidance over which aspects of the draft are under consideration. Rather than side-step the shadow of the CCP, the rest of this chapter relies on a survey effort that makes use of the CCP policy agenda and taps directly into the most public dimension of the regime's consultative architecture. Specifically, I will focus on policy drafts for which policy planners have initiated notice-and-comment consultation procedures, the most generic and broad-based consultative method employed in the PRC,[38] and compare the evolution of these drafts to the outcomes of policy initiatives formulated under more traditional closed-door formats.

Gauging Public Opinion

When Chinese government agencies and administrative bodies invite public comment, they invariably state that inputs acquired during the comment period are carefully reviewed and, when appropriate, incorporated into final decisions. Yet given the highly structured nature of consultation, alongside extensive controls over public discourse, it is hard to ascertain whether or not public input has any bearing on government outputs. In democratic settings, the typical approach is to look for congruence between public opinion and government policy,[39] as measured by priority alignment, that is, whether policy priorities identified by the public are also those advanced by policymakers. A more nuanced approach is to look at within-issue congruence. For instance, if the public favors a public healthcare option over a private one, congruence expects lawmakers to lean toward the public option as well.[40] These approaches, however, are not viable in the Chinese setting. Chinese legislative representatives rarely participate in policy votes and, even when they do, information on individual votes is carefully

---

[38] For a summary of contemporary consultative procedures, see Chapter 3.

[39] Benjamin I. Page and Robert Y. Shapiro. "Effects of Public Opinion on Policy." *American Political Science Review* 77.1 (1983), pp. 175–190.

[40] Jeffrey R. Lax and Justin H. Phillips. "The Democratic Deficit in the States." *American Journal of Political Science* 56.1 (2012), pp. 148–166; Martin Gilens and Benjamin I. Page. "Testing Theories of American Politics: Elites, Interest Groups, and Average Citizens." *Perspectives on Politics* 12.03 (2014), pp. 564–581.

guarded. More generally, fine-grained data on public opinion regarding specific policy priorities and issues is hard to come by.[41]

The same constraints apply to public consultation, which remains a closed-circuit affair. Citizens, like legislative representatives, are encouraged to voice opinions vertically to leaders but not horizontally among peers. While there is evidence that the regime does not censor these prompted debates,[42] barriers to organized discussion and the careful supervision of opinion leaders mean that critical opinions are unlikely to coalesce into discernible popular policy positions. Moreover, while government-run media outlets and think tanks conduct regular public opinion surveys, the raw data from these efforts is not open to the public.[43] In 2015–2016, for instance, the public was consulted on 18 national policy items alongside thousands of other topics raised by regulatory bodies and regional governments.[44] Yet, we know relatively little about what these consultations produced. What we do know is based on interviews with officials on the receiving end of public inputs, who typically point to specific examples of public input contributing to policy design.[45] These anecdotal accounts, however, may not be representative of the full spectrum of public inputs delivered via consultation.

In an effort to tap into public sentiments, I launched a national policy-focused opinion poll, the China Policy Barometer (CPB), in January of 2016.[46] Since then, the CPB has completed three annual waves, reaching roughly seven thousand respondents regarding their views on ongoing policy debates and priorities. The CPB is targeted toward measuring public opinion on policy issues that are deliberately opened to public consultation, as well as those that do not proceed through general consultation. In selecting policy topics for the CPB and demarcating between open and closed items, I relied on two primary sources. First, with respect to open policies, the National People's Congress "Public Consultation" online dashboard provides a list of open policy discussions.[47] Second, the State Council's "Policy" web page documents a broad range of topics

---

[41] Notable exceptions include Shi Tianjian's pioneering surveys on public opinion, as well as surveys conducted by PEW and Gallup.

[42] Gueorguiev and Malesky, "Consultation and Selective Censorship in China."

[43] For example, see the annual "hot-topic" surveys conducted by the *People's Daily*: https://bit.ly/2S90rIR.

[44] See: http://www.npc.gov.cn/npc/flcazqyj/node_8195_2.htm.

[45] He and Warren, "Authoritarian Deliberation: The Deliberative Turn in Chinese Political Development"; Stromseth, Malesky, and Gueorguiev, *China's Governance Puzzle: Enabling Transparency and Participation in a Single-Party State*.

[46] For background on the CPB as well as access to public versions of the data, refer to www.chinabarometer.org.

[47] See: http://www.npc.gov.cn/npc/flcazqyj/node_8176.htm.

under government consideration and discussion, most of which are not open for public comment.[48]

Ideally, the CPB would have covered all possible topic issues, but resource constraints and concerns about respondent fatigue meant that survey length and the range of policy topics had to be kept to a workable minimum. To shorten the list of candidate policies, the CPB focused on policies that garner more public interest and have a higher likelihood of resulting in legislation, regulation, or revealed preference in the near-term future. For example, with respect to the South China Sea issue, it was widely known that a UN ruling would come in early summer of 2016 and that a Chinese response would arrive shortly thereafter. As an indicator of public interest, the NPC open-policymaking website provides statistics on hot topics, as well as the number of public comments received across different policy topics. Since such a tracker is not available for closed policies, interest in closed policies was gauged using Baidu Index, a service that provides indexes of public and media interest across popular search patterns and topics.[49]

From within the sample of popular and timely topics, specific items were chosen based on whether debate could be plausibly positioned along a unidimensional scale, anchored on each end by opposing views. Once a policy item was identified as a candidate survey topic, it was given to research assistants tasked with formulating competing position statements based on the draft policy notice, alongside available secondary sources and public discussion in the press and social media.[50] Policy items for which competing perspectives could be mapped onto a unidimensional spectrum were included in the survey. For example, respondents were informed about tensions in the South China Sea and asked whether China should pursue a *diplomatic* approach, mindful of international law and regional cooperation, or an *assertive* strategy dictated by China's strengths and capabilities. For ease of interpretation, these preferences are anchored along a liberal (internationalist) versus conservative (nationalist) spectrum and distributed across a 10-point scale, with the midpoint reducing to a neutral preference for the status quo. Once an official policy is announced, it is easy to use this same scale to attribute a leaning to the regime and compare it to the public inclination.

[48] See http://www.gov.cn/zhengce/index.htm.
[49] The search index data reported by Baidu is an absolute term index, making comparison across topics and across time possible. See Liwen Vaughan and Yue Chen. "Data Mining from Web Search Queries: A Comparison of Google Trends and Baidu Index." *Journal of the Association for Information Science and Technology* 66.1 (2015), pp. 13–22; Wei Zhang et al. "Open Source Information, Investor Attention, and Asset Pricing." *Economic Modelling* 33 (2013), pp. 613–619.
[50] Source referenced in Chapter 4 Appendix.

To be clear, neither the topic selection nor framing strategy employed by the CPB seeks to factor out the possibility that policymakers are deliberately selecting topics for consultation or that propaganda outlets are framing the boundaries of debate. On the contrary, and consistent with theory of controlled inclusion explored in this book, such controls are fundamental to the process and cannot be ignored. Rather, what the survey design does is help us focus on topics that are highly salient and for which we have good reason to believe public opinion is not homogeneous. As such, the CPB offers a small window onto the public discourse that actually exists, and not what would be the case in the absence of controls. Moreover, what the CPB offers, by directly surveying Chinese citizens about the same topics on which they are being consulted by the state, is a backdoor into the public input generated by consultation. In 2016 this selection and framing strategy yielded twelve policy debates, summarized in Appendix Table A.2. Seven of the twelve items were exposed to public consultation.[51] The remaining five policy items were discussed internally without public input. The 2017 and 2018 waves of the CPB covered ten and seven different policy topics, respectively.

Each wave of the CPB surveys was carried out with the help of Chinese crowd-sourcing services SoJump and Kurun Data, which operate in similar fashion to Amazon's Mechanical Turk but with a narrower focus on survey research. These crowd-sourcing services facilitated access to a large pool of potential respondents, which would have been cost-prohibitive with traditional sampling methods. It is important to stress that this sampling method is not scientific in that there was no attempt to use probability sampling to insure representativeness. Unsurprisingly, the sample is younger and more affluent than the average Chinese citizen (see Appendix Table A.1).

That said, Internet-based surveys have consistently been shown to mirror scientific samples, at least in terms of substance if not composition.[52] It is also worth stressing that the demographic reached through the CPB sampling strategy is probably not too far off from the group of people who might be participating in the regime's actual consultation campaigns. Yet, it is possible to weight unrepresentative data to make it more consistent with what we would expect from a more representative sample. This type of weighting is how large Internet market research firms like YouGov implement their polls in the United

---

[51] Two of these items, amendments to the Environmental Protection Law, and Budget Law, were already decided and do not feature in the main analysis.
[52] Adam J. Berinsky, Gregory A. Huber, and Gabriel S. Lenz. "Evaluating Online Labor Markets for Experimental Research: Amazon.com's Mechanical Turk." *Political Analysis* 20.3 (2012), pp. 351–368, S. Clifford, R.M. Jewell, and P.D.Waggoner. "Are Samples Drawn from Mechanical Turk Valid for Research on Political Ideology?" *Research & Politics* 2.4 (2015), DOI: 2053168015622072; Aniket Kittur, Ed H. Chi, and Bongwon Suh. "Crowdsourcing User Studies with Mechanical Turk." *Proceedings of the 2008 SIGCHI Conference on Human Factors in Computing Systems* (2008), pp. 453–456.

States and Europe. I adopt a similar post-stratification process to weight the CPB data based on its deviation from census statistics on age, education, and income.

Empirical Expectations

If consultative policy planning is heavily controlled, with the regime holding all the cards, where exactly is the public contribution? Here it is important to remember that the instrumental logic outlined in Chapter 2 posits at least two ways by which public consultation might impact governance, namely, via greater policy legitimacy and policy improvement. While the two are often included side-by-side, they actually invoke different mechanisms. Policy improvement explicitly assumes that policy outputs are qualitatively different as a consequence of consultation. By contrast, legitimacy may or may not involve any change to the actual policy output, as long as it is interpreted more favorably by the public. It is possible, however, that these mechanisms operate in tandem. For example, consultation can reveal heterogeneity in public preferences, thereby allowing the regime to stake out and legitimate moderating positions, as they did in the case of the LCL.

In either case, we should expect that policy choices on topics with consultation are more likely to converge with public preferences. To see whether or not this is the case, I rely on the weighted preference distributions as an indicator of where the public leans on each policy item and compare that with the direction the government ultimately took. The determination of whether that direction is liberal or conservative is relative to the status quo policy position. If inputs are being incorporated into the policy formulation process, we should expect the congruence rate for consultation items to be greater than for those items decided without formal public consultation. Moreover, if we assume the regime is simply interested in managing public opinion rather than using consultation for a specific agenda, we should not expect congruence to be ideologically neutral; that is, we would expect government decisions to more closely track conservative (or liberal) public preferences.[53]

Quantitative Results

The results in Figure 4.1 suggest congruence between consultation and policy decisions. In 2016, decisions on all five of the ongoing policy debates for which there was consultation ended up leaning in the direction of public opinion. Likewise, in 2017 and 2018, three out of four and three out of three open policies,

---

[53] I include "liberal" in parentheses because it is unclear whether the public is more liberal or conservative than the Chinese policymaking establishment.

Figure 4.1. Public Consultation and Policy Choices

CPB Survey Wave	Policy Issue	Consultation	Public Leaning (Liberal to Conservative)	Congruence (Regime & Public)
2016				
	Domestic violence	✓		✓
	Wildlife protection	✓		✓
	Counter-terrorism	✓		✓
	Online privacy	✓		✓
	Foreign NGOs	✓		✓
	Media supervision	.		.
	Urban planning	.		.
	South China Sea	.		.
	Stock market	.		.
	Informal lending	.		✓
2017				
	Public surveillance	✓		tbd
	Ridesharing services	✓		✓
	Nuclear energy	✓		✓
	Chinese medicine	✓		✓
	Exchange rate	.		✓
	Foreign aid	.		✓
	Affirmative action	.		.
	South China Sea	.		.
	Capital controls	.		✓
	Domestic passports	.		✓
2018				
	Trade Protections	✓		✓
	National Security Comm.	✓		✓
	Martyrs	✓		✓
	South China Sea	.		✓
	Foreign aid	.		✓
	Capital controls	.		✓
	Term limits	.		✓

Notes: Each policy preference ranges from 1 [most liberal (L)] to 10 [most conservative (C)] based on a sample average of a unidimensional preference scale, with status quo as the midpoint. Congruence is determined by comparing public leaning with final policy direction vis-à-vis the status quo.

respectively, were decided in the direction of public opinion. By contrast, across all three waves of the CPB, we see that public opinion and regime policy choices contrast on six out of fifteen of the closed policy items, or 40 percent of the time. While such crude measures of congruence are not sufficient evidence that policymakers incorporate public preferences into their policy decisions, they are suggestive. For instance, the lone "open" policy from 2017 in which public opinion appears to contrast with regime preferences—about the installation of surveillance cameras in public spaces—has yet to be formally decided. Instead, the regime has proceeded to install surveillance cameras across the country without deciding whether or not it is legal. This indicates that policymakers chose to proceed without regulation rather than adopt an unpopular policy.

The larger proportions of disagreement over closed policy issues nevertheless raises questions about the link between public inputs and regime policy outputs.

The main concern is the question of selection: Why were some topics opened for consultation, while others remained closed? Whenever I have posed this question to government officials and legislative representatives, I get a fairly consistent response: "If the public has an interest, they are consulted, but there are many things about which the public has no clear opinions, so there is no point in asking." One official from the Municipal People's Congress in Shenzhen went a step further, suggesting that, "asking for comments on irrelevant topics would be a burden on the public."[54]

While such explanations are not unreasonable, it is unlikely that citizens lack opinions on topics for which they are not consulted. According to the CPB results, for instance, in 2016 Chinese citizens supported media independence and respect for private property rights during urban planning. But the government sought out a different interpretation of the "public good" by demanding "absolute loyalty" from journalists and added powers for local governments to circumvent property rights when reorganizing urban communities. Similarly, whereas citizens preferred an aggressive strategy in the South China Sea and the stock market, the regime actually dialed down the volume in both cases. The only "closed" item surveyed in the 2016 CPB on which the public and regime did agree was cracking down on informal lenders versus liberalizing the private banking sector.

According to official guidelines, consultation should be offered when the policy in question involves a major interest of the general public and when the general public has major differences on the decision-making plan.[55] Clearly, such guidelines offer almost unconstrained discretion to the policymaker and are thus relatively meaningless in practice. Moreover, even a cursory review of topics that have been opened for public consultation reveals that certain policy arenas, such as foreign policy, are rarely if ever opened for public debate. Yet, even here, there are some exceptions. As noted in Chapter 2, China's government solicited feedback regarding the trade conflict with the United States in 2018, and then again in 2019 concerning the draft Foreign Investment Law.[56]

In short, dealing with the problem of selective consultation is complicated, and the CPB sampling strategy, though helpful, cannot address this problem in full. Instead, I defer the issue of selection for Chapters 7 and 8, where I can leverage more data and experimental randomization to study the direct effects of consultation. For the moment, however, we can assume that at minimum authoritarian policymakers open debate on topics and dimensions for which they are predisposed to some flexibility. This is, after all, precisely what agenda control entails. Importantly, acknowledging that the regime enjoys such agenda

---

[54] Author interview: Shenzhen Municipal People's Congress representative, December 2016.
[55] For example, see: Article 58 of the Legislation Law.
[56] Original call for comment available at: https://bit.ly/2LSwoFS.

control does not obviate the potential impact of consultation on policy and governance. As the Labor Contract Law example demonstrated earlier, it was the process of consultation that helped policymakers tailor the final legislation, not the choice to consult in the first place.

Specifically, the structured and controlled nature of debate allowed policy-makers to demonstrate social disagreement, thereby creating an opportunity for them to foster compromise. Had the government foregone consultation, what turned out to be a compromise would likely have been interpreted as a decree. In a recent journal article, Chen and Xu provide a formal model for how this might work.[57] If decision-makers keep a policy debate private, the public assumes that the policies favor only elites and will be more likely to resist them. By contrast, if a public policy debate is allowed, and it reveals discord in public preferences, policymakers have an opportunity to market their own preferred position as a centrist compromise. The implication of this selective consultation logic is that the regime will keep private those issues on which its preferences diverge sharply from that of the public, and will be open to consultation on issues which the public is itself divided and conflicted.

Taken to the extreme, this logic implies that public consultation is simply a marketing tactic. That is, the regime always pursues its initial preference, and consultation simply serves as tool for disorganizing potential opposition. This highly strategic logic, however, assumes that the regime enjoys prior knowledge about the distribution of public preferences. Such an assumption is somewhat plausible in the case of the LCL, as labor contracting issues are an obvious point of conflict between workers and employers. It is far less plausible when it comes to issues that are relatively more recent or on which prior discussion has been muted by censorship or self-censorship.[58] Moreover, a purely marketing interpretation of consultation presumes that the public is able to observe its own polarization. As argued in Chapter 2, consultation in China is a closed-circuit affair, and only the regime gets to see the full distribution of inputs. The public might hear about disagreement in the news or in op-eds, but it is not clear how such exposure is different from propaganda.[59]

A slightly looser interpretation of Chen and Xu's model is that the consultation process itself reveals the distribution of public opinion, allowing the regime to take advantage of public disagreement or proceed without formal legislation when confronted with public opposition. While we cannot adjudicate these interpretations directly, we can engage in a thought experiment concerning preference distributions. If the regime is simply trying to muddy the waters,

[57] Jidong Chen and Yiqing Xu. "Why Do Authoritarian Regimes Allow Citizens to Voice Opinions Publicly?" *The Journal of Politics* 79.3 (2017), pp. 792–803.

[58] Kuran, "Now Out of Never: The Element of Surprise in the East European Revolution of 1989."

[59] Roberts, *Censored: Distraction and Diversion Inside China's Great Firewall.*

Figure 4.2. Public Preference Distribution

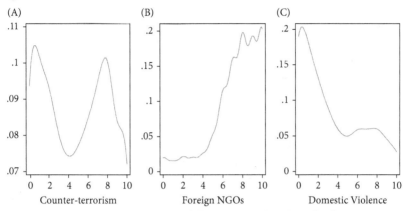

Notes: Each panel reports the kernel density of all survey respondents for each policy topic surveyed in the 2016 wave of the China Policy Barometer. Y-axis represents relative density, totalling 1 for all observations.

we would expect policymakers to target consultation campaigns on issues and policies on which public opinion is divided. The ensuing public debate thereby provides policymakers an opportunity to claim a middle ground, as they did with the LCL. Likewise, policymakers ought to withhold consultation if they expect opinion to be unified, especially if that position is at odds with the regime preference. Put differently, a purely marketing strategy implies that consultation is only offered on topics where public opinion is polarized. By contrast, if consultation is contributing to learning, we should not expect any systematic difference in public opinion distributions for topics that are open versus those that are closed.

Leveraging the CPB data, we can explore this thought experiment empirically. Figure 4.2, for instance, illustrates the public distribution of preferences across three different policy issues: *Counter-terrorism*, *Foreign NGOs*, and *Domestic Violence*, each of which was open to public consultation. Basic visual inspection suggests that public opinion concerning *Counter-terrorism* (Panel A) is sharply polarized, as illustrated by the twin peaks on either side of scale midpoint at 5-value, between those who feel that counter-terrorism operations ought to be restricted to known terrorist groups and individuals, and those who feel authorities should operate with high levels of discretion. By contrast, public opinion toward *Foreign NGOs* (Panel B) was uniformly in favor of treating them as unique and possibly dangerous entities in need of stringent supervision by the state.

There are also topics on which there is neither a single peak nor evidence of polarization. Consider the issue of *Domestic Violence* (Panel C). Whereas

a majority of respondents favor a more liberal interpretation of domestic violence, including violence in nontraditional households, such as those involving
roommates, same-sex partners, and elders, there is a smaller constituency that
favors a more traditional interpretation, which narrowly protects women from
their husbands. To fully assess whether consultation is indeed more common on
polarized issues, I evaluate the distribution of each policy item by constructing
a bi-modality coefficient.[60]

The results of the polarization analysis, as summarized in Table 4.1, provide
only weak support for the idea that consultation is simply about marketing.
Overall, more than half of all policy topics do not seem be polarized, although
some recurrent topics, like the South China Sea item, seem to have become more
polarized with time. Focusing only on consultation topics, roughly half exhibit
signs of polarization. By contrast, about 20 percent of policy topics for which
there is no public consultation also exhibit signs of polarization. The lack of
obvious patterns suggests that consultation strategies are to some extent trial-
and-error attempts at learning. At times, consultation reveals opportunities for
the regime to stake claim to a middle ground that is compatible with its own
preferences. As noted earlier however, however, this is not always the case. At
times, public opinion is fairly uniform. At others, the regime is not prepared to
moderate its policy ambitions. In any case, it is via consultation that the regime
learns where society sits in relation to its own preferred position. Moreover, it
is thanks to careful controls over the consultation process that policymakers are
comfortable learning about what the public thinks and that the public sometimes
disagrees with the regime.

Situating Consultation in the Policymaking Process

One of the biggest challenges in identifying a relationship between public
opinion and policy decisions is the endogeneity that naturally connects both
variables. While it is reasonable to expect that public opinion influences the
decisions of policymakers, it is just as plausible that the views and preferences
of policymakers influence public opinion.[61] The possibility that government
preferences are driving public opinion is even more plausible in the authoritarian

---

[60] I follow established practice and construct the bi-modality coefficient based on Skew and Kur-
tosis features of each preference distribution; See Yphtach Lelkes. "Mass Polarization: Manifestations
and Measurements." *Public Opinion Quarterly* 80.S1 (2016), pp. 392–410. Because the bi-modality
coefficient is sensitive to small deviations from normality and uni-modality, I also inspect each
distribution for signs of polarization (or balanced opposition) using visual inspection.

[61] Gabriel S. Lenz. *Follow the Leader?: How Voters Respond to Politicians' Policies and Performance.*
University of Chicago Press, 2012, p. 327.

Table 4.1 Public Polarization Across Policies

CPB Wave	Topic	Consultation	Bi-modal Coef.	Visual Bi-modal	Polarized
2016	Domestic violence		0.689		•
	Online privacy		0.660		
	Informal lending	•	0.659	•	•
	South China Sea	•	0.631		•
	Wildlife protection		0.618		
	Media supervision	•	0.609		
	Counter-terrorism		0.593		
	Urban planning	•	0.586		
	Stock market	•	0.582	•	•
	Foreign NGOs		0.580	•	•
2017	Nuclear energy		0.619		
	Domestic passports	•	0.596		
	Public surveillance		0.591		
	Ride-sharing services		0.578		
	South China Sea	•	0.570		
	Chinese medicine		0.539		•
	Affirmative action	•	0.536		
	Foreign aid	•	0.501	•	•
	Capital controls	•	0.458	•	•
	Exchange rate	•	0.368	•	•
2018	South China Sea	•	0.538		
	Term limits	•	0.528		
	National Security Comm.		0.462		•
	Foreign aid	•	0.461		•
	Martyrs		0.455		•
	Capital controls	•	0.368	•	•
	Trade protections		0.339	•	•

setting, since mediums for propagating government positions, such as propaganda, are far more prevalent than those for aggregating bottom-up sentiments such as elections, civil society, and a free press. It is hard to tell whether congruence over, say, the need for environmental protection, is evidence of public opinion influencing policymakers or simply recognition by the public that their representatives see environmental protection as a priority.

While my empirical strategy is unable to fully deal with endogeneity, it offers a small improvement over previous studies. For instance, timing the CPB survey in advance of the annual *Lianghui*, a period during which most pending policy decisions are finalized and made public, allows more room for divergence between public opinion and policy decisions.[62] Moreover, by looking at both open and closed policies, we gain at least some dimension of objective comparison. Finally, by decomposing the distribution of preferences, we can begin thinking about the structure of information that policymakers are dealing with when it comes to consultation. Ultimately, this structure has important implications for how the regime translates inputs into intelligence, or what I term "information processing." In this chapter, I have pointed to examples of how the distribution of public preferences reveals competing perspectives. In the following chapter, I generalize this processing logic through a study of competing interests in China's local representative institutions.

---

[62] The pre-NPC timing condition applies to all topics except the Environmental Advocacy and Budget Oversight in 2015, which were chosen deliberately to shed light on previous examples of public consultation efforts.

5

Processing Public Inputs

It has long been a common form of speech that if a good despot could be insured, despotic monarchy would be the best form of government. . . Good laws would be established and enforced, bad laws would be reformed . . . This realization would in fact imply not merely a good monarch, but an all-seeing one. He must be at all times informed correctly, in considerable detail, of the conduct and working of every branch of administration in every district of the country, and must be able, in the twenty-four hours per day which are all that is granted to a king, as to the humblest laborer, to give an effective share of attention and superintendence to all parts of this vast field . . .[1]

— John Stuart Mill, 1861

In critiquing the notion of a benevolent dictator, John Stuart Mill argued that the challenge of governance under autocracy is not merely in selecting benevolent dictators but in finding ones who are "all-seeing." Yet, even if decision-makers are all-seeing, what is to say they can respond accordingly? Consider the case of healthcare in the United States. In 2008, on the heels of a brutal recession and as part of a broader overhaul of the health industry, American President Barack Obama announced, "We will make sure that every doctor's office and hospital in this country is using cutting-edge technology and electronic medical records so that we can cut red tape, prevent medical mistakes and help save billions of dollars each year."[2] Yet ten years and 36 billion dollars later, there is little indication that digitization has reduced either costs or mistakes.

According to an industry report, two key factors stood in the way. First, an already decentralized provider industry meant that records were difficult to move and integrate. According to one study, matching records to current patients was only successful 50 percent of the time. Second, and more importantly, digitization often generates too much information.[3] Surveys showed that doctors

---

[1] Mill, John Stuart. *Considerations on Representative Government.* Henry Holt and Co., 1861.
[2] Radio address delivered by Obama, cited in https://bit.ly/2XNI9yo.
[3] Fred Schulte and Erika Fry. "Death by 1,000 Clicks: Where Electronic Health Records Went Wrong." *Kaiser Health News* 18 (2019).

Retrofitting Leninism. Dimitar D. Gueorguiev. Oxford University Press. © Oxford University Press 2021.
DOI: 10.1093/oso/9780197555668.003.0006

in the intensive care unit were inundated each day with over 7,000 passive notifi-cations, such as automated pop-up warnings about potential drug interactions.[4] Another study found that emergency room providers make around 4,000 mouse clicks per shift as they navigate software intended to facilitate care.[5] In both instances, digitization contributes to information fatigue.

In China, technological innovations have also allowed the state to collect vast troves of information, augmenting the government's already expansive information-gathering capabilities. In 2013, for instance, the National Petitions office established an online petitions portal, resulting in a 280 percent increase in submissions within the first three months.[6] Such increases are dwarfed by the terabytes and petabytes of information generated by new complaint and commenting portals on government-run websites, social media pages, 12345 hotlines, and the online whistleblower sites discussed in Chapter 3. Like the physicians in the hospital, however, even the most competent CCP technocrats might find it hard to process such large quantities of information. Nevertheless, government work reports suggest that most bottom-up messages are indeed processed and almost always responded to. Independent studies confirm that response rates are surprisingly high.[7] How does the regime manage this task?

Information Processing

For the most part, how information is processed and acted upon in China re-mains a black box. This reflects the fact that intelligence agencies mostly operate in secret. While scholars have long known about the ways Soviet surveillance agencies collected information, only recently, and thanks to declassified archives in Eastern Europe, have they been able to systematically study how this surveil-lance was interpreted by agents and leaders.[8] Likewise, the input acquisition side of China's participatory institutions have been studied extensively.[9] How this

---

[4] Vanessa Kizzier-Carnahan et al. "Frequency of Passive EHR Alerts in the ICU: Another Form of Alert Fatigue?" *Journal of Patient Safety* (2016).

[5] Robert G. Hill Jr., Lynn Marie Sears, and Scott W. Melanson. "4000 Clicks: A Productivity Analysis of Electronic Medical Records in a Community Hospital ED." *The American Journal of Emergency Medicine* 31.11 (2013), pp. 1591–1594.

[6] See Xinhua report "Changes in Mass Petitions: Visits Decline, Online Submissions Rise (群众信访新变化: "进京告状"少了, "上网投诉"多了)" October 20, 2016. Available at: https://bit.ly/2LhRgpb.

[7] Tianguang Meng, Jennifer Pan, and Ping Yang. "Conditional Receptivity to Citizen Participa-tion: Evidence from a Survey Experiment in China."

[8] Fitzpatrick, "Suppliants and Citizens: Public Letter-Writing in Soviet Russia in the 1930s."

[9] Stromseth, Malesky, and Gueorguiev, *China's Governance Puzzle: Enabling Transparency and Participation in a Single-Party State*; Rory Truex. *Making Autocracy Work: Representation and*

input is processed into actionable intelligence remains both under-theorized and understudied.[10]

This is a critical omission in that having too much information is hardly more desirable than having too little. In the past, processing was delegated to staff inside control organs who tallied up complaints, summarized hot topics, and delivered reports to superiors. This task has become substantially more complicated. Today, information offices outsource processing to university research labs, private companies and, increasingly, to artificial intelligence.[11] Regardless of who is doing the processing or with what tools, the information challenge can be generalized into a few basic principles. First, the information ought to fill gaps in the autocrat's existing knowledge base. Second, information should be conducive to screening methods of reduction and simplification. Finally, methods of information processing should be robust to distortion. As argued in Chapter 1, authoritarian controls over discourse and communication, though they stand in the way of information acquisition, can facilitate these basic processing principles.

At a most basic level, information generating institutions ought to fill gaps in the leader's existing knowledge base. This principle is both overly general and hard to theorize. As former US Defense Secretary Donald Rumsfeld once cryptically explained, the "unknowns" have many layers, only a few of which are known. When applied to the context of governance, most would agree that Chinese technocrats are primarily concerned with information that helps them push through policy initiatives and monitor subordinates. While such information can be acquired through a variety of methods, the reason China's leaders solicit it from the public is that internally gathered information is likely to reflect and possibly even reinforce the very biases and blind spots the leaders are trying to overcome. By contrast, signals and input from outside the inner circle are more likely to contain "new" information.

In an otherwise top-down and authoritarian administrative system, any sort of bottom-up inclusion ought to bring forth new perspectives, if not new information. However, there are several caveats. For one, not all bottom-up information gathering methods incorporate outsiders.[12] Chinese elections, as

Responsiveness in Modern China. New York: Cambridge University Press, 2016; Jing Chen. *Useful Complaints: How Petitions Assist Decentralized Authoritarianism in China.* Rowman & Littlefield, 2016.

[10] Notable exceptions include Lorenzten's work on protest activity. See Lorentzen, "Designing Contentious Politics in Post-1989 China," and Heurlin's work on responsiveness: Heurlin, *Responsive Authoritarianism in China.*

[11] Interview with Chendgu Information office deputy director, December 2018.

[12] By outsiders, I mean those who lack political connections. For a similar use of this concept, see Lily L. Tsai and Yiqing Xu. "Outspoken Insiders: Political Connections and Citizen Participation in Authoritarian China." *Political Behavior* 40.3 (2018), pp. 629–657.

noted throughout this book, are tightly controlled by the CCP, leaving relatively little room for outside voices. Petitions and protests, on the other hand, are far more likely to involve political outsiders.

Screening and Sorting

Even if the regime is able to fill information gaps with bottom-up input, it is initially unclear which insights demand attention. Like the physician flooded with diagnostics, policymakers and disciplinarians overloaded with inputs may find them hard to digest. This is where the reductive principle—transforming a large amount of nuanced information into a narrower set of priorities—comes into play. In academia, scholars typically judge a colleague's productivity by their number of publications, and their impact on the field by the number of citations. Similarly, democratic vote tallies can translate millions of different aspirations and concerns into one very consequential tabulation.

While the CCP may not rely much on votes, they do structure input mediums in ways that allow for reduction. For example, when citizens petition the government, they do so in a formulaic process which, as discussed earlier, requires them to provide personal information alongside the details of their complaint (online forms now ask petitioners to also choose a topic category(s) that best describes their concern). In turn, the recorder at the petitions office is required to document when a petition is received, where it originated, how many people were involved in bringing it forth, and which administrative branch is most closely involved or should be responsible for dealing with the complaint (See Figure 5.1). Similar forms are filled out every time a citizen lodges a complaint online or on the phone.[13]

Likewise, when deputies in lower-level people's congresses make legislative proposals, they must also specify the discovery process by which the proposal came about. Submission forms ask sponsors to specify the source of input, such as whether the proposal arose from meetings with members of the public, committee, or small-group sessions within the deputy's own delegation (see Figure 5.2). Armed with this information, the regime has a useful set of reductive indicators.

Descriptive indicators are a useful first step, but there are others. One crude but efficient strategy involves imposing costs on those providing the input.[14] Perhaps the clearest example of costly screening can be found in China's petitions system. While the responsiveness of this system is often questioned, it is widely believed that the higher up the ladder one goes with a complaint, the more likely the government will intercede on one's behalf. Presumably, those petitions

---

[13] Interview with the deputy director of the Chengdu Municipal Information Office. Interview Record: CHD122018

[14] Lorentzen, "Designing Contentious Politics in Post-1989 China."

Figure 5.1. Petition Reporting

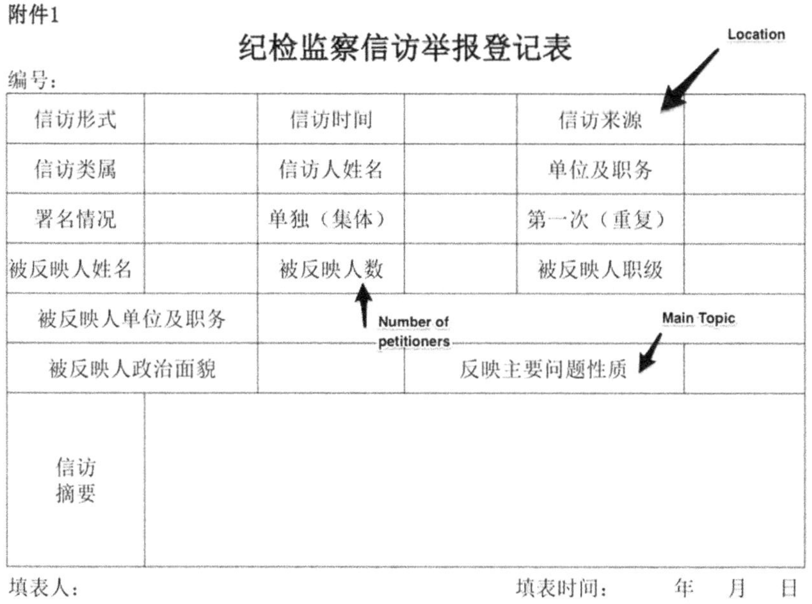

附件1

纪检监察信访举报登记表

编号：

信访形式		信访时间		信访来源	
信访类属		信访人姓名		单位及职务	
署名情况		单独（集体）		第一次（重复）	
被反映人姓名		被反映人数		被反映人职级	
被反映人单位及职务					
被反映人政治面貌				反映主要问题性质	
信访摘要					

Location

Number of petitioners

Main Topic

填表人：   填表时间：   年   月   日

Note: Generic petitions recording form.

that reach Beijing have the highest likelihood of resolution, but the chances of reaching the capital are low. Queues outside Beijing's *xinfang* offices are long, and local governments spend significant resources on convincing their residents, often through coercion, to give up and return home.[15] In effect, the costs and risks associated with petitioning help screen and sort petitions within the administrative process. The same logic is used to explain why Chinese authorities are highly responsive to protest even as they threaten participants with sanction, arrest, and violence.[16]

Imposing blunt costs on input providers, such as material fees or the risk of physical harm, in order to discourage complaints and reduce workload may sound straightforward. But this approach undercuts the CCP's efforts to make input provision cheaper and easier. Indeed, this tension is much like the disconnect between hobbled institutions and reform, which I first raised in the Introduction. Interpreting this tension as a contradiction, however, confuses means with ends. That is, the CCP has a strong interest in not only reducing information flows

---

[15] Kirsten D. Tatlow. "Rights Group Details Abuse in 'Black Jails.'" New York Times, October 20, 2014.

[16] Peter L. Lorentzen. "Regularizing Rioting: Permitting Public Protest in an Authoritarian Regime." *Quarterly Journal of Political Science* 8.2 (2013), pp. 127–158; Lorentzen, "Designing Contentious Politics in Post-1989 China."

Figure 5.2. Suggestion Reporting

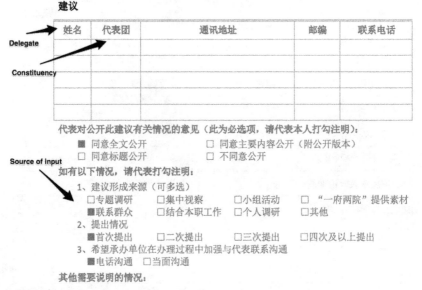

Note: Generic delegate proposal submission form.

but also on isolating high-value information. Imposing blunt costs on input providers, whether aggrieved petitioners or self-interested lobbyists, is unlikely to achieve both goals.

For one thing, imposing blunt costs on input provision has the unfortunate side effect of discouraging future input, aggravating existing grievances and potentially undermining the legitimacy of the input institution. The cynical response to such concerns is that they are not fatal for the CCP, or at least not for the CCP leadership. The logic here is that most of the costs, such as fines, threats, and detentions, are meted out by local hands, so even if local legitimacy suffers as a result, public trust and dependence on the central authorities may actually deepen. This short-sighted view of the problem, however, discounts the fact that most aspects of government are local and that a top-heavy regime is fragile when it rests on brittle foundation (a concern I deal with in Chapter 7).

Another problem with the blunt costs approach is that it, too, is susceptible to bias. For starters, blunt costs are not equally costly for all. Petitioners with more education, more resources, or more political capital are arguably less constrained by blunt costs than the average Chinese citizen. In some respects, this is not a problem for the regime, which arguably has a strong incentive to appease the better endowed portions of society first.[17] With regard to information acquisition and processing, however, the blunt-costs approach risks cultivating blind spots over the most marginalized and arguably most aggrieved portions of

[17] Minxin Pei. *China's Crony Capitalism*. Harvard University Press, 2016.

society. This risks limiting the regime's ability to maintain encompassing control over state and society.

Dis-coordination

One general source of bias arises from asymmetric information, since input providers by definition posses at least some private information vis-a-vis the state. For example, it is plausible that local agents look the other way on local protests because they know the center might offer concessions. Similarly, critics of China's consultative mechanisms point out that powerful interests often skew a debate in their favor.[18] Most explicitly, observers contend that the legislature is often a vehicle for generating private returns for delegates and their associates.[19] This brings us to the third principle of information processing, namely, resilience to distortion. Unfortunately, few indicators are robust to this threat. As Campbell reminds us, the moment any indicator becomes important it also becomes a target for misrepresentation.[20]

In a democratic context, competition over votes helps ensure electoral integrity by promising that efforts to influence votes from one direction will be met by competing efforts from the other. Leninist systems lack political competition, but they do feature internal competition within the state and across society. Specifically, the administrative compartmentalization and social atomization that exist under Leninist control engender group-based competition over resources and privilege. The same boundaries that define administrative and societal interests are also relevant in the input-generating process. In the case of policymaking, for instance, public input is often confined within regime-managed "small groups" along functional, geographic, and sectoral boundaries. As such, modal input tends to be group-centered. Students advocate and agitate on issues pertinent to students, workers for workers, and farmers for farmers. On the rare occasion when a diverse constellation of preferences coalesces on a common position, it signals to the leadership that this position is probably one of encompassing interest. In the next section, I explore this logic through a quantitative examination of bottom-up information generation and processing in local-level people's congresses.

Structured Representation

The Great Hall of the People, just southwest of Tiananmen Square and the Forbidden City in the center of Beijing, is a building of capacious proportions.

---

[18] Wang, "Public Participation and Its Limits: An Observation and Evaluation on Public Hearings as Experimented in China's Administrative Process."

[19] Truex, *Making Autocracy Work: Representation and Responsiveness in Modern China*.

[20] Donald T. Campbell. "Assessing the Impact of Planned Social Change." *Evaluation and Program Planning* 2.1 (1979), pp. 67–90.

Measuring nearly two million square feet in floor space (roughly 400 full-size basketball courts) the Great Hall can host over 20,000 people in its auditoriums and dining halls. Despite its size, it was built in a mere ten months in 1959, along with nine other massive building projects in Beijing designed to showcase China's future glory. The main auditorium has a dizzying panopticon feel; its expansive interior is said to humble even the greatest of egos, rendering the interests of the individual infinitesimal when compared to the common cause of the masses. For two weeks each March, when the "people's representatives" fill the hall during the annual *Lianghui*, delegates give life to this carefully scripted narrative of inclusion and unity.

The script includes strict seating arrangements in the grand auditorium and designated flow patterns for walking around the building, all under the uninterrupted monitoring of surveillance cameras. Indeed, the script extends to every part of the delegates' stay, including where they sleep—which by the way is not in or near the Great Hall.[21] With the exception of those from Macau and Hong Kong, who are apparently allowed to room in the same hotel, accommodations are scattered across the city, usually somewhere within the fourth ring road that encircles the main part of Beijing. Some delegations stay in their provincial missions. As hosts, delegates from Beijing usually stay farthest away, just outside the Fifth Ring Road that circles the capital. Others, like those from Chongqing, move around every year.

Logistically this means budgeting extra time for busing delegates to and from the Great Hall. This basic logistical constraint, combined with mandatory extracurricular activities like hotel screenings of *Crouching Tiger, Hidden Dragon*,[22] means that outside of scripted sessions in the Great Hall, delegates really have no chance to speak or meet with anyone other than their co-delegation members. Indeed, press conferences reveal that some of the most heated debates, such as those concerning policy proposals and work reports, occur within delegations, often inside their hotel's respective conference rooms and not in the Great Hall.[23]

Given that there are nearly 3,000 delegates to the NPC and almost as many to the CPPCC, spreading out participants is perhaps unavoidable. Yet, given that delegates have only eight days during which to review the events of the past year and plan the course for the next, keeping them separated may seem counterproductive. Compartmentalization and fragmentation, however, serves

---

[21] According to one former organizer, Cheng Xiaonong, the goal is to have delegates "eat together, sleep together, and have fun together, but different delegations must do all of this separately." See: https://goo.gl/9Ts5XZ.

[22] The 2000 film, *Crouching Tiger, Hidden Dragon*, directed by Ang Lee, is popular in China. Author's interview with a delegate from Zhejiang delegation, Nov 2011.

[23] We know this by looking at the information provided to journalists who follow provincial delegations during the *Lianghui*, which points to group discussions at individual hotel locations rather than venues in the Great Hall.

a higher purpose. By limiting opportunities for delegates to meet and mingle, the regime also makes it harder for anyone to coordinate opposing positions. It should therefore come as no surprise that delegates almost never challenge anything the Party *proposes* or the government *does*. By the time the Great Hall is filled with representatives, the script proceeds without missing a beat: The Party Committee waves its hand (*hui shou*) . . . the Government gets to work (*dong shou*) . . . the People's Congress votes (*ju shou*) . . . the People's Consultative Congress claps (*pai shou*).

Local Assemblies

The barriers to coordination built into the Great Hall are replicated across thousands of local people's congresses (LPC's). Every five years, LPC delegates are "elected" from around the country to serve as geographic and sectoral representatives. At lower levels, these delegates are elected directly by their constituents. At higher levels, delegates (including those who are nominated to participate in the *Lianghui*) are elected indirectly by lower-level congresses. This system ensures against any popular electoral movement ever breaching anything but the lowest levels of influence. It also means that, regardless of whether delegates are directly or indirectly elected, they are expected to faithfully represent the interests of the group they were selected to represent. In most instances, this group represents a specific geographic constituency.[24]

The primary means by which delegates represent constituencies is by submitting proposals on their behalf (*jianyi*), similar to the submission of legislative motions in democratic legislatures.[25] Proposals in the Chinese legislature encompass a broader set of substantive contents, including legislative proposals, criticisms, and general opinions.[26] Some proposals could end up as a formal motion for a bill (*yi'an*) and placed on the legislative agenda. Most of the time, however, proposals are accepted as non-binding positions circulated to concerned government departments for consideration.

There is little evidence that this highly formulaic mode of information provision is objective or unbiased. On the contrary, delegate motions can be expected to reflect the narrow interests of the delegate's nominal constituents. In his

---

[24] At higher levels there is more specialization, with delegates representing geographic constituencies as well as industrial sectors, functional orders, mass groups, and intellectual affiliations.

[25] I use the term "proposal" rather than "motion" for two reasons: (a) it is a more proximate translation of the Chinese term, and (b) motions are typically defined as formal proposals, and this standard is not met by all proposals in the LPC.

[26] See Article 18 and Article 19 of the Organic Law as well as Article 9 and Article 18 of the Law on Delegates to the National People's Congress and Local People's Congresses.

study of NPC proposals, Cho observes that national delegates see themselves not as "people's representatives" per se, but as a "deputy for farmers," "deputy for workers," "deputy for private businessmen," or "deputy for women."[27] Similarly, in their analysis of the Yangzhou City LPC, Kamo and Takeuchi conclude that delegates, first and foremost, "represent the interests of the constituency of their [geographic] electoral districts."[28] In her extensive study of local delegates, Manion confirms that delegates increasingly perceive themselves as representing geographically defined administrative units.[29] In other words, the inputs being generated by the PCs are parochial in nature and therefore unlikely to be compatible with the more encompassing interests of the CCP.

This observation is neither novel nor surprising, but it carries considerable implications for the study of inclusion, insofar as bottom-up input of this sort also introduces the problem of asymmetric information. Within the context of the LPC, for instance, delegates in possession of valuable private information about their constituencies may choose to relay it selectively and strategically to leaders.[30] Indeed, as long as the interests of the delegate are not fully aligned with that of the leadership, such a scenario is bound to arise. For instance, a delegate may selectively raise proposals informing (or misinforming) their superiors about the risks (or benefits) of a particular policy, with the express interest of extracting special privileges or resources. As agency theory would suggest, unless superiors are able to screen out misinformation, the information potential of the LPC seems tenuous.[31]

Counting Heads

There are several ways the regime might go about screening signals from noise. They could, for instance, put a premium on trusted voices within the legislature, say CCP members and veterans, discounting the proposals submitted by non-CCP members and newcomers. This may, however, backfire if CCP members and veterans are less trusted by their constituents or if they take advantage of their trusted positions. Alternatively, the regime might employ some of the heuristics

[27] Cho, "Public Supervisors and Reflectors: Role Fulfillment of the Chinese People's Congress Deputies in the Market Socialist Era," p. 215.
[28] Tomoki Kamo and Hiroki Takeuchi. "Representation and Local People's Congresses in China: A Case Study of the Yangzhou Municipal People's Congress." *Journal of Chinese Political Science* 18.1 (2013), pp. 41–60, p. 57.
[29] Manion, *Information for Autocrats: Representation in Chinese Local Congresses*.
[30] Whether they chose to do so to benefit their constituencies or enrich themselves is in some respects a moot point, at least from the perspective of the regime.
[31] For further reference on agency theory, see Michael C. Jensen and William H. Meckling. "Theory of the Firm: Managerial Behavior, Agency Costs and Ownership Structure," *Journal of Financial Economics* 3.4 (1976), pp. 305–360.

reviewed in this chapter. In particular, they could study the constellation of interests attached to a proposal. In this regard, the LPC is a microcosm for information processing insofar as interest groups are carefully delineated and proposals can be cosponsored.

Cosponsorship conveys several pieces of information. The number of cosponsors, like the number of protesters or the number of petitioners, conveys level of support. Accordingly, government agents tend to view the number of cosponsors as an indicator of how quickly to respond and with how much detail. "When there is only one name on the proposal, we can simply say 'Thanks, we are looking into it.'" When there are twenty names we have to do a whole report, and it's a real pain."[32]

As discussed earlier, however, such indicators are vulnerable to distortion. In particular, cosponsorship in the Chinese LPC, and really any legislature, is prone to strategic abuse by delegates who trade signatures in the hope of boosting each others' respective proposals.[33] Indeed, Chinese officials recognize that the number of signatures is not always synonymous with information quality, and that many high-signature proposals are on topics that local delegation leaders pushed through to their co-delegates.[34] A group of delegates from Zhejiang, for instance, explained that they sometimes "pass proposals around the table" during their small-group meetings, but contend that only "important" proposals get treated this way.[35] As a result, many highly sponsored proposals turn out to be parochial attempts to get more funding or investment for some local project, without much regard for the community as a whole.

This is where the constellation of interests backing a proposal comes into play. In the case of the LPC, there are several interest groups to consider. In particular, LPC delegates are typically organized according to geographic, sectoral, and partisan affiliation; any delegate associated with one of those affiliations is responsible for "representing" it within the LPC. Consequently, a proposal with signatures coming from different affiliations shows support from a diverse and potentially competing set of interests. As such, I view proposals with diverse cosponsorship as having encompassing support within the legislature. by contrast, a proposal with an equal number of signatures, all hailing from the same interest group, is likely to be more parochial in substance. This distinction is consistent with what Melanie Manion finds in her interviews with LPC delegates:

---

[32] Author interview with Shenzhen transportation official, December 2016.

[33] James M. Buchanan and Gordon Tullock. *The Calculus of Consent: Logical Foundations of Constitutional Democracy.* University of Michigan Press, 1965, p. 361; Thomas Schwartz. "Vote Trading and Pareto Efficiency." *Public Choice* 24.1 (1975), pp. 101–109.

[34] Author interview with Shenzhen government representative, December 2016.

[35] Author interview with Wenling LPC deputy small group, December 2012.

In our delegation of 21 delegates [at the county congress], we see if the problems we want to raise have any common interest for other townships, other delegations. If so, then more delegates and delegations sign onto the proposal...
If a proposal is raised by more delegates and spans more delegations, then it is more powerful—the government knows it really has to take account of it because it is a general problem, not just particular to one township.[36]

It is important to stress that this logic is not China-specific. Indeed, even in the United States, the diversity of sponsors participating in a coalition is the clearest indicator for breadth of support, such that a proposal backed by multiple parties is interpreted as having broader appeal than one backed by only a single party.[37] China only has one party, however, and it is not obvious whether the same political[38] and reputational mechanisms[39] that make bipartisanship costly in the United States are present in the Chinese case.

There are, however, China-specific institutional constraints to diversity. LPC delegates, most of whom are part-time representatives, have no staff or organizational resources through which to lobby peers. During plenary sessions, delegates are typically confined to meeting and sitting with delegates from the same geographic constituency. As noted earlier, outside of the annual plenary sessions, delegates have few opportunities to meet and discuss proposal strategies and attempts to organize independently are illegal. Such barriers can lead to obvious failures in coordination. For instance, when I asked Huang Suning, a nationally renowned advocate for disability rights from Shenzhen, whether she had ever coordinated with Huang Ruiru, another prominent advocate of disability groups from her own municipal legislative congress but a different district, she said she had never worked with him before, explaining that "working with other delegations is very hard."

In addition to the lack of meetings and networking opportunities, working across delegation lines also carries transactional and reputational costs. When asking individual delegates about seeking outside cosponsors, most describe it as "very troublesome" (*hen mafan*). "First, you need a reason to call them or take them out to dinner. Then, you have to wait a while before you remind them about it. Then, they ask who else is signing on . . . . Most people doubt

---

[36] Melanie Manion. "Authoritarian Parochialism: Local Congressional Representation in China." *The China Quarterly* 218 (2014), pp. 311–338, p. 331.

[37] James E. Campbell. "Cosponsoring Legislation in the U. S. Congress." *Legislative Studies Quarterly* 7.3 (1982), pp. 415–422, p. 415.

[38] Daniel Kessler and Keith Krehbiel. "Dynamics of Cosponsorship." *The American Political Science Review* 90.3 (1996), pp. 555–566.

[39] Brian F. Crisp, Kristin Kanthak, and Jenny Leijonhufvud. "The Reputations Legislators Build: With Whom Should Representatives Collaborate?" *American Political Science Review* 98.04 (2004), pp. 703–716.

your intentions, so it's hard."[40] Importantly, legislative leaders recognize the challenges to cosponsorship across delegation lines and use it as an indicator of quality. "If you ask for someone else's signature you are going to make sure it's not garbage first!"[41] The higher up you go in the legislative ranks, the more apparent these barriers to cross-group coordination become, as illustrated with the introductory anecdote about NPC accommodations in Beijing. Yet, at each level, the barriers to coordination are not overt or draconian. They don't bespeak dictatorship, yet they undermine horizontal communication by compartmentalizing and demobilizing organic civil society.

Prioritization

To what extent can the constellation of inputs serve as a useful heuristic? In other words, to what extent is it informative, reductive, and robust to distortion? Given that most LPC members are not political elites and that they represent broader bottom-up interests, we could assume that all proposals are in some sense informative.[42] To be reductive and robust, however, the relative diversity of interests backing a proposal should help distinguish parochial inputs from encompassing ones, allowing leaders to prioritize the latter.

To test this logic, I leverage fine-grained legislative data from the Shenzhen Municipal People's Congress (MPC), an economically diverse and progressive municipality in southeastern Guangdong Province. It is also one of few localities to publish its legislative record in a way that facilitates cosponsorship analysis. This record includes the name of lead sponsors alongside all cosponsors, as well as the full text of the actual proposals. While this level of accessibility makes Shenzhen an outlier, it operates much like other municipal-level people's congresses in other developed parts of China. Moreover, even if Shenzhen is wealthy and admittedly progressive, there is little reason to suspect that these qualities would impact the behavior of delegates within the legislature, which, like all local legislative bodies in China has, at best, nominal influence over local level policy.

At the same time, the digital legislative records from Shenzhen (though no longer accessible) provide a valuable window onto how delegates operate and coordinate within a formalized institution for consultation and information generation. Using the publicly available data on delegate profiles, I was able to replicate the organizational boundaries within cosponsorship groups. With

[40] Author interview with Wenling LPC deputy small group, December 2012.
[41] Author interview with Wenling LPC chairman, December 2012.
[42] Manion, *Information for Autocrats: Representation in Chinese Local Congresses*.

the help of research assistants, I was able to code each individual proposal for the type of information conveyed as well as interests reflected. In particular, coders were asked to identify whether a proposal dealt with the (i) formal legal process, (ii) resource lobbying, (iii) investigation reporting, (iv) grievance letting, (v) criticism, or (vi) empty praise. Coders were instructed to identify whether a proposal fit into any of these categories, with no expectation that any single category was mutually exclusive from the rest. Moreover, within the *Lobbying, Information*, and *Grievance Letting* categories, coders also identified whether a proposal was concerned with parochial, functional, occupational, or encompassing interests based on whether the proposal strictly concerned the lead sponsor's *Geographic, Functional*, or *Occupational* affiliation. A summary of the coding exercise is reported in Table 5.1.[43]

Variables and Operationalization

I operationalize the heuristic quality of the cosponsorship coalition in two ways. First, I construct a "Proportional Index," which takes the identity of the lead sponsor *sl* as a critical anchor relative to every additional cosponsor *sc*. Diversity here is equal to the proportion of *sc* that do not share a common affiliation with *sl*, based on the total number of cosponsors *n*. In instances with only one sponsor, such as *sc = sl*, this equation reduces to zero.

$$Proportional = \frac{\sum_{i=1}^{n}(sc_i \neq sl)}{n}$$

The Proportional Index is intuitive insofar as it captures the key role of the lead sponsor. At the same time, it cannot distinguish between a coalition of say ten sponsors from ten different constituencies versus one with ten sponsors, nine of whom share a common constituency that happens to be different from that of the lead sponsor. Second, as an alternative measure of diversity, I also include an inverse *Herfindahl-Hirschman Index* (HHI), using the following formula:

$$HHI = 1 - \sum_{i=1}^{n} s_i^2$$

Here, s_i corresponds to the share of sponsors attached to a given proposal that belongs to group i, where groups include geographic, sectoral, or partisan affiliation. If the share of sponsors from each of n total groups i is equal, for example, each sponsor comes from a different group, then this formula reduces to $1/n$, with a theoretical minimum of 0. By contrast, if all sponsors originate from a single group, then $HHI = 1$. To make this intuitively consistent with

---

[43] Coding instructions provided in Chapter 5 Appendix.

Table 5.1 Proposal Coding

Category	Subcategory	Frequency	Proportion
Legal Process		206	5.8%
	Local	45	1.3%
	National	60	1.7%
	Constitution	1	0.0%
	Amendments	100	2.8%
Lobbying		1993	55.5%
	Geographic	632	17.6%
	Functional	413	11.5%
	Occupational	122	3.4%
	Encompassing	826	23.0%
Investigation		2314	64.5%
	Geographic	642	17.9%
	Functional	372	10.4%
	Occupational	148	4.1%
	Encompassing	1152	32.1%
Grievances		1754	48.9%
	Geographic	567	15.8%
	Functional	301	8.4%
	Occupational	104	2.9%
	Encompassing	782	21.8%
Criticism		151	4.2%
	Individuals	1	0.0%
	Departments	46	1.3%
	Policies	104	2.9%
	Political	0	0.0%
Empty Praise		30	0.8%
	Individuals	4	0.1%
	Departments	5	0.1%
	Policies	11	0.3%
	Political	10	0.3%

Notes: Categories are not mutually exclusive, and proportions add up to more than 1. Categories were hand-coded based on the full text of each proposal.

the Diversity Index, I subtract the summation from 1, such that higher values indicate a more diverse coalition.

Using these two formulas, I have generated three diversity variables based on the institutionally defined groups within the LPC: *Geographic* according to a sponsoring delegate's home district, *Sectoral* according to their social or economic sector assignment, and *Partisan* according to partisan affiliation. Note that the organizing principle in the LPC is geographic, meaning that a delegate's geographic affiliation is his or her primary group affiliation. A summary of these affiliations and the distribution of delegates is provided in Table 5.2. In addition to the diversity variables, I also include a dummy for *CCP* membership and for prior incumbents *Veterans*, as well as for *Age*, *Education*, and *Gender*, based on the lead sponsor. While I do not have specific expectations for these control variables, it would make sense that CCP members and veterans, whose preferences ought to align with those of leaders, are more likely to submit encompassing proposals.

If the constellation of interests is indeed a viable heuristic, then coalition diversity should predict whether or not the input generated was encompassing rather than parochial. By contrast, the number of sponsors, a far more corruptible indicator, should be more closely associated with parochial input. To test this expectation, I rely on a standard Probit estimator to model whether or not each proposal in the sample dealt with encompassing issues.

$$Pr(Y_i = 1 | X_1, X_2, \cdots, X_k) = \phi(\beta_0 + \beta_1 X_1 + \beta_2 X_2 + \cdots + \beta_l X_k)$$

Where Y refers to the dichotomous dependent variable *Encompassing*; X_1 refers to coalition size, measured as the logged number of sponsors; X_2 refers to each diversity index; and X_k refers to key attributes of the lead sponsor, including whether they are a *CCP Member*, a *Veteran*, their *Age*, *Education* and *Gender*.

Figure 5.3 summarizes the main coefficient effects from the fully specified model, with fixed effects for legislative session and the district of the lead sponsor, as well as robust standard errors clustered on the lead sponsor.[44] The most pronounced effect comes from *Geographic* diversity, the rarest form of diversity. *Partisan* diversity also predicts encompassing proposals, although the effect is smaller than for geography. The fact that *Sectoral* diversity is not a significant predictor of encompassing information is perhaps not surprising, given that some *Sectoral* affiliations are already built into the *Geographic* assignment. With respect to controls, proposals sponsored by a CCP member were less likely, on average, to be encompassing, while in terms of gender, those authored by men were slightly more likely to be encompassing. Whether the lead sponsor was

---

[44] Appendix Table A.3 provides alternative specifications and a complementary set of models using the HHI measure of diversity.

Table 5.2 Shenzhen MPC Delegates

District	Lead	Cosponsor	Sector	Lead	Cosponsor
Futian	1,063	6,707	Democratic Parties	529	3,443
Luohu	801	4,800	Other Labor	507	3,382
Bao'an	639	4,023	Civil Society	442	2,031
Longan	537	4,065	High Technology	268	2,243
Nanshan	431	3,855	Education	216	1,693
Yantian	165	915	Non-Party Affiliates	178	1,129
			Culture	163	757
			Economics	131	1,088
			Industry	126	837
			Municipal Admin	112	1,000
Party			Other Cadre	101	672
	Lead	Cosponsor	SOE Admin	100	774
CCP	2,089	14,576	Commerce	98	633
Non-Party	527	3,074	Other Intellectuals	94	576
Qun Zhong	394	2,543	Finance	90	491
Min Meng	217	1,036	Sanitation	88	706
Unknown	75	581	Justice and law	83	694
Zhi Gong	67	523	Services	81	458
Min Jian	59	382	Mass Organizations	56	372
Tai Meng	50	345	Traffic & Transport	51	313
Min Ge	44	418	District Admin	46	388
Nong Gong	40	310	Farm, Forest, Fish	33	243
Jiu San	39	302	Religious Affiliates	29	351
Min Jin	35	275	Sports	14	91
Total	3,636	24,365		3,636	24,365

an incumbent delegate, their age, and level of education were not statistically associated with encompassing proposals. What is clear, however, is that the coefficient on *Cosponsors* is consistently negative. In short, when it comes to encompassing interests in legislative proposals, what matters is the diversity, not the quantity, of cosponsors. This is true regardless of how the model is estimated or how diversity is calculated.

Figure 5.3. Predictors of Encompassing Proposals

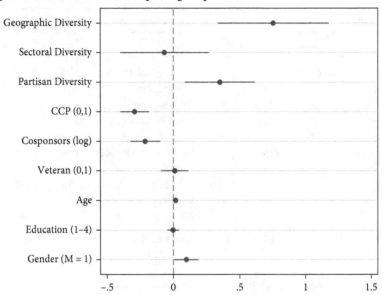

Notes: Estimates based on Model 4 of Appendix Table A.3. Diversity is based on the Diversity Index specification. Points represent coefficient estimates. Bars represent standard error. Estimate includes fixed effects for legislative session and district of the lead sponsor, as well as robust standard errors clustered on the lead sponsor.

Strategic Signaling

Finally, I consider how the behavior of delegates might be impacted by expectations about government priorities. If building diverse coalitions signals encompassing priorities, we should expect delegates to try and coordinate. This is precisely the logic that would compel petitioners to jointly sign a petition or make the perilous journey to a Beijing *xinfang* office. It might also encourage aggrieved residents to coordinate on a street protest, or businesses to collaborate in submitting comments during a consultation campaign. In all instances however, coordination comes with costs. Some costs arise naturally from the need to reconcile disparate and at times competing interests. Yet in China, as discussed earlier, coordination costs are also a function of regime-imposed barriers and penalties to collective action. As such, we should expect input providers to be selective about when they choose to absorb those costs.

In the case of the LPC, it stands to reason that if delegates have gone to the trouble of soliciting cosponsors, they are hoping to have their proposals reviewed by the standing committee. It would make sense for them to behave differently, depending on whether they think their proposals are going to be reviewed by

Figure 5.4. Diversity Discontinuity as a Function of Sponsors

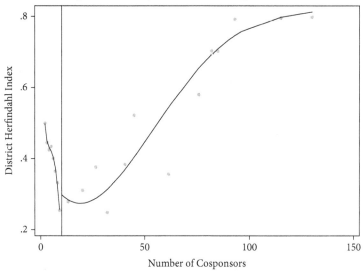

Notes: Vertical line represents discontinuity observed at the ten-cosponsor cutoff. Observation markers represent sample averages within local bins, with 26 and 12 bins to the left and right of the cutoff, respectively. The fitted line is based on fourth order polynomial smoothing function. The sample includes all proposals with more than one sponsor and with a nonzero District Herfindahl Index.

the standing committee, that is, whether they think they can get nine or more cosponsors to sign on to their proposals.

To test this proposition, I conducted a localized test on the data by focusing on proposals just above and below the statutory requirement of ten cosponsors. If delegates are behaving strategically, we should observe a discontinuity around the cutoff, with proposals just above the cutoff backed by significantly more diverse coalitions than those just below the cutoff. Figure 5.4 suggests that the distribution of cosponsor diversity behaves as predicted, with the diversity markedly higher just above the cutoff than below it. Running a McCrary density test on the running distribution of cosponsors confirms this.[45]

One limitation with the discontinuity test is that we cannot be sure that proposals just above and below differ *only* in terms of their prospects for standing committee review. We can, however, examine whether similar sorting results in behavior that is not captured by strategic signaling. Suppose that a delegate's ability to win over more sponsors is a function of political risk, whereby

[45] For more information on the McCrary test, see Justin McCrary. "Manipulation of the Running Variable in the Regression Discontinuity Design: A Density Test." *Journal of Econometrics* 142.2 (2008), pp. 698–714.

Table 5.3 Proposal Diversity Placebo Test

Cutoff=10 (test)	Obs. Below	Above	Means Below	Above	Difference	Std. Error	t-Stat
Geographic Diversity	315	417	.034	.048	-.014	.009	-1.589
CCP Proportion	315	417	.587	.581	.006	.013	.464
Incumbent Proportion	315	417	.298	.319	-.021	.035	-.594
Intellectuals	315	417	.349	.355	-.006	.036	-.160
Cutoff=9 (placebo)							
Geographic Diversity	300	402	.044	.035	.009	.008	1.099
CCP Proportion	300	402	.586	.584	.002	.013	.186
Incumbent Proportion	300	402	.317	.323	-.007	.036	-.188
Intellectuals	300	402	.360	.368	-.008	.037	-.222

the presence of veterans and Party members on a bill signals to prospective cosponsors that the proposal is not risky, as evinced by establishment support. If this were the case, then we might expect a proposal that is aiming to meet the ten-cosponsor threshold to also target more veterans and Party members. Alternatively, it might be that proposals just above the cutoff are qualitatively better-constructed arguments than those below the cutoff. Empirically, such a relationship might involve a greater share of intellectuals in the cosponsorship coalition.

Table 5.3 reports the localized estimates of incumbency CCP, and intellectual coalition proportions just above and below the cutoff, with district diversity measure as a reference. Consistent with the diversity expectation, only district diversity exhibits a significant discontinuity around the cutoff, indicating that sponsors strive to increase diversity if they think they can get at least ten cosponsors. The absence of any effect from alternative coalition attributes supports the main thrust of controlled inclusion, namely that regime-induced barriers to coordination can be leveraged for information. It also provides a useful benchmark for just how salient coalition diversity is. Specifically, the findings suggest that strategic delegates are keener on building diverse, rather than elite coalitions.

Representation by Design

A growing body of scholarship argues that bottom-up institutions help bridge the disconnect between regime leaders and the grassroots of their administration.

In the case of the legislature, delegates representing diverse geographic, sectoral, political, and professional constituencies are believed to feed information up to the legislative body that is then incorporated into future policy.[46] This literature, however, suffers from a fundamental contradiction in that autocrats system-atically cripple their bottom-up institutions, often in ways that seem directly to undermine their informational functions.[47] Much of this crippling is the consequence of political considerations that prevent authoritarian regimes from allowing any institution to operate at its optimal capacity. Openly competitive elections would yield a great deal of information, but they might also get the opposition elected. Allowing delegates to coordinate their proposals could improve policymaking, but it could also encourage organized opposition.

Recognition of these political realities has left scholarship in a bit of a bind, with more pessimistic observers concluding that hobbled institutions are little more than window-dressing, and optimists pointing to evidence that, despite serious flaws, input institutions can still deliver socially desirable governance outcomes. This book's contribution could easily be piled into the latter category, with one exception. Whereas previous literature has identified crippled insti-tutions as a net negative in the information acquisition process, I point to the value of heuristics within these constraints. By making it hard for the public and their representatives to coordinate, the regime is not only reducing the risk posed by a more liberal order, it is also installing built-in noise reducers into the bottom-up process. That is, by making it difficult for citizens to discuss, petition, organize, and participate outside their designated group, coordinated participation becomes informative precisely because it is costly.

These costs are replicated in one form or another across China's partic-ipatory infrastructure. Village leaders are supposed to be popularly elected, but campaigning is illegal. Local delegates are tasked with representing and maintaining close contact with their constituencies but are restricted from engaging in constituency service.[48] Citizens have the right to jointly petition the government, but authorities do everything in their power to prevent them from doing so.[49] Civil society organizations are invited to provide public services but

---

[46] Manion, *Information for Autocrats: Representation in Chinese Local Congresses.*

[47] Pepinsky, "The Institutional Turn in Comparative Authoritarianism."

[48] According to Article 37 of the Organic Law of the Local People's Congresses and Local People's Governments of the People's Republic of China, "Deputies to local people's congresses at various levels shall maintain close contact with the units that elected them or with their constituencies." However, the 2007 revision of the Organic Law that introduced this article also stipulates that the task of maintaining such contact with constituencies can only be pursued by "three or more" deputies, essentially ruling out the possibility that individual deputies set up constituency service offices on their own.

[49] Carl F. Minzner. "Xinfang: Alternative to Formal Chinese Legal Institutions." *Stanford Journal of International Law* 42 (2006), p. 103; Kirsten D. Tatlow. "Rights Group Details Abuse in 'Black Jails'." *New York Times* (2014).

are required to have a government sponsor and are barred from branching out across jurisdictions or issue areas.[50] Across each and every medium for social input, the regime imposes strict barriers to coordination.

At the same time, Chinese authorities actively encourage citizens to participate within designated groups and pre-defined topic issues. In theory, the costs to coordination outside and across these designated groups provide a screening mechanism for the regime as it works to process this bottom-up input for instrumental oversight, planning, and policymaking objectives. In this chapter, I have shown how costly coordination within the legislative forum is indicative of input that represents encompassing interests. This is precisely the type of information the CCP covets as it works to maintain monopoly over a broad governing mandate. Yet even if structured and restricted inclusion is effective in facilitating the production and processing of bottom-up information, it is unclear whether this information has any downstream policy implications. The next three chapters are devoted to this question.

---

[50] Teets, *Civil Society under Authoritarianism: The China Model.*

PART III
DOWNSTREAM POLICY IMPLICATIONS

6

Policy Stability and Avoiding Blunders

The government needs criticism from its people . . . Without this criticism the government will not be able to function as the People's Democratic Dictatorship. Thus the basis of a healthy government is lost . . . We must learn from old mistakes, take all forms of healthy criticism, and do what we can to answer these criticisms.[1]

— Zhou Enlai, 1956

Across the years I have spent going in and out of China, conversations with cabbies have proven a useful source of information and a rough gauge of the public mood. Drivers in some regions are particularly talkative. In Beijing, the proximity to power makes easing into a conversation on politics all the easier. Drivers tend to know what political events are taking place around the city, and at what level of importance, based on the traffic patterns and closures in observance. They are keen to offer background on new construction sites that pop up on the roadside, and are generally unabashed about discussing current events. On my trip in from Capital Airport in January 2013, my driver was more than happy to turn to my usual small talk about the air pollution and the heavy traffic:

"It is bad, an extra 20 minutes to arrive." I am not sure how he knew, as he seemed reluctant to use any GPS assistance. Instead, he handed me his phone, opened to a web page with a cartoon image of an all-red traffic light. The page was from a social media posting about a new policy aimed at deterring drivers from "running yellow lights" (*chuang huangdeng*). Before I could read further, he started complaining about arrogant drivers and incompetent officials. The policy apparently was aimed at reducing congestion, not reckless speeding as I had initially surmised from the headline. The driver pointed at the traffic cameras that lined the expressway and explained how they track everything and fine for the slightest infractions. One loophole was the yellow signal, which drivers took

---

[1] Quoted from Zhou Enlai. "Continue to Exercise Dictatorship and at the Same Time to Broaden Democracy." *Selected Works of Zhou Enlai*. Vol. I. Peking: Foreign Languages Press, 1981, pp. 210–216.

Retrofitting Leninism. Dimitar D. Gueorguiev. Oxford University Press. © Oxford University Press 2021. DOI: 10.1093/oso/9780197555668.003.0007

as an opportunity to enter busy intersections, both to gain ground and keep their place in a line-up of traffic.

During the previous couple of weeks, local traffic bureau officials devised a plan to address this problem by requiring vehicles to stop on yellow, in addition to the traditional red. The new policy was to be enforced entirely by the existing traffic cameras. Penalties would come in the form of six license demerit points, and were to take effect almost immediately, starting January 1, 2013.[2] Though well-intentioned, the policy did not have its desired effect. Indeed, it had no effect. The same day the rule was announced, residents and experts began to lambaste it and its authors. Some raised safety concerns about the increased risk of rear-end collisions, but most pointed to the blatant disregard for basic physics—cars need time to stop. The post the driver was showing me was simply poking fun, suggesting people approved the policy because red was patriotic and so yellow should be happy to have been given the same status. Within a few days, due to much public criticism, implementation was paused and then the policy was permanently shelved.

My driver had found this all quite amusing, but poorly planned policies can have far more dire consequences. In China, history books are replete with examples of disasters caused or exacerbated by bureaucrats.[3] In most instances, the consequences of failed policy are primarily borne by the public, as was the case during China's tragic Great Leap Forward (1957–1961).[4] Blunders can also be damaging for their architects, as was the case with Beijing's traffic fiasco, which was deeply embarrassing for the municipal transportation authorities. Some blunders can challenge the very core of regime legitimacy. In 1990, for instance, Burmese citizens voted in droves against the dominant party after its military leader, Ne Win, pushed for an ill-conceived currency demonetization.[5] In 2015, Sri Lanka's former strongman president, Mahinda Rajapksa, called and lost an early election because his personal astrologer advised him that "the stars were aligned."[6] In 2019, Carrie Lam's government in Hong Kong stoked unprecedented uproar over a poorly organized push for what proved to be a deeply flawed, unpopular extradition law.

Ultimately, policy blunders reflect problems in the policymaking process. With little planning or foresight, laws, rules, and regulations are likely to prove

---

[2] For further background see: https://bit.ly/2Zdh7lq.

[3] See *Zizhi Tongjian* (Comprehensive Guide to Governance) and *Ershisi Shi* (History of the Twenty-four Dynasties).

[4] Dali L. Yang, Huayu Xu, and Ran Tao. "A Tragedy of the Nomenklatura? Career Incentives, Political Loyalty and Political Radicalism during China's Great Leap Foward." *Journal of Contemporary China* 23.89 (2014), pp. 1–20.

[5] David Wallechinsky. *Tyrants: The World's Worst Dictators.* HarperCollins, 2009, p. 368, pp. 61–62.

[6] Author's interview with Rajapaksa 2015 campaign manager, July 2015.

difficult to implement or will result in unintended outcomes. Similarly, if a policy lacks defined responsibilities or public buy-in, it will be easy to ignore and costly to enforce. Even when professionals do the planning and drafting, policymakers still suffer from bounded rationality, since they cannot foresee all the problems and obstacles a policy might encounter once adopted.[7] Instead, even experts tend to muddle their way through by trial and error.[8] In democracies, partisan competition can help preempt downstream obstacles by bringing critical debate to the forefront of policymaking.[9]

Authoritarian regimes are, however, loath to foster such competition, which is, of course, why they are predisposed to blunders in the first place. Instead, feedback control via consultation offers a potential substitute for information and troubleshooting, but only within narrowly defined and more easily controlled issue spaces. At the very least, adding public voices into the mix should slow down the decision-making process, giving policymakers and implementing agents more time to consult among themselves. Observationally, either of these mechanisms should translate into more durable policy decisions.

In this chapter, I test this expectation using an original dataset on sub-national policy and online consultation in China. I find that public consultation during drafting reduces the likelihood that a policy will be repealed or amended in the future. Out of 611 provincial policy items adopted with consultation between 2007 and 2013, none have been repealed. Similarly, amendment rates for policies adopted with consultation are significantly lower than average. These effects, however, depend on the institutional origin of the policy. While consultation appears to have a strong effect on administrative regulations, its impact on formal legislation emerging from representative organs is far more modest.

Soliciting Public Input

As noted in Chapter 3, notice-and-comment consultation offers a close approximation of the feedback control process in that it is aimed at collecting feedback but only within a controlled agenda stipulated by the notice. Moreover, the shift to Internet-based notice-and-comment has amplified this information flow by exponentially increasing the number of potential participants, while also dramatically reducing the costs of participation for all involved.

---

[7] Simon, *Administrative Behavior. A Study of Decison-Making Processes in Administrative Organizations.*

[8] Lindblom, "The Science of 'Muddling Through'."

[9] Bryan D. Jones and Michelle C. Whyman. "Lawmaking and Agenda Setting in the United States, 1948–2010." *Agenda Setting, Policies, and Political Systems. A Comparative Approach* (2014), pp. 36–52.

Notice-and-comment is also attractive from a research standpoint because, unlike expert meetings and public hearings, it leaves behind a digital signature that can be systematically collected and measured. In order to quantify this trail, I visited the web pages of each provincial legislative affairs office as well as a centrally run government website, "Local Legal Network (*difang lifa wang*)", which has since 2006 archived online notice-and-comment solicitations at both national and local levels.[10] In total, this accounting process identified 2,105 instances of online consultation during the observation period (2004–2013), 1,641 of which occurred at sub-national levels.

Selection

Although consultation is now standard guidance for policymaking in China, there is no legal mandate that requires policymakers at any level to follow that guidance. On the contrary, policymakers have wide discretion over what they choose to make public. For example, the national Legislation Law stipulates that any policy may be opened to public consultation but includes no requirements or details on which policies have to be opened or how public consultation should be carried out.[11] Several local administrative procedure regulations (APRs) are more specific, but even then the language suggests that public consultation is only necessary when the policy in question is of "direct public interest."

Hunan Administrative Procedure Regulations, Article 38: *A (public) hearing concerning an administrative decision should be held under any one of the following circumstances:*

1. When it involves a major interest of the general public;
2. When the general public has major differences regarding the proposal;
3. When it might influence social stability; or
4. When laws, regulations or rules stipulate that a hearing should be held.

If policymakers selectively choose to make popular policies public and keep controversial policies private, any relationships between consultation and policy outcome would be confounded. A cursory look at the online notice-and-comment data does not support this conclusion. In particular, more than 30 percent of policies opened up to online notice-and-comment consultation were

---

[10] Because individual websites are sometimes relocated or revamped, and not all information is archived, I rely primarily on the centralized source, using postings on government websites for cross-validation. The centralized website can be accessed from: http://www.locallaw.gov.cn/.

[11] See Article 58 of the Legislation Law.

never adopted. Moreover, many policies put up for comment sit in limbo for much longer than the consultation period, suggesting that the policies in question were not foregone conclusions. Alternatively, policymakers might resort to public consultation when they are uncertain about the policy outcome or when they are concerned about public backlash. Such motives are consistent with China's own experience with policy consultation which, as discussed in Chapter 3, emerged during periods of instability caused by price reforms and mass privatization.[12]

If risk or uncertainty is driving the selection of policies for consultation, then selection should be biased against the main hypotheses because sensitive and untested policies should be more susceptible to reversal and revision. Even if selection bias is not fatal for the analysis, it is still critical to ensure that we are comparing apples to apples. One approach is to analyze the effects of consultation on similar policy initiatives. This is possible when national laws and ordinances are reinterpreted and implemented locally, or when multiple sub-national governments formulate similar policies to deal with the same issue. For example, nearly all of China's 31 provinces passed local interpretations of the Labor Contract Law, some with public consultation and some without it. Based on this logic, I constructed a panel archive of all sub-national legislative and administrative regulations formulated and adopted in China since the 1980s.[13]

By identifying common policy initiatives containing policies of nearly identical content and implication, we can insure that it is not the topic of discussion that is driving any consultation-related effect. However, we are still left with the possibility that the decision to engage consultation, even within common policy arenas, is driven by some unobserved and systematic local factor, or that it is the result of individual-level choices in the local legislative affairs office. Ultimately, how we deal with this problem depends on whether we believe policymakers, tasked with implementing nearly identical policies, are more or less likely to opt into consultation if they anticipate a smooth implementation process.

Structured interviews with administrative officials at provincial Legislative Affairs Offices in Hunan, Sichuan, and Guangdong suggest two primary considerations.[14] The first concerns whether or not the public has an interest in the policy. For example, topics like residential policy, construction, pets,

---

[12] Cai, "Managed Participation in China."

[13] This data was collected using the Beijing University Law Center Legal Archive and corroborated using annual versions of the *Law Yearbook*. In total, the archival data obtained includes over 27,500 administrative regulation-related observations and 19,200 legislative records. While this data provides a detailed description of policy development over the last two decades, only a small portion of it will be used in the main analysis so that it matches the smaller time period covered by the consultation dataset, which does not begin until 2004.

[14] Interview protocols were designed by the author for an unrelated research project and administered by the Asia Foundation's China Administrative Law Research Association (ALRA). For details contact the author directly.

and social security are often opened to public input, whereas economic and industrial policies tend to be decided internally or through expert hearings. According to interviewees, the former categories are more likely to generate public interest and opposition, whereas the public is more deferential on the latter categories.[15] The data on consultation frequencies across policy categories seems to confirm such sentiments (see Table 6.1). Public interest categories like agriculture, construction, and education have received the most consultation, whereas consultation on issues like administration and trade is less common.

The second factor concerns the policymaker's subjective assessment of whether consultation would yield anything useful. A number of officials, for instance, expressed frustration over public hearings, which they viewed as "tedious" and "unhelpful." By contrast, respondents showed higher esteem for comments they receive from academics, lawyers, and professionals. Interestingly, none of the interviewees reported criticism as a factor in determining whether or not to make a policy public. Instead, respondents described their decisions as based on a cost–benefit analysis of how much time and effort it would take to make something public versus the benefit they would get from receiving public comments. This instrumental approach to consultation is consistent with previous work, which finds that concerns

Table 6.1 Consultation Across Categories

Policy Category	Consultation		Consultation Rate
	No	Yes	
Education	91	18	17%
Tax Finance	103	20	16%
Agriculture	238	43	15%
Infrastructure	1039	183	15%
Labor	132	24	15%
Trade	51	8	14%
Use of Land	8	1	13%
Social	323	43	12%
Overall	4610	611	12%
Environment	245	29	11%
Welfare	212	27	11%
Economic	310	35	10%
Industry	353	40	10%
Legal	714	76	10%
Administrative	778	61	7%

Note: Categories created by pooling issue tags for each policy item provided by Beijing Law School.

[15] Interview record: HN.4.p9; JS.2.p5; ST.3.p9.

about policy delay and participant competence are the top concerns among policymakers considering consultation.[16]

Though online consultation is faster and less costly, it is not always readily accessible. According to the most recent provincial numbers, Internet penetration varies dramatically; over 77 percent of Beijing residents have access compared to only 44 percent in Jiangxi.[17] Government website infrastructure also varies significantly. Annual assessments conducted by the China Software Testing Center (CSTC), a research institute under the Ministry of Industry and Information Technology (MIIT), reveals that Chinese governments collectively spend about 500 billion RMB each year on e-governance development, but many of the websites and local servers hosting these e-government platforms are outdated and difficult to operate.[18] At the forefront of the rankings are predictable provinces, such as Beijing and Guangdong, but they are accompanied by Sichuan which, despite being one of the poorest provinces in China, scores higher than Beijing on a number of dimensions, including open government information and public consultation.

If policymakers are making strategic choices on when to utilize online consultation based on information potential and cost, we should expect provinces with higher Internet penetration and good website infrastructure to utilize consultative procedures more often than their counterparts. Leveraging data from the China Internet Network Information Center (CNNIC) on Internet penetration and from CSTC on e-governance infrastructure, I have run a Probit model to estimate the probability that a provincial policy item was opened to consultation. Controlling for the size and wealth of the economy, as well as for provincial expenditures, I find that both penetration and website quality are strong predictors of online consultation. Holding all else equal, moving toward the highest rate of Internet penetration in 2012 increases to about 70 percent the marginal likelihood of using online consultation. Similarly, moving to the top of the website quality ranking increases the predicted probability of consultation to about 55 percent (see Figure 6.1).

Dependent Variables

There are number of ways to think about policy stability. Repeals, for instance, are straightforward, but they may also conflate bad policy with a policy that is

---

[16] Terry H.Y. Li, S. Thomas Ng, and Martin Skitmore. "Public Participation in Infrastructure and Construction Projects in China: From an EIA-based to a Whole-Cycle Process." *Habitat International* 36.1 (2012), pp. 47–56.

[17] Based on the "39th China Internet Development Survey Report (2017)," which is the last time provincial penetration breakdown was reported. Penetration is defined as the share of with access to Internet connections.

[18] Chinese Government Website Performance Evaluation. Accessible from http://politics.people.com.cn/GB/44160/51694/236051/index.html.

Figure 6.1. Internet Infrastructure and Consultation

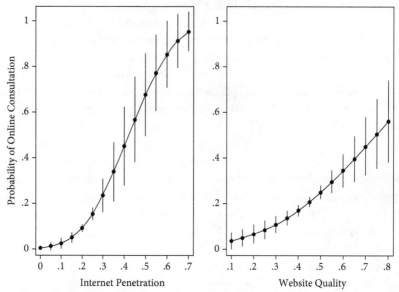

Notes: Figures report the marginal effect of increases in *Internet Penetration* and improvements in *Website Quality* based on Probit estimation of the likelihood that a policy draft is opened to consultation prior to adoption. *Internet Penetration* (share of population with access) data comes from annual CNNIC reports. Measures of *Website Quality* come from the China Software Testing Center CSTC (see text for description).

simply no longer relevant. That said, one could argue that the best policies never lose their relevance. Similarly, frequent amendments may signal a poorly conceived policy, but frequent amendments may also be the indirect consequence of a rapidly changing socioeconomic environment. On the margins, however, policymakers, investors, and citizens ought to prefer policy that lasts to policy that is frequently changing. Practically speaking, a policy that only lasts a few months before it is repealed or revised probably had some fundamental flaws. By contrast, a law or regulation that is repealed ten years down the line was probably a perfectly good policy to begin with but lost its purpose over time.

Rather than adopting a single operationalization, I explore consultation effects under different interpretations of the outcome variable. Specifically, I utilize the policy-specific information and the iterated structure of the dataset to construct three separate dependent variables: policy *Repeal*, policy *Amendment*, and policy *Lifespan*.[19] The first measure, *Repeal*, is simply a dichotomous history of whether or not a given piece of legislation or regulation is ever repealed after

[19] Each observation in the dataset also includes several relational pieces of information; namely the issuing body (i.e., a provincial or local People's Congress in the case of legislation or government

being adopted. The second measure, *Amendment*, is a count of each instance of amendment. Finally, policy *Lifespan* is measured in duration segments, that is, from the point of first adoption up to the first amendment. Once amended, the clock is reset until the next change or until the end of the dataset, which in this version of the analysis is 04/01/13.

How well do these measures capture policy stability? Unfortunately, there are no off-the-shelf measures of policy stability, especially not for authoritarian countries like China, where scholarship on policymaking remains largely qualitative. There are, however, some unique and novel attempts at measuring policy uncertainty using media coverage. In particular, Baker, Bloom, and Davis have constructed a monthly Policy Uncertainty Index for China dating back to 1995 using economic policy–related media reports from the *South China Morning Post*, the leading English-language newspaper in Hong Kong.[20] To test the construct-validity of my measures, I construct an *instability* factor based on amendment and repeal variables.[21] Operationally, this means that in the months in which a higher proportion of policy actions were for amendments or repeals, rather than new policy, the political instability factor will be large. Consistent with this expectation, the correlation between Baker, Bloom, and Davis's policy (Uncertainty) index and my own measure of policy (Instability), as captured by amendment and repeal rates is quite strong, roughly 0.68, and statistically significant to the 95 percent level.[22]

Downstream Stability

Does consultation delay policy adoption? In order to estimate adoption delays, adoption dates were transformed into a single value that begins at zero in Jan-01-1960 and counts forward.[23] As such, larger values correspond to more recent dates and positive coefficients can be interpreted as delays in adoption. For example, the constant on Model 1 of Table 6.2, (18,219), corresponds to Nov-18-2009. The coefficients of the covariates can thus be directly interpreted as the additional number of days it takes to adopt a policy given a one-unit change in the covariate and all other variables held constant. For example, the effect of

---

body in the case of regulations), the time it was adopted and ratified, the topic it covers, and its issue classification.

[20] Scott R. Baker, Nicholas Bloom, and Steven J. Davis. "Measuring Economic Policy Uncertainty." *NBER Working Paper* No. w21633.May (2015), pp. 1–75.

[21] I give equal weight to amendments and repeals.

[22] The correlation is based on comparing monthly rates across the two variables between 1995 and 2013.

[23] The choice of Jan-01-1960 is an arbitrary setting in the Stata statistical package digital date function and has no impact on the analysis.

Table 6.2 Consultation and Policy Deceleration

DV: Adoption Time	Regulations			Laws		
(2007–2013)	Base (1)	Policy (2)	Full (3)	Base (4)	Policy (5)	Full (6)
Consultation	503.2***	408.5***	121.8***	464.2***	410.8***	110.7***
	(38.69)	(59.81)	(32.91)	(35.43)	(61.66)	(27.80)
Draft/Provisional	-180.8***	-245.4**	-52.56	-127.8**	-153.0**	-4.226
	(67.26)	(102.5)	(55.15)	(49.61)	(68.39)	(34.57)
Expend per cap			0.047***			0.087***
			(0.003)			(0.021)
GDP per cap			0.088***			0.047***
			(0.011)			(0.005)
Municipality			75.45			29.77
			(46.17)			(36.98)
Minority			45.03			40.65
			(58.57)			(60.47)
Policy Arena FE	no	YES	YES		YES	YES
Province FE	no	no	YES	no	no	YES
Constant	18,219***	18,661***	17,166***	18,209***	18,942***	17,232***
	(32.86)	(59.81)	(122.2)	(29.91)	(66.91)	(83.50)
Observations	739	739	710	1,072	1,072	1,056
R-squared	0.122	0.470	0.936	0.082	0.319	0.794
Log Likelihood	-5790	-5603	-4616	-8453	-8293	-7532
Clusters	53	53	53	60	60	60

Notes: The DV represents the date when a policy was adopted. The constant on Model 2 corresponds to Jan-10-2007. The coefficient on Consultation can be interpreted as the additional number of days it takes to pass a policy with public participation. Base Models 1 and 3 include no controls or Fixed Effects. Policy models 2 and 5 include a Fixed Effect. (FE) for each policy arena. Full Models 3 and 6 add provincial Fixed Effects (FE). Each of the models is run using OLS due to the large amount of fixed effects. Robust Standard errors are clustered on policy issue: * $p<.10$, ** $p<.05$, *** $p<.01$

having notice-and-comment consultation on a Regulation in Model 3 is a delay in adoption of about 122 days.[24]

Interpreting the results of Models 1 and 4, we see that, on average, policy with consultation is adopted later than policy without consultation. This is

[24] Results are distinguished as Base, Policy, and Full results. The Policy models include a policy-arena fixed effect based on policy roots. Policy-arena fixed effects control for selection bias by identifying unique policy initiatives across provinces. Full models include administrative and economic controls as well as provincial fixed effects. Each model is run using OLS due to the large amount of fixed effects, with robust standard errors clustered on policy issue to capture non-independence across issue topics.

partially due to the fact that consultation rates have been increasing over time. Policy arena fixed effects also absorb a good deal of the underlying variation, as evinced by the increase in R-squared, suggesting that there is a considerable heterogeneity across policy arenas. Models 3 and 6 add provincial fixed effects. Again, the size of the coefficient is reduced dramatically, and the R-squared increases to about (0.94) and (0.79) respectively, suggesting that different provinces have consistently different policy schedules.[25] In particular, wealthier provinces that spend more on their populations tend to be slower in adopting new regulations and legislation. Overall, the results suggest that consultation does delay policy adoption.

Even if consultation is slowing things down, that may not necessarily mean it is helping to produce more durable policy. To try and get a better sense of its contributions, I proceed by looking at the effects of consultation on policy repeal rates. Specifically, if consultation is contributing useful information to the decision-making process, and thereby reducing policy failure, we should observe a negative relationship between consultation and policy repeals. Looking only at policies enacted in the post-2006 period shows that ninety regulations and sixty one laws were repealed; see Table 6.3. However, tabulating these numbers against the presence of public consultation reveals that no openly formulated policy was ever repealed. While this simple tabulation provides deterministic support for our expectations, the relative rarity of repeals and consultation could generate such results simply by chance.

Instead, I proceed with two alternative measures of stability: *Amendment* and *Lifespan*. As noted earlier, policy amendments are usually enacted in order to fill gaps in the original policy or as updates to articles and statutes that are no longer relevant. Taking this perspective, frequent revisions should suggest a lack of completion and foresight in the original document. Table 6.4 evaluates this logic using OLS regression.[26] Overall, we observe a negative relationship

Table 6.3 Consultation and Policy Repeal

Regulations (2007–2013)				Legislation (2007–2013)			
Consultation	Repeals	Amend	Total	Consultation	Repeals	Amend	Total
No	90	272	2557	No	61	131	2088
Yes	0	13	273	Yes	0	9	338
Total	90	285	2830	Total	61	140	2426

[25] The high R-squared values may seem suspicious. However, given that policy adoption follows a fairly uniform process, there is not a great deal of variation across observations, especially once all policy arena fixed effects are taken into consideration.

[26] Ideally, a negative binomial count model would have been used. However, concerns about using numerous fixed effects in nonlinear equations make OLS a more appropriate, albeit less accurate, substitute. That said, negative binomial estimates were conducted and provide similar results.

Table 6.4 Consultation and Policy Amendment

DV: Amendment	Regulations			Laws		
(2007–2013)	Base (1)	Policy (2)	Full (3)	Base (4)	Policy (5)	Full (6)
Consultation	-0.078***	-0.056**	-0.062*	-0.021	-0.026	-0.022
	(0.025)	(0.024)	(0.033)	(0.015)	(0.022)	(0.021)
Provisional	0.074*	0.090**	0.082	0.047**	0.048	0.047
	(0.038)	(0.041)	(0.051)	(0.021)	(0.032)	(0.033)
Expend per cap			5.2e-06			-2.6e-06
			(1.7e-05)			(6.1e-06)
GDP per cap			-7.6e-07			-4.5e-06
			(5.3e-06)			(4.1e-06)
Municipality			0.021			0.038
			(0.031)			(0.026)
Minority			0.007			0.0207
			(0.045)			(0.046)
Time			9.7e-06			-3.6e-05
			(8.3e-05)			(8.7e-05)
Time^2			4.0e-08			3.81e-10
			(3.8e-08)			(2.2e-08)
Policy Arena FE		Y	Y		Y	Y
Province FE			Y			Y
Constant	0.105***	0.056**	0.054	0.025***	-0.022	0.149
	(0.021)	(0.024)	(0.172)	(0.006)	(0.014)	(0.147)
Observations	739	739	710	1,068	1,068	1,052
R-squared	0.016	0.472	0.561	0.008	0.259	0.311
Clusters	53	53	53	60	60	60

Notes: Dependent variable measures the total number of amendments each policy experiences. Each model is based only on policy arenas that have included consultation. The Policy Models 2 and 5 include a fixed effect for each policy arena to control for heterogeneity between policies that were or were not opened to public consultation. The Full Models 3 and 6 include economic and administrative controls, as well as province and year fixed effects. Each model uses OLS due to multiple fixed effects. Robust standard errors clustered on policy issue: * $p<.10$, ** $p<.05$, *** $p<.01$

between consultation and policy amendment. Unsurprisingly, provisional drafts are significantly more likely to be amended. Yet, while the effect of consultation on reducing amendments is large and robust for regulations, it is smaller and not significant for legislation. Holding all else equal, the substantive impact of consultation in Models 3 and 6 yields a roughly 2 percent reduction in the likelihood of undergoing an additional amendment for regulations, while the effect on legislation is not significant. The reason this effect is so small is that the underlying probability of amendment for policies enacted since 2007 is already very small. A further possible explanation for why consultation does not appear to affect legislative amendment is that the legislative process is institutionally more complicated and rigorous, which reduces the additional information value provided by consultation.

Examining *Lifespan* allows us to further decompose policies into segments, from birth until amendment, and subsequent amendment or repeal. In so doing, we capture more variation, including instances of consultative revision as well as policies that are revised or abandoned very shortly after adoption.[27] One challenge to estimating lifespan is that the sample period artificially cuts short policies that start late or are never repealed or amended. To account for this, I also included a time and time-squared component that tracks the number of days between the policy adoption date and the dataset terminus represented by April 1, 2013. An alternative approach is to censor policies that end with the sample period using a Cox Proportional Hazards specification.

In the case of regulations, results in Table 6.5 suggest that consultation is significantly associated with longer lifespan. In the OLS Models 1 and 2, the coefficient can be interpreted directly as the additional number of days a policy lasts, or about 45 days in the Base Model 1 and 42 days in the Policy Model 2. The negative coefficient in the Survival models represents a reduction in the proportional hazard of a policy ending in amendment or repeal.

Substantively speaking, consultation increases the lifespan period from about 950 days to 995 days. As with policy amendments, we see that the estimated effect of public consultation on policy lifespan length is larger and more significant for regulations than for legislation. This might be due to the fact that legislative sessions are more regularized, which reduces variation in lifespan. Alternatively, however, it again suggests that public consultation is most effective in regulatory decision-making, where institutional constraints are weaker.

---

[27] As with the analysis on amendment, OLS was chosen as the primary model specification due to the need to include multiple policy fixed effects, and the "Policy" models include policy-arena fixed effects to identify unique policy initiatives across administrations.

Table 6.5 Participation and Policy Stability

DV: Lifespan	Regulations				Laws			
	OLS		Hazard		OLS		Hazard	
(2007–2013)	Base (1)	Policy (2)	Base (3)	Policy (4)	Base (5)	Policy (6)	Base (7)	Policy (8)
Consultation	45.840**	42.960*	-0.793**	-1.012**	32.600**	31.06	-0.741	-0.550
	(18.550)	(22.200)	(0.308)	(0.423)	(15.780)	(19.490)	(0.484)	(0.635)
Draft/Provisional	-59.890**	-73.330**	0.614*	1.262**	-29.640**	-26.420	-0.0108	0.0610
	(26.900)	(28.380)	(0.318)	(0.538)	(14.160)	(18.730)	(0.520)	(0.663)
Expend per cap	-0.003	-0.009	0.001	-0.001	0.007*	0.008*	-0.001***	-0.001**
	(0.006)	(0.008)	(0.000)	(0.000)	(0.004)	(0.004)	(0.000)	(0.000)
GDP per cap	-0.001	-0.001	-1.6e-05	7.4e-06	0.003**	0.004**	0.000***	0.000***
	(0.003)	(0.003)	(3.7e-05)	(4.6e-05)	(0.002)	(0.002)	(5.1e-05)	(6.6e-05)
Municipality	9.401	11.500	-0.094	-0.290	5.680	0.373	-0.274	-0.193
	(13.600)	(20.030)	(0.241)	(0.399)	(8.863)	(9.047)	(0.328)	(0.416)
Minority	14.180	20.120	-0.191	-0.209	6.375	20.53	-0.548	-0.919
	(29.800)	(34.920)	(0.510)	(0.884)	(28.230)	(26.670)	(0.605)	(0.820)
Time Controls	Y	Y			Y	Y		

Table 6.5 (*continued*)

DV: Lifespan (2007–2013)	Regulations				Laws			
	OLS		Hazard		OLS		Hazard	
	Base (1)	Policy (2)	Base (3)	Policy (4)	Base (5)	Policy (6)	Base (7)	Policy (8)
Policy Arena FE		Y		Y		Y		Y
Province FE	Y	Y	Y	Y	Y	Y	Y	Y
Constant	59.520 (58.30)	19.990 (121.0)			-172.6** (73.26)	-181.5** (82.81)		
Observations	1,160	1,160	1,160	1,160	1,724	1,724	1,714	1,714
R-squared	0.872	0.895	0.042	0.217	0.943	0.949	0.096	0.293
Log Likelihood	-7860	-7745	-709.2	-579.6	-10999	-10900	-1627	-283.5
Clusters	60	60			63	63		

Notes: Dependent variable measures the number of days a policy segment lasts between creation and amendment and amendment/repeal, or amendment to next amendment/repeal. Base Models includes all controls and provincial Fixed Effects. Policy Models includes a Fixed Effect for each policy arena, to control for heterogeneity between policies that were or were not opened to public participation. Models 1, 2, 5, and 6 use OLS with robust standard errors clustered on policy issue. Models 3, 4, 7, and 8 use a Cox Proportional Hazards Model. Robust standard errors clustered on policy issue: * $p<.10$, ** $p<.05$, *** $p<.01$

No Need for Speed

Though the effects of consultation are highly significant, it is worth considering them in the broader context. At minimum, it appears that consultation carries a classical trade-off between decisiveness and resoluteness.[28] Here, however, it is essential to remember that authoritarian leaders have ample opportunity to be decisive. That is, after all, their comparative advantage. By contrast, the aim of consultation in the policymaking process is more about quality and process than it is about quantity or speed.

There are also political and reputational trade-offs involved, and they are more difficult to quantify. Unforced policy errors, or what in China are sometimes referred to as *yiwai*, like the traffic debacle referenced earlier or the many other blunders referenced in previous studies,[29] are embarrassing for a political regime that claims to be all-knowing and infallible. Put simply, having to repeal a previous policy is tantamount to admitting a mistake, and the CCP is not in the business of admitting mistakes.

The analyses presented in this chapter demonstrate that consultation can help the CCP avoid mistakes and unforced errors. Building on the previous chapters, the evidence increasingly points to public inclusion as an information-generating exercise, the benefits of which accrue as a result of learning on the part of decision-makers. The mechanisms behind this effect need not be mono-causal, however. As suggested in Chapter 5, public inclusion can also be seen as a political move aimed at dispelling public mistrust by marketing government policy as inclusive and deliberative—a topic that I turn to in the next chapter.

---

[28] Gary W. Cox and Mathew D. McCubbins. "Political Structure and Economic Policy: The Institutional Determinants of Policy Outcomes." *Presidents, Parliaments and Policy.* Ed. by Stephen Haggard and Mathew D. McCubbins. Cambridge University Press, 2001, pp. 21–63.

[29] Stromseth, Malesky, and Gueorguiev, *China's Governance Puzzle: Enabling Transparency and Participation in a Single-Party State.*

7

Spending Together

> We will improve the open administrative system in various areas
> and increase transparency in government work, thus enhancing the
> people's trust in the government.
>
>   — Hu Jintao, Report to 17th Congress of the CCP, 2007

A "nail house" (*dingzi hu*) is a name given to the most tenacious of house-holds that resist China's incessant drive for demolition and transformation. The households hold out to the very end, often sticking out in the middle of busy construction sites or, as was the case in Daxi town, in the middle of a brand new roadway that conspicuously snaked around Luo Baogen's four-story home. Mr. Luo, like millions of others across China felt the compensation offered by the local government for his home, reported at 260,000 RMB (approximately 40,000 USD), was not enough to cover his losses, and he was determined to stay put until the government upped its offer. The ordeal lasted over a year, forcing higher levels to intervene and undisclosed concessions to be made, in order to convince Mr. Luo and his family to abandon their home. On one level, the nail house is a product of weak property rights that allow local governments to exploit collective land for development projects.[1] On another, these standoffs reflect festering mistrust and animosity between Chinese residents and their local governments.

Nail houses like Mr. Luo's are, in some respects, the best possible outcome of local tensions. In many other instances, protests break out, and lives are lost. Just a year earlier, a popular village leader in next door Yueqing County was found mysteriously crushed by a tractor after leading a group of villagers to protest a land confiscation by the county government.[2] At times, such as when the police officers are killed in broad daylight for trying to enforce eviction notices the victims are on the government side.[3] Nationwide, an overwhelming majority of protests that occur in China each year are attributed to altercations with local

---

[1] Mr. Luo's house, for example, stood in the way of road networks built alongside a new high-speed rail station in the neighboring town.
[2] See: https://nyti.ms/2KwQcMA.
[3] See: https://bit.ly/2Kv9UrR.

Retrofitting Leninism. Dimitar D. Gueorguiev. Oxford University Press. © Oxford University Press 2021.
DOI: 10.1093/oso/9780197555668.003.0008

governments over land grabs, and these numbers are growing.[4] The remaining portion of protests, though not about land per se, are almost always directed against local government actions.

Yet not all disagreements between citizens and government devolve into conflict, and local governments are able to push through development projects at far faster rates than they might in more democratic environments. To be sure, coercion plays a large role, as do backdoor negotiations and payoffs. Often it relies on both, with local residents recruited to help nudge their neighbors into agreements. In either case, social surveys confirm that animosity and mistrust toward local government in China is growing. Still, there are some instances in which decisions, including land sales, are made through consultative means whereby residents are incorporated into the decision-making process. In this chapter, I explore one prominent site of such consultations, just 20 miles northeast of Daxi, where residents are regularly invited to participate in major government decisions and spending plans. In particular, the experimental nature of consultations explored in this chapter will help us make sense of whether and how structured consultation impacts perceptions of government.

Rebuilding Trust

Despite apparent tensions at the grassroots level, public approval for the Chinese leadership is higher than that in many Western democracies.[5] In understanding how this can be, it is again helpful to abandon the unitary version of the Chinese state and think in terms of layers. The uppermost layer, inhabited by the Party leadership, claims credit for nearly four decades of uninterrupted growth. This is the layer that is recognized internationally for China's gleaming skylines, its unmatched high-speed rail network, and its soaring global profile. Yet for many Chinese, the deeper you descend, the closer you get to a rotten base. As discussed in Chapter 2, this layering allows the central leadership to deflect blame for governance failures—environmental disasters, food scares, and health outbreaks.[6] When problems arise, a hyper-responsive leadership is able to intervene, demonstrating not only that it has the public interest at heart, but also the capacity to protect citizens from venal local officials.[7]

---

[4] In 2005, the last year that the Chinese government published official statistics, there were over 87,000 "mass incidents," as compared with roughly 5,000–10,000 per year in the early 1990s and fewer than 1,000 a year in the 1980s.

[5] Tang, *Populist Authoritarianism: Chinese Political Culture and Regime Sustainability.*

[6] As discussed in Chapter 3, public opinion in China sharply discriminates between local and central authorities, exhibiting far less trust in the former than the latter; see Lianjiang Li. "Reassessing Trust in the Central Government: Evidence from Five National Surveys." *The China Quarterly* 225 (2016), pp. 100–121.

[7] Tang, *Populist Authoritarianism: Chinese Political Culture and Regime Sustainability.*

There is a problem with this Machiavellian logic, however, as constantly putting out fires sends a problematic set of signals. First, responsiveness can encourage collective action against local authorities as a way of provoking central government intervention.[8] As of late, it has become nearly impossible for local governments to address basic servicing, like sanitation, without a small Not in My Backyard (NIMBY) protest breaking out. All the while, repeatedly sanctioning local authorities only reinforces concerns about state corruption,[9] and potentially discourages local officials from exercising their economic options.[10] At the end of the day, it is the localities that govern China, implement national policies, sell bonds, build infrastructure, and, increasingly, it will be local authorities who collect revenue from taxpayers.

CCP leaders are not blind to such dangers, and the issue of grassroots governance failures is a frequent subject of concern. In the past, Beijing has often opted for reactionary solutions focused on increasing control. For instance, fiscal tightening in the mid-1990s,[11] and the abrogation of the agricultural tax system in 2005,[12] were clear attempts at recentralizing control over how public revenue is collected and distributed. Similarly, the more recent anticorruption campaign reflects the center's desire to reassert control over the Party and bureaucracy. Such solutions, however, are not ideal. Recentralization reduces the loss of agency but only by undermining delegation. Likewise, disciplining corrupt officials may be popular, but it probably does not help to resolve underlying levels of mistrust toward the government.

Instead, scholars, both foreign and domestic, argue that China's local legitimacy crisis requires more participatory solutions that address mistrust and grievances between local communities and their governments.[13] But what if the participatory process is controlled, if the focus of inclusion is narrow, and if decision-makers face no formal incentives to listen? According to Fewsmith, these are the "limits" to reform in China, but it is unclear what these limits preclude.[14] As argued in the previous four chapters, regime controls over the way

[8] Yanhua Deng and Guobin Yang. "Pollution and Protest in China: Environmental Mobilization in Context." *The China Quarterly* 214 (2013), pp. 321–336.

[9] Dan Chen. "Local Distrust and Regime Support." *Political Research Quarterly* 70.2 (2017), pp. 314–326; Yuhua Wang and Bruce Dickson. "How Corruption Investigations Undermine Regime Support: Evidence from China." Available at SSRN 3086286 (2018).

[10] Luyao Wang. "The Impacts of Anti-corruption on Economic Growth in China." *Modern Economy* 7.02 (2016), p. 109.

[11] Yasheng Huang. "Central–Local Relations in China during the Reform Era: The Economic and Institutional Dimensions." *World Development* 24.4 (1996), pp. 655–672.

[12] Kai-yuen Tsui. "Local Tax System, Intergovernmental Transfers and China's Local Fiscal Disparities." *Journal of Comparative Economics* 33.1 (2005), pp. 173–196.

[13] Keping Yu. *Democracy Is a Good Thing: Essays on Politics, Society, and Culture in Contemporary China.* Vol. 1. Brookings Institution Press, 2009, p. 219; Joseph Fewsmith. *The Logic and Limits of Political Reform in China.* Cambridge University Press, 2013; He and Warren, "Authoritarian Deliberation: The Deliberative Turn in Chinese Political Development."

[14] Fewsmith, *The Logic and Limits of Political Reform in China.*

citizens and their representatives participate have not prevented the process from generating useful information for the regime. On the contrary, the controlled nature of participation can in some respects facilitate information processing. This chapter proceeds along a similar course by asking whether there is any legitimacy to be gained from controlled inclusion?

Before I proceed, it is important to clarify what I mean by "legitimacy." In Soviet systems, legitimacy is commonly interpreted as an affirmation of good performance,[15] or what some political theorists refers to as "output" legitimacy.[16] The extent to which this kind of legitimacy relates to inclusion, however, is limited. The Soviet Union frequently boasted of mass participation, but as Roeder points out, Soviet-era participation amounted, at best, to a system of "coproduction," whereby citizens were systematically disassociated from decision-making but were enlisted in production and implementation.[17] To be sure, coproduction of this sort could bring legitimacy, but that would be contingent on the performance of the policy being implemented. Instead, this chapter will focus on public perceptions of the governing process itself, irrespective of the outcomes it delivers, or what is sometimes referred to as "throughput" legitimacy.[18]

As outlined in Chapter 2, extant literature offers a range of plausible mechanisms for how controlled forms of inclusion might contribute to throughput legitimacy. At the very least, including someone who otherwise feels ignored could simply change their mind about the government's level of concern and responsiveness.[19] When citizens take the next step and interpret the decision-maker's invitation for input as credible and genuine, it tends to increase satisfaction with government in a general sense.[20] Even when citizens disagree with the ultimate policy decision, participation in the process that formed it can increase understanding and thus decrease resistance.[21] In the rest of this chapter, I evaluate these mechanisms through the lens of participatory budgeting.

---

[15] Stephen White. "Economic Performance and Communist Legitimacy." *World Politics* 38.3 (1986), pp. 462–482; Yuhong Zhao. "Assessing the Environmental Impact of Projects: A Critique of the EIA Legal Regime in China." *Natural Resources Journal* 49.2 (2009), pp. 485–524.

[16] Fritz Scharpf. *Governing in Europe: Effective and Democratic?* Oxford University Press, 1999.

[17] Roeder, "Modernization and Participation in the Leninist Developmental Strategy."

[18] Vivien A Schmidt. "Democracy and Legitimacy in the European Union Revisited: Input, Output and 'Throughput'." *Political Studies* 61.1 (2013), pp. 2–22.

[19] King, Feltey, and Susel, "The Question of Participation: Toward Authentic Public Participation in Public Administration."

[20] Ruscio, "Trust, Democracy, and Public Management: A Theoretical Argument."

[21] Thomas, "Maintaining and Restoring Public Trust in Government Agencies and their Employees"; Warren, "Democratic Theory and Self-transformation"; Benjamin Barber. *Strong Democracy: Participatory Politics for a New Age.* University of California Press, 1984.

Participatory Budgeting

The concept of participatory budgeting, a process that combines transparency with citizen input on spending decisions, originated in Brazil during the late 1980s. At the time, Brazil was transitioning from military dictatorship to civilian democracy, and participatory budgeting was an attempt by a new left-wing Workers' Party to mobilize poor voters.[22] Since the first participatory budgeting event held in Porto Alegre, Brazil in 1988, over one thousand cities across Latin America have started holding annual participatory budgeting meetings.[23] Beginning with the initial Porto Alegre meetings, participatory budgeting throughout Latin America has retained a redistributive tone, usually taking place in low-income neighborhoods and attracting a mix of young, poor, and predominantly female participants.[24] By contrast, participatory budgeting in Europe, having expanded during the 2008 financial crisis, has served mainly as a mechanism for prioritizing spending preferences amid tightening local budgets, and not for redistribution.[25]

Participatory budgeting, as it operates in the Chinese context, resembles the European case insofar as coproduction is confined to prioritizing items from within predetermined spending menus. This development, however, is relatively recent, and some background on fiscal relations is helpful. In particular, the CCP has often struggled to balance a desire for central control with the benefits of decentralization.[26] During the Mao era, central government laid claim to nearly all revenue.[27] Beginning in the 1980s, the fiscal relationship between the center and localities began shifting, with provincial and local authorities progressively gaining greater autonomy over revenues.[28] This period of rapid decentralization has been credited with instilling market incentives among local officials,[29] as well

[22] Joan Lamaysou Bak. *Militants and Citizens: The Politics of Participatory Democracy in Porto Alegre (review)*. Vol. 42. 2. Stanford University Press, 2006, pp. 166–169.
[23] Brian Wampler. *Participatory Budgeting in Brazil — Contestation, Cooperation, and Accountability*. Vol. 54. 5. Penn State Press, 2010, pp. 294–294.
[24] A. Marquetti, C.E. Schonerwald da Silva, and A. Campbell. "Participatory Economic Democracy in Action: Participatory Budgeting in Porto Alegre, 1989–2004." *Review of Radical Political Economics* 44.1 (2012), pp. 62–81; World Bank. *Toward a More Inclusive and Effective Participatory Budget in Porto Alegre*. Tech. rep. 40144. World Bank, *Public Expenditure Review (PER)*, 2008, pp. 1–106.
[25] Yves Sintomer et al. "Learning from the South: Participatory Budgeting Worldwide–An Invitation to Global Cooperation." *Dialog Global* 25.25 (2010), p. 86.
[26] Oksenberg and Tong, "The Evolution of Central–Provincial Fiscal Relations in China, 1971–1984: The Formal System."
[27] P.T. Wanless. *Taxation in Centrally Planned Economies*. Routledge, 2018.
[28] For a political perspective on the evolution and logic of these reforms, see Shirk, *The Political Logic of Economic Reform in China*, pp. 147–196.
[29] Barry Weingast. "The Economic Role of Political Institutions." *The Journal of Law, Economics and Organization* 7.1 (1995), pp. 1–31; Weingast, "The Political Foundations of Democracy and the Rule of Law."

Figure 7.1. Local Revenue and Expenditure

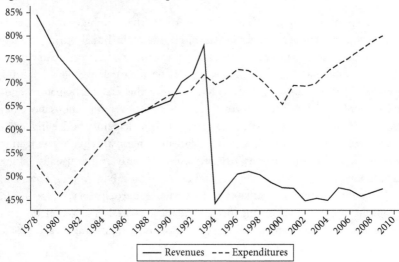

Note: Data compiled from the *China Statistical Yearbook* (various years).

as misallocation and corruption.[30] The effects of decentralized fiscal authority were, however, most pronounced in a rapidly dwindling central budget.[31] In reaction, the leadership reasserted fiscal control in the mid-1990s. Between 1993 and 1995, local revenue as a share of national revenue fell from roughly 78 percent to about 44 percent, while local expenditures stayed constant at about 70 percent of the national total, a severe structural imbalance that persists to this day (see Figure 7.1).[32]

On one hand, central authorities covet the power to mobilize and allocate resources for grand policy objectives. On the other, it is local officials who are tasked with utilizing fiscal resources and who are in a privileged position to discriminate between competing priorities. The central leadership would prefer that local officials spend resources in ways that contribute to the national policy objectives, but alas, this is not always the case.

Recentralization helped recapitalize central coffers, but the pressure it imposed on local budgets helped spring new leaks in the national fiscal cauldron. Under new fiscal constraints, local governments were forced to get more creative in generating, hiding, and repurposing revenue. These methods included an

[30] Christine P.W. Wong. "Central–Local Relations in an Era of Fiscal Decline: The Paradox of Fiscal Decentralization in Post-Mao China." *The China Quarterly* 128 (1991), pp. 691–715.

[31] Albert Park et al. "Distributional Consequences of Reforming Local Public Finance in China." *The China Quarterly* 147 (1996), pp. 751–778.

[32] See Huang, "Central–Local Relations in China During the Reform Era: The Economic and Institutional Dimensions," for a review of fiscal recentralization in the 1990s.

increase in local extraction through taxes and fees, extra-budgetary financing, and convoluted accounting schemes that funneled resources across departments and through SOEs. In an attempt to further strengthen top-down control, the PRC established a centralized treasury in 2001, national procurement rules in 2002, and a new classification system for within and outside budget revenues in 2005.[33] To help monitor the budgetary process, central authorities also strengthened audit procedures and imposed stricter requirements for the early submission of budget plans.[34] In an attempt to address inequalities and shorten lines of delegation, the government began earmarking funds for national policy priorities that would be delivered via direct central transfer. Finally, in a blunt-force attempt to end local predation, the central government eliminated all local agricultural taxes and levies.[35]

As local governments were losing their revenue collection rights, however, central authorities were also announcing bigger and more expansive public spending mandates, including free rural education, a rural medical cooperative system, and a national basic pension scheme. Even mandates that are funded through transfers trickle down the administrative hierarchy, leaving ample opportunity for manipulation along the way.[36] Moreover, and unsurprisingly, strained local governments naturally sought further and ever more creative methods of finance, including selling off public land and piling up debt. Since 2006, land expropriation has emerged as the single largest source of social unrest, accounting for over 66 percent of all mass protests.[37] Likewise, government debt, a substantial portion of which is owed by local governments, has ballooned to near 50 percent, according to official figures from the Ministry of Finance, or around 300 percent based on estimates by independent researchers.[38] While these developments cannot be attributed to budgeting alone, the Chinese public and even top Chinese leaders see the fiscal system as rife with problems:

> [T]he defects have become increasingly apparent: the budget management system is not standardized, transparent, or suited to the requirements of modern

[33] Victor C. Shih, Luke Qi Zhang, and Mingxing Liu. "When the Autocrat Gives: Determinants of Fiscal Transfers in China." *Department of Political Science, Northwestern University Working paper.* 2010.

[34] Yang, *Remaking the Chinese Leviathan: Market Transition and the Politics of Governance in China*; Jun Ma. "The Dilemma of Developing Financial Accountability without Election - A Study of China's Recent Budget Reforms." *Australian Journal of Public Administration* 68 (2009), S62–S72.

[35] John James Kennedy. "From the Tax-for-Fee Reform to the Abolition of Agricultural Taxes: The Impact on Township Governments in North-west China." *The China Quarterly* 189.1 (2007), pp. 43–59; Kai-yuen Tsui. "Local Tax System, Intergovernmental Transfers and China's Local Fiscal Disparities." *Journal of Comparative Economics* 33.1 (2005), pp. 173–196.

[36] Christine Wong. "Paying for the Harmonious Society." *China Economic Quarterly* 14.2 (2010), pp. 20–25.

[37] Based on figures from a 2013 report in the *Legal Daily*, available at: https://bit.ly/2Y4ZIKQ

[38] Victor Shih. *Financial Instability in China*. Tech. rep. MERICS Mercator Institute for China Studies, Klosterstraße 64, 2017.

governance; the tax system . . . is not conducive to supporting the shift to the new development paradigm, social fairness, or market integration. The division of responsibilities between the central and local governments is unclear and unreasonable. (Lou, 2014).[39]

Institutionally speaking, oversight responsibility lies in the halls of the people's congresses. Unfortunately, neither the Law on Budgets (adopted in 1995) nor the Law on Legislation (adopted in 2000) gives assemblies the legal power to determine tax rules or amend government budgets, only the power to approve or reject government proposals. In an effort to discourage backdoor debt financing and increase transparency, the NPC adopted a long-awaited revision to the Budget Law in 2014, giving provincial governments authority to sell bonds, but once again it stopped short of giving congresses full oversight authority of these sales. Rather than strengthening institutional oversight, the leadership has more often looked to bottom-up supplements to oversight. As Premier Zhu Rongji explained in 2000, transparency "facilitates public access to government information and public services, so that the people could supervise the government more easily," and "effectively check on 'passive corruption' by officials."[40]

Responding to the call in 2002 for bottom-up oversight, Guangzhou became the first major city to issue open government information (OGI) regulations, similar to the Freedom of Information Act in the United States, in 2002, paving the way for similar regulations in Shanghai and a number of other big and small cities soon thereafter. Then, in 2007, the State Council adopted a national OGI statute, resulting in a cascade of provincial and local-level regulations beginning in 2008.[41] Around the same time, several localities in Shanghai and Zhejiang began experimenting with participatory budgeting.[42] By far, the largest participatory scheme occurred in Chengdu, where an estimated 2,300 villages held deliberative budgeting meetings between 2009 and 2013.[43] Many of these sessions were, unfortunately, one-off events that took place informally and without specific record. In the next section, I detail one case that has been sustained for over a decade.

---

[39] Lou, Jiwei was Minister of Finance between 2013 and 2016. He currently chairs the National Social Security Fund Council. See: Lou, Jiwei, 2014, "Deepening the Fiscal and Tax Reform to Establish a Modern Fiscal System (深化财税体制改革 建立现代财政制度)," Qiushi (Seeking Truth), Vol. 57, No. 20, pp. 24–7. Ungated copy available at: https://bit.ly/2Y3crgR.

[40] General Office of the Communist Party of China Central Committee, "Notification on the Nationwide Promotion of Open Government Initiative in Towns and Townships of China," Document No. 25, Section 1 (Beijing: December 2000).

[41] Jamie P Horsley. "China Adopts First Nationwide Open Government Information Regulations." Freedominfo.org (Online) (2007), pp. 1–13.

[42] Baogang He. "Civic Engagement through Participatory Budgeting in China: Three Different Logics at Work." Public Administration and Development 31.2 (2011), pp. 122–133.

[43] Y. Cabannes and Z. Ming. "Participatory Budgeting at Scale and Bridging the Rural–Urban Divide in Chengdu." Environment and Urbanization 26.1 (2014), pp. 257–275.

An Unlikely Experiment

Zeguo is a coastal town in Zhejiang Province, just east of the high-speed rail linking the main provincial cities of Hangzhou and Wenzhou. Residents of Zeguo are wealthier than the average rural Chinese citizen and are well known for their entrepreneurial spirit across a broad range of economic activities, from aquaculture and textiles to small engine manufacturing. As in many other coastal regions, Zeguo residents are slightly outnumbered by migrants, attracted by the numerous light manufacturing enterprises dotted across Zeguo and the surrounding townships. Some of these, in particular several battery plants, contribute to some of the worst freshwater pollution in the country—which is ironic given the town's name, which literally means "a land that abounds in rivers and lakes."[44] Since the early 2000s the local government has also had trouble funding environmental cleanup, as well as other public services, including health care and education. At the same time, local authorities spent large sums on administrative buildings and infrastructure; some of was related to the high-speed rail line, which passes through Wenling with a stop just on the outskirts of Zeguo. But, as in neighboring Daxi, local projects have drawn public ire over costs and perceived misuse of collectively owned land.

Zeguo's central administration building, equipped with an elevated drive-through entrance and an expansive parking lot, towers above all others in Zeguo. When the building was first proposed, locals demonstrated, accusing the government of profiting from the construction. Eventually, however, people made peace with the building, its parking lot, and the officials who sponsored its construction. The turnaround in opinion, according to Deputy Mayor Liang Yunbo, had much to do with Zeguo's approach to planning and implementation. "The building proposal was very unpopular to begin with, but after multiple public hearings, administrators and business representatives were able to convince residents that the town as a whole would benefit from a central landmark to attract domestic and foreign investment." Deliberations, according to Liang, were also crucial for reaching a compromise on compensation for the collective land absorbed in the construction and for an agreement that opened the square surrounding the building for public use after working hours and on holidays.[45]

This was not the first consultative session in Zeguo. In fact, Zeguo had been conducting similar procedures for a nearly a decade. This proclivity toward participation owes much to the efforts of several innovative officials in the Wenling government who, in coordination with superiors, sought mechanisms

---

[44] Around 97 percent of the freshwater in the area is unsafe for human consumption. Author's interview with Wenling County People's Congress Standing Committee members in August 2012.
[45] Author's interview with Deputy Mayor Liang Yunbo in August 2011.

for improving public relations via inclusion. In particular, Chen Yimin, a local theory officer in Wenling's Propaganda Department, organized the region's first deliberative meeting in his hometown of Songmen in 1999.[46] Such experiments do not, of course, emerge out of thin air. They need a nudge from above. The initial deliberation meeting in Songmen was devised shortly after central leaders designated Wenling, along with nearby counties, as a testing ground for advancing sustainable development and good governance.[47] Around the same time, the Taizhou Propaganda Department issued directives to carry out education campaigns for modernizing the rural economy in Wenling. Both of these moves coincided with dramatic reductions in the local revenue shares.

Had it not been for the personal and political capital invested by Mr. Chen, however, it is doubtful whether the meetings would have progressed. Most of Wenling's localities held deliberations around the same time as Songmen, but they were poorly attended, consisting mainly of local assembly representatives and several handpicked residents. Mr. Chen was not impressed.[48] In Songmen, Chen worked with village leaders and local media to publicize the event as an opportunity for residents to lob questions directly at government representatives. Over one hundred local residents responded to the invitation. Positive media coverage encouraged town authorities to hold three additional meetings that same year, which over 600 people attended altogether, offering 110 suggestions, 80 of which were responded to, with 20 leading to promises of action.[49] In 2001, the Wenling Party Committee officially endorsed the consultative model, giving Mr. Chen credit for his efforts and more latitude to push the model forward.

Recognized for his efforts, Mr. Chen began frequenting academic and professional conferences on good governance and public participation.[50] One of the lessons he took was the advantage of a narrowly themed program. Back in Wenling, the Local People's Congress had formally recognized democratic consultation (*minzhu kentan*) as a standard policymaking tool and designated the towns of Wenjiao, Songmen, Zeguo, and Xinhe as pilot sites for further

[46] The first meeting was dubbed the Rural Modernization Conference (农业农村现代化建设论坛, *Nongye nongcun xiandaihua jianshi taolun*). For background, see Yifei Mu and Yimin Chen. "*Democratic Consultation: Creation of the People of Wenling*" (*Minzhu Kentan: Wenling Ren de Chuangzao*). Beijing: Central Translation and Compilation Press, 2005, p. 306.

[47] In 1997, Wenling, along with 77 other counties across China, was designated as a provincial-level social development experimental zone (浙江省社会发展综合实验区). See http://wlnews.zjol.com.cn/wlrb/g_g/2012/9/wljs/2004.html. Wenling was subsequently awarded national-level status in 2004.

[48] Interview with Chen Yimin in August of 2011.

[49] See X. Wu, "Citizen Participation, Deliberative Democracy, and the Deconstruction of Rural Public Order (公民参与、协商民主与乡村公共秩序的重构)," Ph.D. Dissertation (Zhejiang University, 2008), p. 50.

[50] Wenling first received the China Innovations Award in 1999 (see Chapter 3).

innovation.[51] With this institutional backing, Chen was able to hold focused consultation meetings on public transport and road construction in 2004. Later that year, Mr. Chen attended a conference in Hangzhou on participatory budgeting, a theme he immediately wanted to bring to Wenling.

Organizing a budget meeting, however, would prove considerably more complicated. As budget items affected administrative bodies, all government departments had to accept the same process. Here Chen solicited the help of Zhang Xueming, chairman of the Wenling County People's Congress. Importantly, the People's Congress had the authority to examine budgets along with the capacity to coordinate multiple administrative departments. Moreover, for Zhang, a Wenling native and career representative, budget meetings seemed like an excellent way to engage his deputies with local residents.[52]

With Chen and Zhang on board, the next step was to select a suitable location for holding the budget deliberations. As Mr. Chen recalls, Zeguo's Party secretary, Jiang Zhaohua, had recently expressed frustration with unending funding requests from both administrative organs and local grassroots social organizations. "Nobody believes us when we tell them: we really don't have the resources."[53] The problem was that the town and the local economy were growing, but discretionary funds, for reasons described in the previous section, were actually decreasing. Secretary Jiang wanted to "empty out his pockets" so that everyone could see that there really was no money available. Chen and Zhang felt they had a way to make that happen.

Zeguo would not be the first locality to hold budget deliberations. Previous experiments had taken place, most notably in Shenzhen, but these deliberations were limited to members of the Local People's Congress. In Zeguo, Mr. Chen was determined to make deliberations open to the general public. This presented a serious challenge. If deliberations relied on self-selecting participants, there was a risk that some group might take advantage of the process. Or, as Chen explained, that would be the public perception. Likewise, if the organizers recruited participants, it would tarnish the legitimacy of the process. To deal with this problem, Chen invited the help of professors He Baogang, a Zhejiang native, and James Fishkin, an American political scientist known for his work on deliberative polling.[54] Their solution was to select a small random sample

[51] Y. Lin, "Democratic Consultation and the People's Congress (民主恳谈与人大工作, *Minzhu kentan yu renda gongzuo*)," National People's Congress of the People's Republic of China, 2009, https://bit.ly/2Jzc3m7.

[52] Interview with Zheng Xueming in August of 2011.

[53] A Local People's Congress finance committee delegate corroborated the frustration concerning funding requests.

[54] Deliberative polling involves taking a random, representative sample of citizens engaging in small-group deliberations on competing policy options. He and Fishkin were presenters at the 2004 participatory budgeting conference, which Chen attended in Hangzhou.

(a core feature of deliberative polling) of local residents to participate in the budget deliberations. The solution was attractive not only because it solved the representation problem but also because it scored points for Zeguo's innovations for being "scientific."

The first Zeguo budget deliberations took place in March 2005, involving 270 randomly selected residents,[55] a panel of independent experts and academics, and representatives of the Zeguo government. At the start of deliberations, participants received an informational lecture on thirty different spending proposals with the knowledge that only ten could be implemented from within an allocated budget of 40 million RMB.[56] Following several rounds of small-group deliberations, participants ranked their preferences from among the proposed projects and also stipulated whether or not they believed the amount of funding proposed by the government for each item was too little, too much, or just about right. Critically, no vote or open discussion takes place in the full meeting. Instead, all critical discussions and debates occur within the designated small groups.

The results were encouraging. Surveys showed dramatic improvements in the participants' understanding of the budgeting process and spending constraints. The deliberations also provided useful information for the government. For example, evaluations suggested a strong public preference for spending on environmental protection and cleanup over other public works projects.[57] In addition, government officials were said to have been particularly satisfied because the results apparently "gave them grounds for turning down several unpopular construction projects promoted by the county government."[58] That same year, similar experiments took place in towns neighboring Zeguo, most notably Xinhe.[59] Provincial leaders, including Xi Jinping, who was provincial party secretary at the time, visited Wenling in 2005 and publicly endorsed the consultation model as an exemplar for "building social harmony," highlighting Zeguo's efforts.

Budget deliberations in Zeguo have continued annually, and while the basic format has not changed, there are several notable modifications. First, whereas sampling in 2005 was based on household lists, successive iterations have relied on voter registration lists, with the hope that this would reduce gender

---

[55] According to H.W. French, 257 participants attended, resulting in a response rate of about 95 percent. See Howard W. French. "China's New Frontiers: Tests of Democracy and Dissent." *New York Times*, June 19, 2005.

[56] All thirty spending items totaled almost 137 million RMB.

[57] Fishkin et al., "Deliberative Democracy in an Unlikely Place: Deliberative Polling in China."

[58] Author's interview with Wenling LPC delegates and standing committee members (August 2012).

[59] Joseph Fewsmith. "Exercising the Power of the Purse? Zeguo Reform." *China Leadership Monitor* 19 (2006).

disparity, which was an issue in earlier sessions. Second, the 2005 sessions deliberately excluded government officials from the small-group deliberations, but that condition was relaxed for subsequent consultations. In the 2012, for instance, two to three delegates from Zeguo's LPC delegation participated in each small group. Yet, the most significant change has occurred with respect to the budgets themselves. In 2005 participants were provided with information on spending proposals, but the comprehensive budget itself was not public, which generated suspicions among some participants. In response, town officials began publishing draft and final budgets in 2008; they have continued to do so since.

Survey Sampling and Design

The propitious circumstances behind the Zeguo experiment make it a very unique case. In the year I spent building a network of collaborators and gaining the trust of local officials, I did not hear of a single instance of similar experiments elsewhere in the country. To the best of my knowledge, Zeguo remains the only place in China with a publicly accessible, randomized field experiment in participatory governance. As such, Zeguo, and Wenling more generally, have received considerable domestic and international attention, winning coveted innovation awards, and have served as the focus of more than a dozen academic studies. Yet, even the most rigorous studies have all relied on pre/post evaluation.[60] Such an approach is a perfectly good way to gauge the impact of the deliberative session itself, but not the social experiment bringing citizens into a part of the governing process. Up to this point, researchers have been interested in how the session impacted the invited participants on dimensions such as efficacy and government satisfaction, among others. The problem is that even when respondents are randomly selected, pre/post evaluations introduce something called "a pre-treatment bias" because part of the treatment effect is the invitation itself.[61] This is particularly problematic in the authoritarian setting, where citizens almost never get invited to anything remotely democratic.

To capture a more complete picture of what was taking place in Zeguo, I had to reverse-engineer the experimental design in order to establish a pure control group with which to compare treated participants. While I provide a more detailed account of my methods in the Chapter 7 Appendix, a few key features are important to note here. For one thing, I was able to rely on the sampling strategy adopted by the Zeguo government for identifying treated participants. As mentioned earlier, this sampling process is based on a town-wide

---

[60] Fishkin et al., "Deliberative Democracy in an Unlikely Place: Deliberative Polling in China."
[61] Brian J. Gaines and James H. Kuklinski. "Treatment Effects." In *Cambridge Handbook of Experimental Political Science* (2011), pp. 445–458.

lottery using voter registration forms that aims for representation across all 97 villages within Zeguo. The same sampling strategy was not feasible for the control group for two reasons. First, contacting specific individuals would have compromised anonymity and the likelihood of gauging genuine perceptions. Second, navigating the spread of villages to reach specific individuals was simply time- and cost-prohibitive. Instead, control group participants were identified using a modified random walk design, which is well suited for Zeguo's semi-urban geography.

In 2012, the year I conducted my study, 156 randomly selected participants attended the annual budget deliberation session. A total of 134 of these individuals agreed to participate in the study and complete post-treatment surveys, contributing to a response rate of about 86 percent. This resulted in two separate samplings. By comparison, the control group sample, made up of 136 non-participants, was based on a random cluster of ten villages (see Figure 7.2), selected using a population-proportional-to-size sampling rule, meaning that larger villages were more likely to be sampled than smaller ones.[62] To ensure there was no pre-treatment contamination in the sample, all nonparticipant respondents were asked about their knowledge of budget participation.

The two sampling strategies, though employing some differences, produced relatively comparable sub-samples, as summarized in Table 7.1. Although both treatment and control groups produced samples of respondents with age and income profiles consistent with those of the local population,[63] representation on gender was off in both sub-samples, and education levels were not balanced across the two groups. In particular, male participants comprised about 70 percent of the treatment group and about 60 percent of the control group. After I inquired about the gender balance, Zeguo officials explained that on the day of the forum, spouses were allowed to substitute for one another in the event that the original selectee was unable to attend. This meant, in effect, that husbands were more likely to attend.[64] Similarly, non-response rates for female control group respondents were almost 20 percent higher than for males.[65]

Imbalance on the education variable is harder to explain. One speculative explanation is that participants with higher education levels are more likely to be employed in areas outside Zeguo. This might explain why the treatment group, which received advance notification, had a higher mean education level.

---

[62] All control-group surveys were concluded during the same week as the budget participation forum.

[63] The modal occupation in the sample was agriculture (53 percent), and the modal household income (38 percent) was under 30,000 RMB (around 4,000 USD) per year.

[64] Author's correspondence with Zeguo deputy mayor.

[65] Enumerators reported that, on average, 1 out of 3 men declined to participate in the survey when approached, while about 1 out of 2 women declined.

Figure 7.2. Sampled Villages

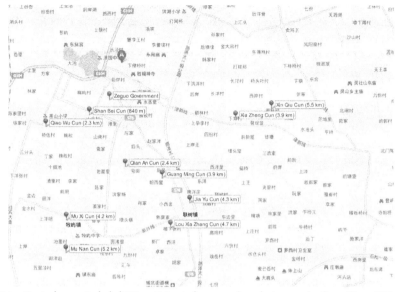

Notes: Control group included 136 participants from a random cluster sample of ten villages. Village distances from the Zeguo government administrative center are reported in parentheses.

Table 7.1 Zeguo Sample Demographics

	Average		Standard Deviation			
	Treated	Control	Treated	Control	p-Value	t-Statistic
Age	47.1	44.4	14.967	10.832	0.1	-1.65
Gender (M)	0.728	0.597	0.471	0.043	0.026*	-2.237
Education	3.471	3.059	1.481	1.246	0.013*	-2.492
Income	1.961	1.841	0.799	0.891	0.254	-1.144
Retrospect	2.171	2.233	0.893	0.777	0.557	0.588
Prospect	1.934	2.075	0.724	0.735	0.125	1.539
Total	≈ 134	≈ 136				

Invitees, including those residing outside of the town, had more time to make arrangements. Unfortunately, if the advance invitation explanation is correct, it might also mean that some of the treated participants, due to their outside employment, are less interested in local government. To address such biases, I include robustness tests on the main findings using controls for gender and education, as well as interactions with those variables and the treatment category.

The survey instrument itself was designed to be as brief as possible, so as to avoid survey fatigue and to increase response rates.[66] As part of the Oral Consent statement delivered prior to each survey, enumerators made it clear that the survey would not last for more than eight minutes. With this limited amount of time, only essential questions were included in the survey. Questions of particular interest include those concerning satisfaction with government performance and perceptions of government integrity.[67] For both satisfaction and integrity, two versions of the question were included—one directed toward the local and the other toward the central government.[68] Consistent with the expectations laid out in Chapter 2, inclusion in the policymaking process ought to boost public attitudes concerning both satisfaction and integrity.

> Satisfaction: "Some people are not very satisfied with the *local/central* government. Others are very satisfied. What about you?"[69]
> Integrity: "To what extent do (*local/central*) government officials utilize public resources for the benefit of the people and not themselves?"[70]

Questions about interest in politics, electoral participation, views on political participation, and the role of political elites in guiding the public were also included. While these questions are not central to the analysis, they provide additional insight on the main results and opportunities for robustness tests. Moreover, although every effort was taken to ensure consistency across treatment and control group surveying environments, there is always some risk of social desirability bias among treated versus control group, that is, participants who feel pressure to respond or behave positively just by the fact of their inclusion in the experiment.[71] Importantly, if this were the case, we would expect to see inflated responses across all of the subjective variables. I address this possibility after the primary analysis in the next section.

---

[66] A copy of the survey can be found in the Chapter 7 Appendix.

[67] Question wording was refined based on focus group meetings with local students attending Zhejiang University.

[68] Local and central government versions of the question were randomly ordered so as to eliminate the risk of ordering bias.

[69] Higher values on the response variable represent greater satisfaction: 1=not very satisfied, 2=satisfied, 3=very satisfied. A fourth option, not listed here, allowed respondents to abstain from the question.

[70] Higher values on the response variable equal more integrity: 1=almost never, 2=some of the time, 3=almost all the time. A fourth option, not listed here, allowed respondents to abstain from the question.

[71] Eleanor E. Maccoby and Nathan Maccoby. "The Interview: A Tool of Social Science." *Handbook of Social Psychology: Vol. 1.* 1954, pp. 449–487.

Analysis

The most straightforward way to assess the impact of a randomized treatment effect is a simple difference-in-means test. This approach focuses on the distribution of sample means along a single dependent variable for both treatment and control groups. I perform the difference-in-means test on dependent variables concerning both the central and local government. Specifically, I focus perceptions of government *Integrity* and *Satisfaction* with government at both levels. I also examine generalized effects on perceptions of citizen *Efficacy* and *Policy Improvement*, which are not tied to levels of government. Finally, I include attitudes toward *Elite* decision-making and the need to *Obey* leaders as variables that we should expect to decrease or at least remain unaffected by inclusion. Figure 7.3 summarizes the difference-in-means results, with point estimates representing the difference in attitudinal means for treatment and control group respondents.

What is immediately apparent is that while each of the responses directed toward the local government exhibit a significant positive treatment effect, responses directed toward central authorities reveal slightly negative but overall insignificant effects. Interestingly, participation did not significantly increase

Figure 7.3. Participation and Political Attitudes

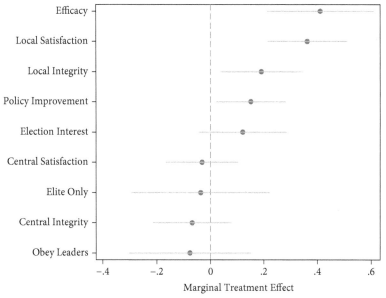

Notes: Point estimates are equivalent to difference in attitudinal means for treatment and control group respondents. Bars represent the 95% confidence interval for the difference. Crossing the dashed line indicates an insignificant treatment effect, i.e., no difference.

Figure 7.4. Local vs. Center Effects

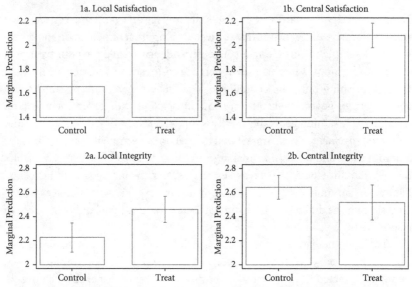

Notes: The dependent variable on satisfaction ranges on a scale from 1=not very satisfied, to 3=very satisfied. The dependent variable on integrity ranges on a scale from 1="government *rarely* uses resources in the public interest," to 3="government almost *always* uses resources in the public interest." Bars represent the marginal prediction; whiskers represent the 95% confidence interval for the prediction.

a respondent's interest in local elections, suggesting that inclusion is not an obvious gateway for further democratic demands. Moreover, perceptions of efficacy increased dramatically, as did general perceptions of policy improvement. Importantly, inclusion did impact respondents' beliefs about politics being elite-led or about the virtues of obedience, which we might have expected if inclusion were simply performative or indoctrinated. To control for potential imbalance across samples, I also ran a linear probability model with interaction effects between the treatment category and the gender and education variables. The estimates from these models, summarized in Figure 7.4, show that public consultation bolstered satisfaction and integrity for the local government, but that the effects did not spillover to help the central government. Put simply, when the Zeguo government invites residents to participate in the budget process, residents are more satisfied with and less suspicious of the Zeguo government. Opinions of the central leadership remained largely unaffected.

Raising Expectations

A core proposition advanced by optimistic observers is that by engaging the public on matters of governance, the CCP is making a small step toward liberal democracy, even if it is not intentional.[72] The logic underlying this proposition is that participation translates into more interest in, and thus more demand for, democracy.[73] This logic is sensible and probably correct in principle, but it nevertheless conflates good governance with the democratic process. That is, inclusion may very well increase a participant's interest in and expectations for better governance, but it does not lead them to democratic elections as the path to accountability. In the previous section, for instance, we saw that participation in the Zeguo budgeting process, arguably a very strong inclusion treatment as Chinese standards go, did not substantially increase a participant's interest in elections.[74]

To gain additional traction on how inclusion might impact expectations, the Zeguo survey also included questions aimed at capturing governance priorities. To home in on a reasonable set of governance priorities, I conducted two focus group sessions (one with students in Zhejiang University and one with local residents in Zeguo).[75] As a result of these sessions, the number of priorities was ultimately narrowed down to three broad dimensions: *Performance, Responsiveness, and Accountability*.[76] Focus groups were also used to formulate brief and simple definitions for each of the three governance dimensions, which were included in the oral script of the questionnaire.[77] To avoid any ordering bias, the placement of each item was randomized.

- *Performance*: Use public resources efficiently to promote economic growth
- *Responsiveness*: Respond to the needs of the people
- *Accountability*: Take public responsibility for actions and policies

Table 7.2 summarizes preference across each of the governance qualities, across both treatment and control groups. With regard to the control group, we see that respondents are roughly equally split on *Performance* and *Responsiveness*. This is consistent with the conventional China studies literature, which identifies performance and, more recently, responsiveness as the twin pillars of CCP legitimacy.[78] *Accountability*, the quality most closely associated with

[72] He and Warren, "Authoritarian Deliberation: The Deliberative Turn in Chinese Political Development; Fishkin, *When the People Speak: Deliberative Democracy and Public Consultation*.

[73] Larry Jay Diamond. "Liberation Technology." *Journal of Democracy* 21.3 (2010), pp. 69–83.

[74] Respondents did express greater interest in township politics, but not in the electoral process.

[75] Manuals and guidebooks published by international organizations with programs dedicated to good governance were also consulted; see Chapter 7 Appendix.

[76] Adding more than three dimensions resulted in more than half of participants confusing concepts or forgetting the items listed first.

[77] The oral script covered information on consent as well as definitions and directions for specific questions. All response options were also read out loud for respondents who could not read them. Chinese and English versions of the questionnaire are available in Chapter 7 Appendix.

[78] Dingxin Zhao. "The Mandate of Heaven and Performance Legitimation in Historical and Contemporary China." *American Behavioral Scientist* 53.3 (2009), pp. 416–433; Heurlin, *Responsive Authoritarianism in China*.

Table 7.2 Participation Effect on Governance Evaluation

Most Important Quality				Z-test	
	Control	Treatment	Difference	2-tailed	1-tailed
Performance	37.6%	23.7%	-13.9%	0.029	0.014
Responsiveness	37.6%	40.8%	3.2%	0.626	0.313
Accountability	24.8%	35.5%	10.7%	0.087	0.043
N=	93	125		218	

democratic theory, comes in a distant third, with only 24.8 percent.[79] Preferences, however, shift quite noticeably among treated respondents. While prioritization of responsiveness remains relatively stable, participants overwhelmingly gravitate toward accountability rather than performance. The right-hand columns of Table 7.2 present the statistical difference of this shift produced by a difference-in-proportions test. In the two-tailed version of the test, the shift away from performance and toward accountability is significant at the 95 and 90 percent level, respectively; both differences are significant at the 95 percent level in the one-tailed test.[80]

What does the shift toward accountability tell us about the participation effect? One implication is that the reason only local government approval is increasing is that participants are changing not only their perceptions of local governors, but also the metrics they are using to make those evaluations. As discussed previously, the literature on performance legitimacy places highest emphasis on economic growth, which is usually tied to the central government. Similarly, regime responsiveness is also highly monopolized by the central government. The central leadership, however, is not really accountable to anyone.

What the budget sessions in Zeguo may have accomplished is to remind participants that accountability is important. Indeed, for the better part of two hours at the start of the session, local government representatives accounted for how they had spent money in the previous year and answered questions over why so many projects had not been funded, admitting that few of those outstanding ambitions would ever be realized. Over the following six hours, participants were transported into the roles of the budget planners themselves—weighing options, arguing about priorities, and thinking about long-term consequences.

[79] For instance, see the volume on *Elections and Representation* by Bernard Manin, Adam Przeworski, and Susan C. Stokes. *Democracy, Accountability, and Representation*. Cambridge University Press, 1999.

[80] The two-tailed version of the test is more restrictive, insofar as it allows differences to move in either direction. The one-tailed test only considers difference in the observed direction.

In the end, two things appear to have happened. First, as noted above, these participants came back with a different set of metrics for evaluating government. Yet while economic growth was still important to them—roughly 24 percent thought it was key—many were now concerned about *how* growth would be achieved rather than simply *if*. Second, participants used this metric to evaluate their local government and gave it a higher ranking than did non-participants.

Robustness and Generalizability

The findings presented in this chapter concern one experiment, in one town, in one corner of China. To say that they should be interpreted with caution is an understatement. While it would be impossible to deal with every threat, we can review some of the most outstanding limitations to drawing conclusions from a single field experiment. First, what is the endurance of the observed effects? Second, how generalizable is the Zeguo experiment for our broader exploration into controlled forms of inclusion?

The budget deliberation process described in this chapter amounts to a fairly strong treatment. Participants were asked to give up a substantial portion of their time and energy, only to be rewarded with a crash course in finance and budget constraints. As with most treatment effects, however, even strong ones, shelf-life tends to be short. To try and get a sense of the durability of the treatment effect in Zeguo, I also contacted 247 prior participants who attended budget deliberations the previous year and compared their responses to the non-participant sample.[81] In total, I was able to retrieve 55 complete responses. These additional observations suggest that the approval effect observed in the main analysis was relatively short-lived. Whereas roughly 39 percent of randomly sampled non-participants were unsatisfied with the local government, about 42 percent of prior participants were. In other words, prior participants seem more unsatisfied with the local government than non-participants, though the difference is nowhere near statistical significance. Prior participants were also more likely to be dissatisfied with the central government than non-participants, 11 vs. 7 percent respectively. One interpretation here is simply that Zeguo residents do not like being surveyed on the phone.

Surprisingly, reaction to the question about governance qualities resembles the pattern observed in the main results. Specifically, prior participants prioritize *Accountability* over *Performance* at roughly the same rate as participants

---

[81] These respondents were contacted by phone and not in person; most attempts at making contact failed; refusal rates were high, and survey completion quality was lower, than for the face-to-face survey.

surveyed in the 2012 experiments: 31.6 versus 21.1 percent, respectively. Put differently, even though the participation effect on government approval seems fleeting at best, the impact on how participants internalize good governance appears durable. Another way to think about this is that the benefits of public engagement under autocracy need to be nurtured in order to be sustained. One-off invitations to participate in budget decisions are not going to make citizens trust the government's spending choices indefinitely. On the contrary, being invited one year but not again the following might aggravate feelings further.

Budgeting is an admittedly narrow slice of policy, but within the scope of authoritarianism it exhibits precisely the type of informational challenges that would concern a control regime. Budgeting is extremely complicated, rife with distributional conflicts, and highly constrained by bounded rationality, since investments must be made with long-term forecasts in mind. Budgeting is also characterized by extreme informational asymmetries, as local officials have broad discretion in not only how they use public resources, but also how these these choices are reported to superiors. Moreover, the consultation experiment in Zeguo typifies a controlled inclusion format. First, the government sets the agenda for inclusion by outlining the budget items open for deliberation and makes the final decision on how allocations will be distributed. Second, the government controls the discourse of consultation by organizing and compart-mentalizing participants into small groups that serve as the setting for critical debate and discussion.[82] In concert, these controls ensure that the inclusion process never goes off the rails. Yet despite these controls, the survey findings suggest that citizens still appreciate the process and that it impacts how they view the government.

Finding a Balance

To reiterate, The principal means by which controlled inclusion could improve public perceptions of legitimacy, the theme of this chapter, are via information and persuasion. In Zeguo, for example, participatory budgeting provides the local government with information on public preferences about budget items that they already have an interest in funding. Armed with this information, the local government is in a better position to achieve its own spending priorities. Moreover, by engaging public citizens in coproduction framed around fiscal constraints and spending priorities, the government can dispel concerns about misuse and corruption and bolster the legitimacy of its broader spending agenda.

---

[82] During the 2011 and 2012 sessions, which I was able to attend, these small-group meetings took place in classrooms and were mediated by volunteer teachers.

By focusing on the public participants of this process, it is possible to test the latter persuasion mechanism. However, as argued in the previous section, even if participation does bolster legitimacy it is unclear to whom this legitimacy accrues. It could potentially resonate throughout the entire political regime, or it might be focused on the local government that is engaging in the participatory activity. Previous work has ignored this distinction, but it does so at the risk of overstating and/or misrepresenting the benefits and political motives for pursuing public participation under autocracy.

We have seen that, in Zeguo at least, public engagement in budgeting led to marked improvements in perceptions of the local government, but not the central authorities. At the same time, engaging citizens in policymaking was not all roses for the local government. In particular, participating in the budgeting process did not fully satisfy respondents, at least not for long. It did alter the way they thought about government and how they evaluate its legitimacy. Participants updated their priorities, placing greater emphasis on the importance of accountability. This should not be interpreted as an obvious invitation for more democracy. The Zeguo experiment suggests that inclusion had little impact on participant interest in elections. In other words, Chinese citizens want better governance, not just growth. Yet, just as in the case of economic growth, Chinese citizens are not particularly interested in *how* good governance is delivered.

More broadly, this finding also offers a possible explanation for why citizens in authoritarian countries place a premium on economic performance: they are typically excluded from substantive matters of governance. The more a regime opens up, whether politically or procedurally, the more it exposes itself to public scrutiny. This logic is not unlike what occurs in the relationship between companies and shareholders. A shareholder with no voice and no access to company meetings will focus on stock performance. Some companies, however, go to great lengths to engage shareholders through transparency, meetings, and even poll votes.[83] Shareholders in this latter category are much more likely to scrutinize corporate behavior in addition to stock performance.[84] Extending this logic to authoritarian governance suggests that participatory decision-making is not a free lunch. Instead, the findings presented here indicate that public inclusion, though it can improve the government's public image, also raises expectations.

In theory, this is all well and good. Returning to the framework presented in Chapter 2, heightened expectations are part of a feedback loop that keeps the

[83] James E. Gruning and Todd T. Hunt. *Managing Public Relations*. Holt, Rinehart and Winston, 1984, p. 550.
[84] Blake E. Ashforth and Barrie W. Gibbs. "The Double-Edge of Organizational Legitimation." *Organization Science* 1.2 (1990), pp. 177–194.

system moving and improving. Politically speaking, it is not so clear that the CCP would necessarily want to raise its own bar. If the effects are concentrated on local officials, however, as the results presented seem to indicate, the logic seems more plausible. As noted in the introduction of this chapter, China's leaders have long sought to improve governance at the local level and if limited forms of apolitical participation contribute to that goal, it seems like a worthwhile investment. That said, as stressed earlier, the Zeguo experiment is highly unique and extremely localized. In the next chapter, I explore ways by which inclusion, with the help of technology, can be scaled up at the national level.

8

Remote Control

> One of the longstanding fears for the [Chinese] party-state is not that
> it will go out with a bang but that it will fold quietly in a whimper of
> irrelevance.[1]
>
> — Damien Ma, 2012

The Qingdao Refrigerator Corporation was incorporated in 1984 as a Township and Village Enterprise.[2] At the time, the company was deeply indebted, overstaffed, and notorious for its poor-quality products. Today the company, better known as Haier, remains a murky "collective" enterprise, still owned in part by the Qingdao municipal government.[3] Yet, Haier is hardly the lethargic, politically pliant relic of the planned economy—a common trope among critics of China's state-owned sector. Instead, Haier is now the leading white goods manufacturer in the world, with 16 percent share of the total market and an annual turnover of over 250 billion RMB.[4] Haier's success has inspired numerous books, articles, and nearly two dozen *Harvard Business Review* case studies dedicated to understanding and learning from this unique corporate model.

Those who have studied the company attribute its success to something Haier Chairman and CEO Zhang Ruimin—the same chairman who led the initial collective in 1984—calls *rendan heyi*, or "zero distance to customers."[5] There are two core features of this management model. The first is a deluge of consumer input. Before Haier designed its Tianzun air conditioner, for instance, it surveyed 30 million online consumers on Chinese social media platforms like

---

[1] Ma, Damien. "Beijing's 'Culture War Isn't About the US—It's About China's Future." *The Atlantic* 5, January 5, 2012.

[2] The original factory dates back to at least 1955, when it was formed around a commune organized by the municipal government. Ling Liu. *China's Industrial Policies and the Global Business Revolution: The Case of the Domestic Appliance Industry*. Routledge, 2005, p. 90. 1984 was also the year the city of Qingdao was designated a special economic and trade zone by China's State Council, allowing collectives like Qingdao Refrigerator to form.

[3] The name change resulted from the transliteration of the name of a joint venture between Qingdao Refrigerator and a German refrigerating company called Liebherr.

[4] Based on *Haier Corporate Report 2018*.

[5] The terminology of "zero distance to consumers" was adopted based on usage in existing publications, many of them aimed at management audiences. A literal translation of (*rendan heyi* 人单合一) would be "integration of people and goals."

Retrofitting Leninism. Dimitar D. Gueorguiev. Oxford University Press. © Oxford University Press 2021.
DOI: 10.1093/oso/9780197555668.003.0009

Q-Zone and WeChat, with open-ended questions like, "What do you want in air conditioning?" They also set up a public discussion forum, throwing out ideas for potential designs and observing what got the most attention. Participants debated whether or not they preferred "cold" or "cool" on knobs and buttons, the placement of lights and indicators and, of course, what they would like to see in the companion mobile app.[6] Naturally, this app also reports how the equipment is used and how the app is used, as well as a summary of communications with other devices linked to the app. According to managers, this information allows the corporation to increase responsiveness and to incorporate the tastes and tendencies of consumers into its own innovation strategy.[7]

The second aspect of *rendan heyi* is organizational. The Haier Corporation embodies an "iceberg" structure, with three broad tiers. At the bottom there are 4,000 or so micro-enterprises, or *xiaowei qiye*, composed of small working groups of 10 to 15 employees who interact directly with suppliers, distributors, and consumers.[8] The middle tier supports the first, providing design and systems maintenance functions with which the bottom tier and consumers interact. The top tier includes supervisors and division managers who set out corporate plans and strategy.[9] At the base, the bottom tier is the largest, but it is mostly submerged. The top tier, like the tip of an iceberg, is narrow but highly visible. Although the middle tier serves as an interface, the uppermost tier can interact with the base via direct and indirect columns of communication. According to Chairman Zhang, this convoluted bottom-heavy organizational structure allows Haier's leadership to circumvent bottlenecks and avoid bureaucratization, which he sees as anathema to complex organization.[10]

By now, the reader will notice parallels in how Haier conducts itself in the business of profit and how the CCP has gone about the business of power. First, Haier's *rendan heyi* model echoes Mao's theory of the "mass line" (*qunzhong luxian*). The cornerstone of both doctrines is maintaining constant contact with end users, namely the public. In Haier's case, consumer inputs inform

---

[6] See: *The Haier Road to Growth, Strategy+Business*, at: https://bit.ly/2W9Eevr.

[7] Yazhou Hao and Yong Hu. *Haier Purpose: The Real Story of China's First Global Super-Company.* 2017; Bill Fischer, Umberto Lago, and Fang Liu. *Reinventing Giants: How Chinese Global Competitor Haier Has Changed the Way Big Companies Transform.* John Wiley & Sons, 2013.

[8] Prior to 2014, micro-enterprises were previously formed as *zizhu jingying ti* (自主经营体) ZZJYTs, independent operating units funded by the central corporation. The shift to *xiaowei qiye* (小微企业) or micro-enterprises has made it easier for outside investors to selectively hold ownership stakes in the small enterprises. See Gary Hamel and Michele Zanini. "The End of Bureaucracy," *Harvard Buisness Review* (2018), pp. 3–11.

[9] Jedrzej George Frynas, Michael J. Mol, and Kamel Mellahi. "Management Innovation Made in China: Haier's Rendanheyi." *California Management Review* 61.1 (2018), pp. 71–93.

[10] Ruimin Zhang. *Haier is the Sea: Zhang Ruimin's Selected Essays (海尔是海：张瑞敏随笔选录).* Mechanical Industry Press, 2015.

engineering, investment, and marketing decisions. In the CCP's version, informants, constituents, and representatives inform oversight, policymaking, and administrative agencies. Organizational parallels are equally relevant. Administrative decentralization and compartmentalization, for instance, play a key role in how the CCP is able to harvest and process information for the purpose of political and socioeconomic control. Like Haier, the PRC's administrative structure of highly decentralized Party-run lines of communication—whether through disciplinary authorities, consultative committees, or neighborhood informants—provide a potential link between the grassroots and Party leaders, even if these links are not utilized in normal operations. Similarly, Haier's heterarchical management structure offers peak leadership options for bypassing an otherwise complex and fragmented corporate structure.[11]

The ideological and organizational parallels between Haier and the CCP are not entirely surprising. Born on the same year as the PRC's founding, a young Mr. Zhang had lived through the failed attempts at total control during the Great Leap Forward and then, as a Red Guard in the Cultural Revolution, the chaos that accompanies the breakdown of control. By the time Mr. Zhang began his career in Qingdao's state-run economic bureaucracy, he was well-versed in Leninism and Maoism but would not earn his management degree until well after taking over Qingdao Refrigerator in 1984. As director of the company that would soon become Haier, Mr. Zhang was given wide latitude to make the company competitive and, maybe one day, even profitable. This was a time when capitalist reforms were just taking hold in China and generating much excitement. Yet, Mr. Zhang's mobilization techniques—including an infamous incident in which he smashed to pieces dozens of the company's low-quality refrigerators in front of staff and workers—and organizational strategies like *rendan heyi*, were inspired by his formative experience in a Leninist-run China.[12] Moreover, Chairman Zhang has, throughout his career, maintained a close connection with the CCP; this includes his Party membership since 1975, status as an alternate member of the Central Committee (CCOM) between 2002 and 2017, and most recently, serving as a representative in Shandong's Provincial Party Congress.

Perhaps more interesting, however, is how leaders in both organizations have profited from blending and integrating Leninist management principles with technological innovations to facilitate faster, more seamless, and more information-rich contact with end-users. Indeed, it is likely that Haier's unorthodox franchise structure would have failed were it not for data-driven adaptation

---

[11] Heterarchical organizations are neither purely hierarchical or fully decentralized, resulting in unranked modes of network communication (McCulloch, "A Heterarchy of Values Determined by the Topology of Nervous Nets").

[12] Based in part on the author's discussion with a researcher at Haier University, a business school affiliated with the corporation and located in Qingdao China.

brought forth by the "smart-device" revolution. Similarly, it is unlikely that China's antiquated and logistically limited system of analog consultation and surveillance would have been sufficient to get the country through the last decade of unprecedented investment, migration, and pandemic response. At the same time, the fact that both organizations, at their core, remain rooted in a state-dominated and centrally orchestrated leadership stands as testament that Leninism and innovation are not directly incompatible.

Unlike Haier, however, the political landscape on which the CCP operates dictates that public inclusion must be meticulously controlled. Chinese citizens can report on corrupt officials, voice complaints, and provide input in planning, but their options are restricted to the CCP brand, their criticisms are only tolerated within prescribed issue spaces, and their input is only welcome when invited. There is no end-user agreement for members of the Chinese public, no refunds, and absolutely no exchanges. As underscored at the beginning of this book, the state and society relationship underpinning such a system is not immediately obvious. Why do Chinese citizens participate in their own entrapment? What does the Party do with the terabytes and petabytes of data they compile on average people, businesses, and even their own rank-and-file?

These are not rhetorical questions. Social and organizational control in China has arrived at a point where questions like this present themselves in daily life. Chinese citizens are now being integrated into a state-run framework for social evaluation whereby their actions and inactions, their history and their potential, their attitudes and their character, are each subject to peer review and autonomous quantification—all in the service of "stability and harmony," which is CCP-speak for regime control. Over the last seven chapters I have offered some insights on how this type of system works, but not why. Perhaps "why" is not a very relevant question. Perhaps people have no choice: control, and their participation in it, is forced upon them. The more provocative proposition is that the public, at least to some extent, consents to control.

This chapter explores the nature of consent in China's inclusive control system. Borrowing from the corporate example, Haier's customers stick with the product and consent to its feedback architecture for many reasons—value, convenience, and most importantly trust. Indeed, Haier ranks as one of the most trusted brands in its market, both in China and beyond. Similarly, China's leaders enjoy an enviable amount of trust from their citizens. Then again, in the absence of political competition, trust in the CCP has never faced a real test, which is why the Party has always operated from a position of insecurity.

Another, less appreciated dimension of trust operates in the other direction. Haier's users take for granted that they are trusted and valued by the corporation. "The customer is always right." Customers can take such matters for granted because of the readily available exit options a market provides. Citizens of the

PRC, of course, do not enjoy the same privilege when it comes to governance. But does that imply that China's citizens do not also feel valued, needed, and appreciated by their leaders? The average participant in the Chinese inclusive control paradigm does so, at least in part, voluntarily. Informants, representatives, and even petitioners are thus in some regards collaborators. The secret sauce of inclusive control has always, and I will argue continues to be, the regime's capacity to make willful collaborators out of average citizens and even potential opponents. As theorized in Chapter 2, collaboration is a feature of the Party's traditional ability to compartmentalize Chinese society and pit groups and individuals against one another.[13] What are the prospects for this type of contrived consent in an increasingly technology-driven control architecture?

From Hardware to Software

Since its founding, the CCP has, true to Leninist fashion, served as the chief interlocutor between state and society. Whereas this function has traditionally been the purview of rank-and-file cadres, we are now witnessing technology complement and even supplant the role of humans. This evolution has allowed the CCP to interface with the masses faster and more seamlessly than ever before. In this respect, the CCP is on its way to realizing Soviet visions of feedback control, whereby oversight, planning, and implementation are assisted by the speed and processing power of computers and fed by real-time and broad-reaching input from society.[14] If that is the case, what then is the role of the Party? Is it possible that in advancing and refining feedback control, the Party undermines its own part in the process?

To better appreciate this question, it is helpful to return to some of the basic features of feedback control, as outlined in earlier chapters. Among those, a high degree of regime embeddedness within society is a critical component. In the days of the Jiangxi and Yan'an soviets, embeddedness involved sending thousands of cadres into village homes where they penetrated family and communal networks.[15] During the formative years of the PRC, it meant relying on an army of Party representatives and informants embedded within labor, industrial, civil,

[13] Whyte, *Small Groups and Political Rituals in China*; Schurmann, *Ideology and Organization in Communist China*; Andrew G. Walder. *Communist Neo-traditionalism*. University of California Press, 1986.

[14] Slava Gerovitch. *From Newspeak to Cyberspeak: A History of Soviet Cybernetics*. MIT Press, 2004.

[15] Whyte, *Small Groups and Political Rituals in China*; Hua, *Hong taiyang shi zenyang shengqi de-Yan'an zhengfeng yundong de lailong qumai* (How the Red Sun Rose: The History of the Yanan Rectification Campaign).

and spiritual organizations.[16] Today, the Party is rooted in millions of village and residential committees; a much larger number within party cells implanted within factories, classrooms, board rooms, and professional organizations; and all alongside an unknown quantity of informal "volunteers" who patrol the streets, alleys, and corners of urban centers. In Beijing alone, for instance, there are over 1.4 million of these volunteers, organized in groups with names like the "Dongcheng Watchmen" or "Haidian Network," each with its own designated beat.[17] During special events, or any instance of public unrest, numbers can surge overnight.

These individuals penetrate social networks—whether as members of a neighborhood watch, leaders of a legal house of worship, or workers in a Party cell of a private company—to find out who is saying what, where the problems and problem-makers are, and how the community is responding. As such, this mass of individuals and operatives represent the physical frontline of control. Such numbers, however, are difficult to sustain—even volunteers appreciate in-kind incentives.[18] In 2017 alone, China spent over 1.2 trillion RMB on public security, or over 300 billion USD after correcting for purchasing power.[19] With a slowing economy, odds are that massive investments in physical grassroots control will become increasingly hard to finance. Already, local governments throughout the country are struggling to fund their staffed positions, turning instead to temporary, non-traditional (*bianwai*) staff members.[20] Even for the CCP, which still has about 90 million members, the numbers look unsustainable. As early as 2013, the Organization Department substantially reduced enrollment targets in order to "improve quality," but this has apparently not helped them recover unpaid dues from members or spur more youth applications.[21] While it is still too early to tell what the long-term consequences may be, it is perhaps telling

---

[16] Schurmann, *Ideology and Organization in Communist China*; Gerry Groot. "Managing Transitions: The Chinese Communist Party's United Front Work, Minor Parties and Groups, Hegemony and Corporatism." PhD thesis. 1997.

[17] See Beijing News Report citing statistics from deputy director of the Beijing Political and Legal Affairs Commission, dated August 12, 2017, available at: https://bit.ly/2wc1Ww0.

[18] Those who have spoken to me mention material perks as well as indirect benefits for themselves and their families.

[19] For central government expenditures see: https://bit.ly/2LWtekE; public security expenditures, however, can only be estimated by including regional expenditures, which are about five times that of the central government. See Adrian Zenz estimates and conversions here: https://bit.ly/2SBpepp.

[20] Non-traditional staff (编外人员) are not processed through the civil service system, do not enjoy civil service benefits, and are not subject to the same career incentives. Yet they increasingly represent the majority of local government administrative personnel.

[21] Since 2013 the CCP has initiated at least three campaigns aimed at forcing members to provide unpaid fees. Though the problem of unpaid dues is a perennial concern, and the Party deliberately restricts membership for symbolic reasons, it is notable that the number of '35 and under' members has been in absolute decline since at least 2016. For reference see annual Organization Department statistics, the most recent from 2018, available at: https://bit.ly/2LDDkpt.

that the 19th Party Congress featured the oldest cohort of leaders in nearly three decades.[22]

Technology is a game-changer in this respect. According to market consulting firm IHS Markit, by 2016 the Chinese government had installed over 176 million surveillance cameras, with 626 million slated for 2021.[23] That is more than one camera for every three citizens. Combined with facial recognition technology, biometrics, and GPS live-trackers on phones, this network of surveillance provides the state unprecedented clarity about who is where and when.[24] While these numbers are ominous, it is important not to overstate the surveillance capacity of the Chinese state. There is no all-seeing eye. Like much of the Chinese bureaucracy, surveillance is siloed and fragmented across jurisdictions and within a multitude of private companies who are providing a hodgepodge of intelligence services.[25] Nevertheless, the control potential of modern surveillance technology is obvious, and there is a strong national effort by the state to integrate and centralize digital surveillance. If, or rather *when*, successful, this will mean that tasks that currently involve millions of individuals spread across numerous agencies and organizations could one day be managed passively, through a centralized surveillance architecture and ever-more efficient software solutions.

The CCP's grassroots presence, however, is not simply about control. As stressed throughout this book, grassroots connections also serve as a two-way interchange, where top-down directives are circulated to the masses and where bottom-up inputs are "distilled" and redirected upward to superiors. Moreover, the fidelity of this interchange is proportional to the amount and diversity of input it is able to generate. Attracting large numbers of diverse participants, let alone critical ones, involves both technical and political challenges. Logistically, this kind of participation can be extremely costly for both participants and the state. In China, for instance, a typical public hearing can cost between 5,000 and 10,000 USD and about a day's worth of time for the individual.[26] By contrast, soliciting feedback online is almost costless. It is therefore no surprise that both national and local authorities are aggressively taking advantage of e-government technologies to facilitate interaction with the public.

---

[22] Dimitar D. Gueorguiev. "Dictator's Shadow: Chinese Elite Politics Under Xi Jinping," *China Perspectives* 1.2 (2018), pp. 17–26.

[23] See reference story in *QDaily* available at: https://www.qdaily.com/articles/47431.html.

[24] Authorities in Xinjiang, for instance, have been collecting biometric data, including voice, fingerprints, and iris scans from residents between the ages of 12 and 65. See Human Rights Watch Report, *China: Minority Region Collects DNA from Millions*, available at: https://bit.ly/2VHnmeu.

[25] Based in part on author's interviews with leaders of private data aggregation and analytics contractors in Shanghai, who provided background information on surveillance data gathered by local authorities in Shanghai and nearby municipalities.

[26] Author's estimates based on discussions with local officials in Wenling and Shenzhen.

There are strong indications that the Chinese government is hoping members of the public will participate. Those who commute in today's urban China, for instance, will find it hard to pass through any public space without being reminded, by wall poster or digital screen, of the opportunity to contact authorities with comment or information. The government is not simply soliciting information; it is putting it out in large quantities. As noted in Chapter 2, in 2013, the Supreme People's Court moved to publish all civil, administrative, criminal, and commercial case records on its website, and the Ministry of Land and Resources began publishing urban land transactions going back into the 1990s.[27] Other types of information, including government leadership structures (power lists) and government budget and spending figures are also being standardized and released in mass quantities.

How do these investments in technology-enhanced governance interact with teched-up modes of control? Presumably, investments in digital consultation combined with increased government transparency ought to contribute to higher public participation rates, especially given China's rapidly expanding

Figure 8.1. NPC Consultation Participation Rates

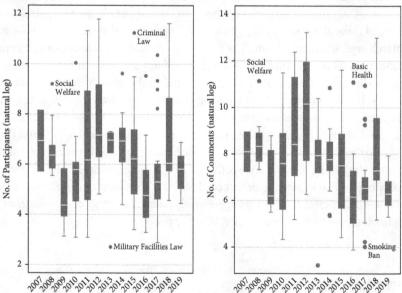

Notes: Black bars represent the 25 to 75 percentile around the median values for each year. Dots represent what appear to be outlier cases that attracted either a great deal (or uncharacteristically little) participation.

---

[27] See Chapter 3, footnotes 21 and 23.

Internet population. Looking at broader trends, however, it is unclear if feedback rates are indeed increasing. In Figure 8.1, I plot public participation rates from 2007 through 2019, as reported by the National People's Congress's online consultation platform. Regardless of whether one focuses on the number of participants or the number of comments they provide, there is no evidence that participation is increasing. Indeed, on both measures, the high point was in 2012, just around the time that digital surveillance investments started increasing. In the absence of sustained growth in voluntary participation rates, one cannot help but wonder if China's digital consultation campaign has passed its zenith, and that the input authorities are receiving is increasingly coming from a common pool of participants rather than the population at large.

The challenge of mass participation under authoritarianism bears some similarity to the paradox of voting in democracies, where going through the effort of turning out to vote is not always rational.[28] Now compare that to composing a letter to comment on a draft policy proposal, which is not only more arduous but also nearly impossible to valuate in terms of efficacy. One way to make sense of public participation, whether it involves sitting in a town hall or casting a ballot at a polling station, is to consider ideational features of constructed behaviour.[29] Participation represents the confluence of multiple factors, each of which play some part in contributing to the behavior. Among the many contenders, we may consider civic-mindedness, private grievance, social pressure, or simply convenience. Most generally, however, it is widely believed that political participation is a function of interest, specifically interest in politics and government.[30]

Interest in politics is a trait that you (as the reader) and I (as the author of this monograph on Chinese politics) clearly possess, perhaps at a level higher than what is good for us. For most people, however, political interest spikes in response to a specific trigger. In China, millions tuned in to the revision of the Labor Contract Law because the terms of the amendment would very likely impact their lives. It is plausible that future "hot-button" issues, such as those concerning property rights, raising retirement age, and immigration policy will result in similar spikes in targeted interest. Another, more durable type of interest, what Prior refers to as "dispositional interest," extends far beyond the immediate trigger and is a critical feature of stable politics.[31] Citizens with dispositional interest in politics participate not because they anticipate a

---

[28] William H. Riker and Peter C. Ordeshook. "A General Theory of the Calculus of Voting." *American Political Science Review* 62.1 (1972), pp. 32–78.

[29] Markus Prior. *Hooked: How Politics Captures People's Interest.* Cambridge University Press, 2018.

[30] Sidney Verba. *Participation and Political Equality: A Seven-Nation Comparison.* Chicago: University of Chicago Press, 1978, p. 394; Robert A. Dahl. *Poliarchy: Participation and Opposition.* Vol. 54. Yale University Press, 1971, p. 257; Prior, *Hooked: How Politics Captures People's Interest.*

[31] *Ibid.*

personal benefit but because they believe their participation contributes to a collective profit. If we accept socialism as a collective theory of political economy, then the dispositional interest of the public ought to be a prized feature of the feedback control system. Looking to the future, however, there is reason to suspect that public engagement will increasingly be taken for granted.

Passive Control

Already, there are concerning trends in China's participatory model. Public interest in politics, for instance, is lower today than at any point since polling began. According to the World Values Survey, thirty years ago roughly 66 percent of Chinese citizens considered politics to be "somewhat" or "very important."[32] More recent surveys put the figure at about 45 percent.[33] Similarly, Netizen data collected by Professor Ma Deyong of Renmin University shows that public interest in politics has dropped from around 24 percent expressing "a great deal of interest" in 2014, to less than 13 percent in 2017.[34]

While it is beyond the scope of this book to evaluate the determinants of this decline, probable causes are readily available in journalistic and academic accounts. Under the current Xi administration, a resurgence of censorship and political indoctrination may be driving individuals away from politics. Another possibility is that the regime's desire to make society legible and controllable is pushing elements of the population further into self-imposed obscurity. Still, it could be that perceptions about the state being omnipresent and omniscient may simply discourage people from contributing further input. In addition, the lack of anonymity, onerous codification and identification procedures, and the broad range of issues on which citizens are asked to provide information may prove daunting and discouraging. Taken together, the shrinking distance between the reach of the state and the individual is likely be more and more stifling.

Yet China and the CCP have always been stifling in some way. As in most authoritarian regimes, self-censorship is a survival instinct, and the strategic misrepresentation of true preferences is a social habit.[35] What makes China

---

[32] WVS is a global social science survey effort spearheaded by political scientist Ronald Ingelhart.

[33] Comparative statistics taken from the 1989–1993 (n=1000) and the 2010–2014 (n=2300) waves of the the World Values Survey.

[34] Based on Question 9 of the Netizen Opinion Survey (网民"阅读与态度"调查). Text of question: "Overall, how interested are you in current political affairs?" "总体来说，您对时政类信息感兴趣吗？" See: China National Survey Database project, available at http://cnsda.ruc.edu.cn/index.php?r=projects/view&id=69084413.

[35] Perry Link. "China: The Anaconda in the Chandelier." *The New York Review of Books* (2002), April 11, 2002, http://tiny.cc/hm9ehy; Kuran, "Now Out of Never: The Element of Surprise in the East European Revolution of 1989."

slightly different is that the CCP has consistently made the effort to provide citizens with channels by which to provide input and participate, despite pervasive impediments to doing so. Curiously enough, what has sustained these channels, as noted throughout this book, is the Chinese public's apparent willingness to participate and provide that voluntary input to government leaders. Such behavior ultimately boils down to an abstract notion of trust—trust that someone on the regime end will listen and respond. Inevitably, however, such faith reflects its own personal conceit: that the individual is trusted by the regime. Moves toward computer-assisted feedback control have important implications for trust as well.

The Social Crediting Frontier

As alluded to in previous chapters, China's emerging "social crediting system" (SCS) is poised to transform the country's feedback control architecture, both technically and conceptually.[36] Despite its revolutionary potential, most of what has been written about the SCS has focused narrowly on individual credit "scores" and the prospect of individuals being "black-listed" (sanctioned) or "red-listed" (rewarded) for their quantifiable behavior. The SCS, however, is far more complex and extends to businesses, corporations, and even government entities.[37] More broadly, Chinese scholars depict the SCS as a massive social experiment in increasing systemic "trustworthiness."

For all its complexity and emphasis on trust, the irony is that the SCS is based on a traditional CCP framework for coopting society into the service of state control by cultivating social mistrust. Some of the data used to compile credit scores, for instance, will come from mandatory disclosures from creditors, employers, and Internet Service Providers (ISPs). Like traditional methods of feedback control, however, the SCS will also feed on the voluntary contributions of colleagues, neighbors, friends, and family members.[38] Likewise, businesses will be scored based on their compliance with official regulations and standards, and local governments on their procurement transparency and debt solvency. In each instance, the voluntary reviews, complaints, and disagreements logged by individuals will also be factored into the scoring mechanism. In effect, participation in the system will help the regime exert serious influence over mobility, finance, and the pursuit of livelihood.

Nevertheless, roughly 80 percent of Chinese citizens either strongly or somewhat approve of the SCS approach, according to a recent national survey

---

[36] Local versions of the SCS framework are already in place in a most Chinese cities and are slowly being integrated as part of a national implementation plan.

[37] For a breakdown of the various features of the planned SCS as they stand today, see the China Law Translate discussion of *State Council Release* (2014) No. 21, which outlines the institutional framework and goals, available at: https://bit.ly/2Jnah8r.

[38] This includes Party members and government officials.

conducted by a European-based survey company.[39] As with statistics on government approval, we should worry that these measures are inflated. What is perhaps more interesting about the survey findings are the individual-level determinants of support. According to the study's author, Genia Kostka, citizens justify their support for social crediting on the grounds that it will increase accountability among individuals: "People with bad credit will be less likely to be employed and it will not be easy for them to access more funds in the future. Such punishments provide feedback to people with bad behavior to restrain themselves. Step by step, the SCS will create trust in society."[40] In other words, Chinese citizens consent to participating in the crediting system because they do not trust one another.

Even if citizens do not trust one another, surely they must at least trust the system. For citizens to participate in the process of oversight, planning, and implementation, there must be some degree of faith in the regime's willingness to incorporate that input into its final decisions. To be sure, propaganda authorities go to great lengths to convince the public that its input does make a difference, and I have provided empirical evidence in Chapters 4 and 5 to suggest that it does. The thing about trust, however, is that it is not a one-way street. For the public to have trust in its leadership, it follows that the leadership ought to have trust in the public. This is a touchstone of democracy, whereby the will of the people is ultimately paramount—even if the people sometimes prefer politicians and policies that might be detrimental to their interests. This, however, is not a feature of Leninism. On the contrary, as laid out in Chapter 2, the need for social control is premised on the belief that the public is not capable of exercising its own best interest. Put differently, the social control dimensions of Leninism are grounded in a fundamental mistrust of the public.

Though fundamental, the regime's lack of trust in the public is not an overt feature of the system. Indeed, the mass-line has long served to obscure this fact by giving the impression that the masses are the core and inspiration of the CCP's mandate to rule. The tactic is effective in part because of how the party bifurcates the masses into friends and enemies, thus giving certain groups and individuals the feeling that they are entrusted by the regime to influence the fate of others.[41] This tendency to fragment society into trusted and untrusted categories, as noted in previous chapters, was a critical feature of Chinese politics throughout the Mao period,[42] even after class-based categories had lost much

[39] Kostka, "China's Social Credit Systems and Public Opinion: Explaining High Levels of Approval."
[40] Chinese citizen interviewee cited in ibid., p. 21.
[41] Lyman P. Van Slyke. *Enemies and Friends: The United Front in Chinese Communist History.* Stanford University Press, 1967.
[42] The strategic logic of social bifurcation goes back to Mao Zedong's "Analysis of the Classes in Chinese Society" (March 1926), *Selected Works*, Vol. I, p. 13.

of their relevance.[43] Indeed, it was only in the 1980s that formal enumeration categories of friends and enemies were partially dismantled.[44] Yet even today, top leaders continue to divide society between "patriots" (*aiguo zhe*) and so-called "bad elements" (*huai fenze*).[45]

An updated version of the same strategy is part of the SCS and its goal of increasing "trustworthiness" in Chinese society by sanctioning the bad apples. Similar to previous mass campaigns, the SCS will allow and indeed encourage individuals to report on and denounce one another. What makes the SCS unique, however, is the ubiquitous nature of its application. During Mao's reign, CCP campaigns against bad elements tended to target narrow bands of the popula- tion.[46] While the SCS is ostensibly more benign, it is near total in coverage, thus giving the impression that no group or individual is in a privileged or trusted position.[47] This is, after all, precisely what the cybernetic version of feedback control entails: every one and every entity is integrated into a system of input and correction. When this realization sinks in, especially among those who have not considered themselves vulnerable in the past, it will likely undercut their own sense of entrustment.

Empirical Strategy

To get a sense of whether this expectation about eroding trust plays out in public perceptions of the SCS and public attitudes toward the regime, the 2019 China Policy Barometer (CPB) incorporated a series of questions about the SCS into its pilot round, which was conducted on a national sample (n=2703) of online respondents. Respondents were asked about their familiarity with the SCS and their support for its further implementation, as well as follow-up questions concerning trust. Importantly, the questions concerning trust were organized in two ways. Consistent with previous surveys, the CPB asked about trust in government. In addition, the CPB asked whether the respondent felt trusted by the government, a formulation which, as far I am aware, has not been asked before in any Chinese public opinion survey.

The breakdown of the response variables is summarized in Figure 8.2. Con- sistent with Kostka's estimates, the CPB results suggest overwhelming support for the SCS, with around 72 percent of the sample reporting "some" or "strong"

[43] Kraus, "Class Conflict and the Vocabulary of Social Analysis in China"; Stuart R. Schram. *The Political Thought of Mao Tse-tung*, Praeger. 1969; Martin King Whyte. "Inequality and Stratification in China." *The China Quarterly* 64 (1975), pp. 684–711.

[44] Alvin Y. So. "The Changing Pattern of Classes and Class Conflict in China." *Journal of Contemporary Asia* 33.3 (2003), pp. 363–376.

[45] Recent examples of this rhetoric pertain to critical voices in Xinjiang and Hong Kong.

[46] Van Slyke, *Enemies and Friends: The United Front in Chinese Communist History*.

[47] This is of course a rhetorical position, since those with resources have options for affecting their scores in a positive way. But they are still under the same microscope.

Figure 8.2. Social Crediting and Public Trust

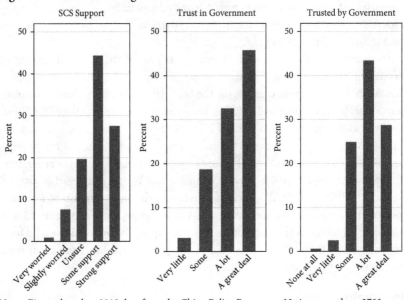

Notes: Figures based on 2019 data from the China Policy Barometer. Netizen sample n=2703.

support for further implementation.[48] Also consistent with other surveys, the results reveal extensive trust in the Chinese government, with roughly 78 percent of respondents expressing "a lot" or a "a great deal" of trust in the central government.[49] Interestingly, 72 percent of respondents also believe that the government has "a lot" or "a great deal" of trust in them. Unsurprisingly, each of these measures is positively correlated with the others.[50]

To drill down deeper into the correlates of public support for the SCS, I estimate the association with trust conditional on additional covariates, including gender, income, and urban registration status. These covariates are important insofar as they may capture different expectations about personal utility (or liability) resulting from the SCS. I also include alternative dimensions of trust, such as trust in local government, trust in and from friends, colleagues, and neighbors, along with self-reported familiarity with the SCS system. The results from this regression, illustrated in Figure 8.3, reveal an important set of correlations. Those who support the SCS are those who feel they are trusted by

[48] Forty-four percent expressed "some" support, 28 percent expressed "strong" support.

[49] The Chinese translation for "a great deal" was "非常信任" and "比较信任" for "a lot."

[50] The correlation coefficients: between *SCS Support* and *Trust in Central Government* is = .16, between *SCS Support* and *Trust by Government* is = .31, between *Trust in Central Government* and *Trust by Government* is = .36.

Figure 8.3. Support for Social Crediting System

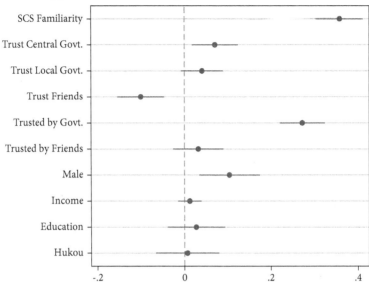

Notes: Point estimates are based on a linear probability model with robust standard errors. Whiskers represent 95 percent confidence interval around the estimates.

the government but have low trust in their friends, colleagues, neighbors, and family. In other words, these are people who consider themselves "good" citizens among an otherwise not-so-good population.

This dynamic is consistent with what we might expect under China's paternalistic version of authoritarian control, whereby social capital is low and dependence on the regime is high. However, as mentioned earlier, the critical innovation of the SCS is the ubiquity of its targeting and ranking process. Under previous campaigns it was not obvious, at least not for all citizens, that they themselves could one day be the target of monitoring and sanction. Even today, a substantial portion of the population seems unconcerned with the SCS, explaining that it will only hurt those who deserve it.[51] Is this simply confidence, or is it possible that some have not really thought about how seamlessly the SCS applies to them as well?

To try and communicate the inherent personal liability involved with participating in the SCS, the survey also included a priming experiment, whereby respondents were provided with additional information concerning the SCS before expressing their sentiment about the system. Specifically, respondents were randomly assigned to five different categories (see below), four of which

[51] Kostka, "China's Social Credit Systems and Public Opinion."

highlight the fact that the respondent could easily become a target of the system. While all the information items correspond to factual features of the SCS, they are not widely known across the population. If the treatments are working as expected, one should expect respondents to reevaluate their prior beliefs about the government, or at least about how the government sees them. The overt nature of SCS control ought to remind respondents that the state might not trust them all that much.

- **Control**: No additional information.
- **Donation**: You can improve your score by donating money to charity.
- **Government Donation**: You can improve your score by donating money to a government charity.
- **P2P**: Friends, colleagues, and neighbors can make reports that affect one's score.
- **Dang'an**: Scores are kept by the government, similar to *dang'an* records.

Importantly, such an experiment must also consider the prior knowledge of respondents concerning the SCS, which can be considered a form of pre-treatment bias. Accordingly, each treatment in the experiment was introduced in the form of a question, inquiring whether the respondent was aware of that information. Overall, about 50 percent of respondents understood that the SCS system would rely on citizen informants and would involve government controlled records for all citizens, akin to China's *dang'an* system,[52] while only 46 percent were aware that individuals could make donations in order to try and improve their record and score. With this background, I can incorporate prior knowledge about the SCS when considering treatment effects.

The effects of this experiment on trust in the regime and beliefs about being trusted by the regime are summarized in Figure 8.4. Several aspects are worth highlighting. First, the results are strongly driven by prior knowledge. If prior knowledge is not accounted for, there is no significant treatment effect, as indicated by the gray "saturated" treatment estimates.[53] This is unsurprising, as it would be difficult to change anyone's attitude by telling them something they already know. Focusing on the unsaturated and properly "treatable" portion of the population suggests that beliefs about government trust (panel A) are significantly depressed by informing respondents that they are both participants and targets of control. Interestingly, however, the right-hand panel B suggests

---

[52] The *dang'an* system is a dossier system for archiving one's life history and behavior, but in its analog form it rarely penetrated beyond a narrow segment of the population working in the public sector. It lost much of its relevance with market reforms in the 1980s and 1990s.

[53] The gray bar estimates are "saturated" in the sense that respondents were saturated with prior information, thus neutralizing the intended effect of the treatment.

Figure 8.4. SCS Effect on Trust

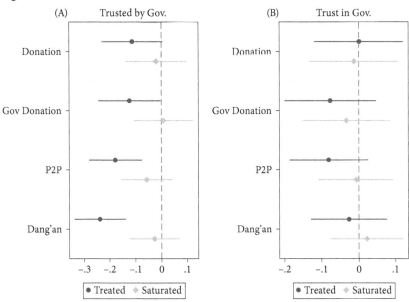

Notes: Point estimates are equivalent to difference in attitudinal means for treatment and control group respondents. Bars represent the 95% confidence interval for the difference. Crossing the dashed line implies an insignificant treatment effect, i.e., no difference. Gray bar estimates are based on the entire sample, including "saturated" respondents who reported prior knowledge of treatment items. Black bar estimates focus on respondents for whom the treatments represent new information.

there is no treatment effect, saturated or otherwise, on trust in the regime. In other words, learning more about the how SCS control works reminds individuals that they are not special and that they too are not fully trusted by the state. This is true even if trust in the regime remains unshaken.

Taken together, the results in Figure 8.4 reveal a dimension of political culture rarely discussed in studies on China. The reason that most studies focus on unidirectional trust toward the leadership and governing, as noted earlier, is that trust in government has long served as a proxy for state legitimacy and stability. According to most estimates, including my own with the CPB, the Chinese state enjoys a high degree of trust—upwards of 80 percent—from the people.[54] Yet, as I have argued throughout this book, integrated control also requires that members of society feel entrusted by the state. As Figure 8.2 indicates, this sense of entrustment is generally high among Netizens, but it is also more fragile than trust in the state—as it should be. Indeed, there are few objective reasons why Chinese citizens should feel trusted. If they were, we might as well imagine

---

[54] Tang, *Populist Authoritarianism: Chinese Political Culture and Regime Sustainability*.

that they would be given real voting rights, consume unfiltered information, and be allowed to invest their savings where they see fit. Instead, this sense of inclusiveness is aspirational at best. As technology redefines how the Chinese state integrates society, however, these aspirations may fade.

The Political Disconnect in Technical Control

Like the Haier corporation, the CCP has, over the last two decades, used technology to shorten the distance between governing institutions and the general public. As recounted in Chapter 2, smartphone apps and digital "drop boxes" are making it easier for citizens to submit applications, file complaints, and connect with administrative agents. Online consultation platforms and Internet polls are making it easier for the regime to calibrate policy, while also giving citizens an opportunity to provide feedback and feel invested in the process. At the same time, technology is also transforming how the regime exercises control over the population. Social media, for instance, is helping make citizens more legible to the propaganda and public security authorities, while smartphones Smartphones are making it easier to track communications and movements, and soon a state-backed blockchain ledgers will make nearly every economic transaction infinitely traceable.

While it is easy to disparage the "Big Brother" nature of China's technology fetish, one should not ignore the possibility that a Chinese surveillance state will contribute to better governance, more compliance, and a more ordered society in general. Indeed, this is the stated goal of the regime. It is also one that the Chinese citizen has implicitly endorsed by supporting the CCP's platform for a stable, "harmonious" society. At the same time, the shift to digitization has not only augmented the Chinese state's control capacity, it is shifting the way in which it is being conducted. In particular, passive modes of surveillance through security cameras and an ever increasing bank of biometrics are now omnipresent features of state control. Likewise, passive indicators of public opinion are now extracted each time someone conducts a search on Baidu, posts on Weibo, or opens a message on WeChat. Perhaps most dramatically, an automated SCS system is poised to seamlessly integrate control and inclusion by enrolling citizens in the task of monitoring and evaluating one another. To be sure, China's ability to integrate and centralize its growing surveillance capacity remains questionable, but expanding this capacity is a frequently espoused national effort and thus not easily discounted.

Success in digitizing control and participation, however, might be thinning out the intricate network linking the Party and the people. Take, for example, future investments in grassroots cadres to monitor and interface with residents

in China's villages, streets, and communities. As discussed earlier, these investments are substantial, especially for cash-strapped local governments that are
finding it increasingly difficult to hire and retain staff. Presumably, China's aging
population will continue to provide a steady stream of "volunteers" to keep
watch on their communities, as is already the case in large cities like Beijing and
Shanghai. Yet, as surveillance technology proliferates and the software running
it continues to improve, it is likely that the physical arm of the party-state will
gradually shift toward passive, digital alternatives. How this might impact the
public's connection to the CCP remains an open research question.

Consider the best-case scenario, one in which a benevolent technocracy,
replete with big data analytics, makes informed policy choices and addresses
social grievances. Where exactly does the value of the CCP lie within such a
system? If passive, data-driven control is operating in the background, it will
likely be more efficient and more comprehensive than the current agent-based
system. In addition to giving authorities unprecedented surveillance power, such
a system would likely also lead to genuinely pro-social outcomes including
less crime, fewer traffic accidents, and generally less risk in day-to-day affairs.
Suppose the system works precisely as the CCP advertises. What role then does
the CCP play? Does it matter which political entity sits behind the software
and the algorithm? Does it matter what ideology it represents or who chairs its
leadership? Ironically, one of the outcomes of automated control is that political
identity becomes rather remote. To put it simply, the CCP's success in automating
Leninism may one day render the Party, as the epigraph in this chapter suggests,
politically irrelevant.

Such a possibility represents a serious threat to inclusive control. Each governance achievement documented thus far has relied on an engaged Chinese public
that has invested its time and faith voluntarily in the participatory process. Why
they did so is by no means obvious, but it is safe to say that people participate in
part because they believe in the system. An underlying premise of this chapter
has been that participants must have some degree of trust in the regime, and they
must also have some article of faith that the regime trusts them. One strategy
for forging such beliefs relies on fracturing society and entrusting some but not
others. In the past, the rhetorical lines of division were based predominantly on
class and ideas.[55] There are still deep cleavages along the lines of religion and

---

[55] I say "rhetorical" because there is little evidence to suggest that the CCP was genuinely
interested in eradicating inequality or denigrating intellectuals, but pursuing these stated goals
served party interests; See Whyte, "Inequality and Stratification in China." For a general review of
divisions and classifications, See Kraus, "Class Conflict and the Vocabulary of Social Analysis in
China"

ethnicity,[56] but overall the nature of inclusion and exclusion has become more fluid and opaque.[57]

With the arrival of the SCS, these remaining divisions might be subsumed by a more atomizing framework, whereby each individual is both a participant and a target of control. As the surveys explored in this chapter indicate, this ubiquity of control undercuts the degree to which Chinese Netizens feel trusted by the regime. The implications here are profound. If the public believes that it is under constant surveillance, what is the motivation to voluntarily contribute further information? Likewise, if the public believes that its actions, preferences, and biases are being passively mined by authorities, should we not expect them to be even more cautious in revealing precisely those critical opinions that authorities need for the purposes of oversight and planning? Finally, if authoritarian control in China is reduced to that of a social credit score, what is the nature of party loyalty beyond that which is purely instrumental?

[56] Thomas Cliff. "The Partnership of Stability in Xinjiang: State–Society Interactions Following the July 2009 Unrest." *The China Journal* 68 (2012), pp. 79–105.
[57] So, "The Changing Pattern of Classes and Class Conflict in China."

Conclusion

> Information is information, not matter and not energy. Any materialism that cannot allow for this cannot exist in the present.
>
> — Norbert Wiener, 1948

Sea vessels moving at high speed generate turbulence in their wake. As long as they move swiftly enough, the disruption is unlikely to threaten those aboard. If the vessel slows too fast or tries to change course too suddenly, however, the forward ripples cast from the stern risk swamping its rear or broadside. The bigger the ship, the bigger the risk.[1] During the first three decades of the post-Mao period, 1978–2008, China's economy was a giant speedboat. This dramatic run, however, is reaching an inflection point. Rising wages, overcapacity, debt, and an aging population are slowing China down. The recent setbacks resulting from a prolonged trade dispute with the United States and the Covid-19 pandemic have only hastened this slowdown. As a consequence, an informal social contract offering economic opportunity in exchange for political stasis is becoming increasingly tenuous.[2]

To stay in power, China's leaders must do more than just steer the ship. The regime has to convince the public that it can mend cracks and navigate swells better than anyone else. To be sure, this argument is made easier by the fact that there is no viable political opposition, no openly critical media, and few obvious benchmarks from which to evaluate the CCP's leadership or the efficacy of its policies. Nevertheless, China's maturing economy has raised new challenges and forced unpopular decisions, like raising individual taxes and retirement ages, without the buffer of high growth to ease the pain. The principal challenge for China's current and future leaders will thus be to articulate, implement, and sustain difficult but unavoidable reforms. This is how the CCP thinks about governance, or at least how it presents itself in public.[3]

---

[1] I thank Brian Yang (杨扬), Deputy Director of the Foreign & Overseas Chinese Affairs Committee of the Shenzhen Municipal People's Congress, for sharing this wonderfully apt metaphor with me.

[2] For background on the "informal" economic bargain, refer to Richard Baum. *Burying Mao: Chinese Politics in the Age of Deng Xiaoping*. Princeton University Press, 1996.

[3] He Li. "The Chinese Discourse on Good Governance: Content and Implications." *Journal of Contemporary China* (2020), pp. 1–14.

Retrofitting Leninism. Dimitar D. Gueorguiev. Oxford University Press. © Oxford University Press 2021.
DOI: 10.1093/oso/9780197555668.003.00010

Self-righteous as it may sound, there is reason to suspect that the CCP's rhetoric on governance is at least partially sincere. As previous work has shown, China's leaders are keenly sensitive to public opinion and see performance as a basis for sustainable legitimacy.[4] In terms of promises, the current administration has committed to bold investments in poverty reduction, renewable energy, and improved living standards, in a broad-sweeping effort to raise the Middle Kingdom's status to that of a "moderately prosperous society," and a prosperous global leader. To be sure, the CCP's ability to achieve these bold targets will be aided by its control over statistical output and relentless propaganda, and there are those who remain convinced that pro-social ambitions are untenable under the current political system.[5] Nevertheless, it is worth reflecting on how China's leaders have committed themselves to economic and governance targets, especially given a slowdown that is already underway and the emergent challenges.

One recent explanation for how China has managed to achieve rapid development with remarkably few setbacks is found in Ang's theory of "directed improvisation," whereby central leaders establish abstract development goals but leave local governments and communities to figure out how to get them done. The adaptive potential that underpins directed improvisation helps explain how the Chinese people and economy succeeded without many of the institutional prerequisites—property rights, legal independence, and credible constraints on executive power—that economists and political scientists have come to consider critical for development.[6] Nevertheless, Ang's theory leaves open questions about how much direction the center commands and how much autonomy the grassroots have for improvisation. As Slater and Fenner stress, authoritarian states are often underappreciated regarding how much influence and constraint they impose on political, economic, and social possibilities.[7] In the case of the PRC, the Chinese party-state is exceptionally pervasive, and its modus operandi has always been and continues to be that of control. Pragmatism, improvisation, and perseverance at the grassroots have no doubt been critical for China's improbable success, but these bottom-up forces have always operated within the bounds of state control. Moreover, as I have elaborated upon over the previous eight chapters, effective state control in China involves sustained feedback, not simply delegation, between leaders and masses.

---

[4] Tang, *Populist Authoritarianism: Chinese Political Culture and Regime Sustainability*; Dickson, *The Dictator's Dilemma: The Chinese Communist Party's Strategy for Survival*.

[5] Pei, *China's Crony capitalism: The Dynamics of Regime Decay*.

[6] Douglass C. North. *Institutions, Institutional Change, and Economic Performance*. Cambridge University Press, 1990, p. 152.

[7] Dan Slater and Sofia Fenner. "State Power and Staying Power: Infrastructural Mechanisms and Authoritarian Durability." *Journal of International Affairs* (2011), pp. 15–29.

In particular, I have shown how the regime seeks out, aggregates, and exploits public-provided information for use in oversight, planning, and implementation. Technology has served as a powerful amplifier in this effort, and computer-assisted modes of inclusion have provided the regime with a near–seamless ability to interface and collect information from the public. Yet, information for information's sake may not be enough. When Soviet cyberneticists published their first article on information control in 1955,[8] they borrowed heavily from Norbert Wiener's 1948 classic on the subject.[9] But, as noted by Peters, they only quote Wiener once: "Information is information, not matter and not energy. Any materialism that cannot allow for this cannot exist in the present."[10] The choice of reference (the quote that opens this chapter), underscored the Soviet authors' challenge in introducing what was at that point a Western theory of information science into a system of Marxist-Leninist dialectics. It also emphasized a core Leninist principle: information control in the absence of political connection is little more than bureaucratization.

After years of war, targeted violence, and dogged guerrilla resistance, the Chinese communists came to power with stronger grassroots connections than most other authoritarian regimes, even more than their institutional archetype in the Soviet Union.[11] Routine political campaigns served to further entrench and refine the CCP's links to Chinese society.[12] Even during prolonged periods of chaos, such as the Cultural Revolution, local CCP cells were never abandoned and ultimately proved to be the last line of defense.[13] Most recently, CCP-affiliated grassroots organizations helped mobilize local communities as the frontline of Covid containment.[14] Furthermore, the CCP appears deeply committed not only to mobilizing the public but also to understanding, appeasing, and influencing public opinion.[15]

China's society is, however, becoming more sophisticated, and the people are growing ever more ambitious.[16] Appealing to public opinion is getting harder and appeasement more expensive. At the same time, new, digital forms of surveillance and engagement are getting cheaper. As suggested in the previous chapter, this confluence of factors may move the CCP in the direction of technology-driven control, whereby artificial intelligence increasingly takes the

[8] Sergei Sobolev, Alexey Lyapunov, and Anatoly Kitov. "The Main Features of Cybernetics (Основные черты кибернетики)." *Problems of Philosophy (Voprosy filosofii)* 4 (1955), pp. 136–148.
[9] Wiener, *Cybernetics or Control and Communication in the Animal and the Machine.*
[10] Peters, *How Not to Network a Nation.* p. 39.
[11] Schurmann, *Ideology and Organization in Communist China.*
[12] Whyte, *Small Groups and Political Rituals in China*; Walder, *Communist Neo-traditionalism Work and Authority in Chinese Industry.*
[13] Koss, *Where the Party Rules: The Rank and File of China's Communist State.*
[14] See the discussion of China's efforts to contain the spread of Covid-19 in the Introduction.
[15] Tang, *Populist Authoritarianism: Chinese Political Culture and Regime Sustainability.*
[16] Evan Osnos. *Age of Ambition: Chasing Fortune, Truth, and Faith in the New China.* Macmillan, 2014.

place of grassroots, human connection. All the while, we are also witnessing a stark departure, or rather reversion, away from pure technocracy toward strongman idolatry.[17] Considered in tandem, these two developments are contradictory. How can the CCP improve governance by optimizing information control, while at the same time stoking the passions of personalism?

This conclusion engages this contemporary paradox both as a critique of my theory on inclusive control and a potential but unanticipated consequence of the same logic. One clear takeaway from this exercise is that whatever China's technology-augmented governance may bring forth, it is unlikely to move in a democratic direction. Looking forward, coming to terms with China's non-democratic trajectory is an important step in understanding China's domestic politics and in resetting US foreign policy toward the PRC, especially after four years of a Trump-led approach that has largely ignored the Chinese public in favor of brinkmanship, bigotry, and hyperbole against the country's "socialist" background. I also consider the implications of the logic of inclusive control for other control-minded regimes that may look to China as a model. I conclude with some final thoughts on what the book suggests about China's citizens and why more research on Chinese public opinion is needed.

Double Hedging for the Future

One of the perks of running a noncompetitive regime is the ability to reflect on the past and present, as well as to plan well into the future without having to factor in routine political or ideological transition. Nonetheless, noncompetitive regimes are prone to uncertainty and they are vulnerable to sudden breakdown.[18] This fact only makes the PRC's economic achievements and relative political stability all the more worthy of analysis. As students of Chinese politics, both foreign and domestic, have long noted, the prism through which the CCP reflects on its past and future is that of political insecurity.[19] Similarly, I view the CCP's utmost emphasis on control and stability as emanating from a common

---

[17] Susan L. Shirk. "China in Xi's 'New Era': The Return to Personalistic Rule." *Journal of Democracy* 29.2 (2018), pp. 22–36.

[18] Stathis N. Kalyvas. "The Decay and Breakdown of Communist One-Party Systems." *Annual Review of Political Science* 2.1 (1999), pp. 323–343.

[19] Susan L. Shirk. *China: Fragile Superpower*. Oxford University Press, 2008; Minxin Pei. "China's Coming Upheaval: Competition, the Coronavirus, and the Weakness of Xi Jinping." *Foreign Affairs* 99 (2020), p. 82; Sulmaan Wasif Khan. *Haunted by Chaos: China's Grand Strategy from Mao Zedong to Xi Jinping*. Harvard University Press, 2018; M. Taylor Fravel. "Regime Insecurity and International Cooperation: Explaining China's Compromises in Territorial Disputes." *International Security* 30.2 (2005), pp. 46–83.

well of insecurity. My thoughts on China's future thus start by highlighting periods of instability in China's recent past.

The most notable periods of past instability for the CCP are the Cultural Revolution (1966–1974) and, to a lesser extent, the first decade of opening and reform (1979–1989). As discussed in Chapter 3, personality cult and ideological fervor hyper-mobilized grassroots society during the Cultural Revolution, bringing system control to the brink of outright collapse. During the late 1980s, decentralization and privatization undercut grassroots, legal, and social welfare platforms, thus allowing bottom-up pressure to bubble into mass opposition.[20] Given the Party's chronic insecurity and preference for risk aversion, one would expect the CCP to avoid repeating both mistakes by committing to good governance and firmly eschewing personalism and populism. This is partially what we are seeing, but with some notable exceptions and caveats.

Hedging Against Technocracy

With regard to governance, China's leaders face a slew of third- to first-world challenges, ranging from poverty and pollution to culture wars with Chinese characteristics and cybercrime on Chinese scale magnitudes. Thanks to long-term investments in inclusive control, along with good fortune and timing, China's decision-makers now operate in an incredibly information-rich environment from which to address these challenges. Arguably the most consequential example of this technological revolution in governance is China's new social crediting system (SCS), which I see as a descendant of a century-old Leninist vision of information-based control. To this end, the SCS will likely help the regime overcome systemic weaknesses in a number of areas, including a bloated and antiquated state-run banking system and a grossly inadequate consumer protection infrastructure. As discussed in Chapter 9, however, the SCS, alongside other computer-assisted modes of surveillance, is also poised to impact state–society relations in China in at least two ways.

First, the move to algorithms will facilitate passive forms of surveillance and control, thus reducing the need for grassroots investment and cooptation.[21] Second, pitting citizen against citizen within a depoliticized, algorithm-driven framework will atomize the politicized grouping of Chinese society that the CCP has long exploited in its favor.[22] Such developments may, as I have argued in Chapter 9, undermine the "good citizen" connection that underpins Leninist

[20] Minxin Pei. "Citizens vs. Mandarins: Administrative Litigation in China." English. *The China Quarterly* 152.152 (1997), pp. 832–862.
[21] Xu Xu. "To Repress or to Co-opt? Authoritarian Control in the Age of Digital Surveillance." *American Journal of Political Science* 65.2 (2021), pp. 309–325.
[22] Whyte, *Small Groups and Political Rituals in China*; Walder, *Communist Neo-traditionalism*; Ching Kwan Lee and Yonghong Zhang. "The Power of Instability: Unraveling the Microfoundations of Bargained Authoritarianism in China." *American Journal of Sociology* 118.6 (2013), pp. 1475–1508.

state–society relations and the voluntary participation that this framework facilitates. Second, digital innovations in information control may encourage leaders at all levels to consider targeted repression as an alternative to broad-based social spending.[23] This is undoubtedly attractive from the authoritarian vantage point, but if it were to undermine public perceptions of the regime's commitment to social progress it could further undercut an already diminished CCP legitimacy. In this respect, the digitization of information control carries opportunities for greater control as well as some risks.

One way to hedge against this possibility is to set in stone bold commitments, such as the Party's stated plan to eradicate poverty, expand public health and pensions systems, and sharply transition away from fossils to renewables. Whether the CCP can make good on these ambitions is unclear, although, state control over the media insures that progress toward these goals is presented in the best possible light. Yet, we should be not too cynical. Just before Xi Jinping first announced China's bold poverty eradication program in 2012, the State Council also went ahead and raised its own bar by nearly doubling the official poverty line to 2,300 yuan (approximately $350 USD) per annum.[24] Such moves are not consistent with the "performative" governance line of criticism, which contends that the CCP's performance achievements are mostly show with little substance.[25]

Even so, it is worth noting that in outlining bold commitments, the CCP also sets its own agenda and benchmarks for evaluation. Rather than evaluating overall gains in standards and quality of life, the focus is now on poverty targets. Rather than exposing itself to criticism over the poor quality and gross inequality of healthcare and retirement planning, the CCP has instead redirected attention to more crudely quantifiable coverage goals. Furthermore, in the spirit of meeting targets, the CCP has also indirectly sanctioned new forms of repression, including forced resettlement, mandatory education, and obligatory charity.[26] Finally, by imposing bold targets and novel forms of repression to reach them, the CCP has given new life to some of its more antiquated grassroots infrastructure, such as posting "first secretaries" (young up-and-coming CCP cadres) from urban centers to rural development residencies.[27] Between 2012

---

[23] Xu, "To Repress or to Co-opt? Authoritarian Control in the Age of Digital Surveillance."

[24] This increased threshold brings China in line with global standards after adjusting for purchasing power parity.

[25] Iza Ding. "Performative Governance." *World Politics* 72.4 (2020), pp. 525–556.

[26] For example, it is not uncommon for well-off households, particularly those with connections to the state, to be paired and tasked with helping a poorer household.

[27] Xingmiu Liao, Wen-Hsuan Tsai, and Zheng-Wei Lin. "Penetrating the Grassroots: First-Secretaries-in-Residence and Rural Politics in Contemporary China." *Problems of Post-Communism* 67.2 (2020), pp. 169–179.

and 2016, around 775,000 well-off officials were sent to the countryside under programs like this.[28]

Hedging Against Populism

As discussed in Chapter 3, Mao's personal power has arguably been the single greatest threat to systemic control ever faced by the CCP, and Party incumbents carry a deep-seated aversion to the rise of new charismatic populists.[29] This is why, in 1980 the CCP Central Committee explicitly advised that "Portraits of the current Communist Party leader are forbidden to be displayed in public; no personality cult will be tolerated." Consistent with this caution, Chinese leaders, including Deng Xiaoping, Jiang Zemin, and Hu Jintao, have each abided by this collectivist norm and avoided building personality cults, even as they worked to augment their own individual authority. In restraining their own populist potential, however, China's stoic managers may have inadvertently raised the risk that a less scrupulous leader might arise to seize the opportunity.[30] This risk has only increased alongside the Party's gradual departure from socialism, as well as the growing rivalry in its relations with the United States. Seen in this light, the creeping return of a personality cult since Xi Jinping's rise to power in 2012 is deeply troubling.

A return of idolatry and personalism in China suggests that Xi Jinping is aggrandizing individual power at the expense of the CCP's institutional power. Yet, there is reason to suspect the Party might be a willing accomplice. For one, Xi Jinping was dealt a strong hand before he ever took office. In particular, the outgoing Hu-Wen administration signed off on a full handover of powers to Xi, and to a smaller and weaker cohort of co-leaders expected to constrain him.[31] Furthermore, it is well known that the CCP identified moral shortcomings, both within the Party and among the public, well in advance of Xi's rise.[32] More generally, the Party's grand theorists have long sought to reestablish a more religious connection between the Party and the masses; ideological indoctrination campaigns started to gain momentum around 2008.[33] One could argue that the

---

[28] Ding Dou. "China's Ambitious Path to Poverty Eradication." *Global Asia* 11.2 (2016), pp. 22–26.

[29] Shirk, "China in Xi's 'New Era': The Return to Personalistic Rule."

[30] Dimitar D. Gueorguiev and Paul J. Schuler. "Collective Charisma: Elite–Mass Relations in China and Vietnam." *Problems of Post-Communism* (2020), pp. 1–12.

[31] Dimitar D. Gueorguiev. "Dictator's Shadow: Chinese Elite Politics Under Xi Jinping." *China Perspectives* 1.2 (2018), pp. 17–26.

[32] David L. Shambaugh. *China's Communist Party: Atrophy and Adaptation.* University of California Press, 2008.

[33] Frank N. Pieke. "Party Spirit: Producing a Communist Civil Religion in Contemporary China." *Journal of the Royal Anthropological Institute* 24.4 (2018), pp. 709–729; Willy Lam. "The Maoist Revival and the Conservative Turn in Chinese Politics." *China Perspectives* 2012/2 (2012), pp. 5–15; David Shambaugh. "Training China's Political Elite: The Party School System." *The China Quarterly* 196 (2008), pp. 827–844.

relatively lower scale of ideological fervor during the late Jiang and early Hu administrations (1997–2007) was perhaps more of an exception than a rule.

Nonetheless, this recent ideological shift seems to have provided a foundation for a populist turn in Chinese politics, and Xi Jinping has in many ways personally profited politically from the effort. Even if Xi had kept politics impersonal, however, that in no way guarantees that a populist challenger would not have emerged. Chongqing's former and now imprisoned Party Secretary, Bo Xilai, presented precisely such a threat.[34] Yet, it is one thing for a political entrepreneur like Bo Xilai to go it alone, and another for propaganda offices and cultural agents around the country to be engaged in the effort, which is what was happening in the background of Bo Xilai's drama.[35]

As President of the CCP Central Party School (CCPCPS), between 2007 and 2012, Xi Jinping was tasked with overseeing the latter effort by synchronizing Confucian, Marxist, and Maoist ideas. This effort to bolster the Party's footing within Chinese tradition, to appropriate credit for the people's achievements, and to bury its past failings has been, and continues to be, a systemic, institutionally driven one aimed at extending the CCP's lease on power. Put differently, for all the parallels one can draw between current ideological revival and that of the Mao era, one clear contrast is that in today's statist campaign, control and stability trump all other considerations, and there is no apparent interest by Xi or his loyalists in stoking revolutionary passions.

This is perhaps why, even as the Xi administration pursues its war on liberals and Western sympathizers, it is equally concerned about the rise of leftists and ultra-nationalists.[36] As then PBSC member Wang Qishan reiterated in 2016, "guard against the Right, but guard primarily against the Left."[37] Accordingly, authorities have targeted and arrested Marxist activists across China,[38] and Marxist student societies have been routinely barred from registration at major universities[39] This should not be surprising, given what we know about control systems that, above all, are organized around the pursuit of self-calibrating

[34] Dimitar D. Gueorguiev and Paul J. Schuler. "Keeping Your Head Down: Public Profiles and Promotion Under Autocracy." *Journal of East Asian Studies* 16.01 (2016), pp. 87–116.

[35] Shambaugh, "Training China's Political Elite"; Lam, "The Maoist Revival and the Conservative Turn in Chinese Politics".

[36] Jessica Chen Weiss. *Powerful Patriots: Nationalist Protest in China's Foreign Relations*. Oxford University Press, 2014; James Reilly. *Strong Society, Smart State: The Rise of Public Opinion in China's Japan Policy*. Columbia University Press, 2011.

[37] Listen to the full speech here: https://youtu.be/CS8z-SEWeK4; accessed 08-24-2016. The slogan a is direct quotation from a speech Deng Xiaoping made in 1992. The message is also enshrined in the CCP Charter, "The Party must ensure that reform and opening up are carried out in unity with the Four Cardinal Principles, put its basic line into effect in all fields of endeavor, and combat all mistaken tendencies of the 'Left' and Right, maintaining vigilance against Rightist tendencies, but primarily defending against 'Leftist' tendencies."

[38] See: https://bit.ly/2EITAAT; Access 06-18-2018.

[39] See: https://bit.ly/2C0GwVW; Accessed 10-25-2018.

equilibrium. The homeostasis of such systems is threatened by extremes in any direction, and the most likely ideological future in China is one that is carefully calibrated and moderated by the CCP establishment.

Opportunity Costs

As with any hedging strategy, there are also opportunity costs to consider. In pledging to eradicate poverty, insure all, and lead the world in renewables, the CCP is committing scarce resources that could have been deployed in other areas. We are already seeing China pull back on some of its foreign investment ambitions,[40] and there is widespread concern that Xi's administration has overextended China's capabilities. Priorities aside, we are also seeing more belt-tightening in Beijing, which may temper optimism about the economy. Consider, for instance, the night-and-day contrast between how Beijing responded to the Global Financial Crisis in 2008 with that of the Covid-19 pandemic in 2020. During the former, China was the big spender, injecting nearly 600 billion (USD) into the economy in record time, while its peers in North America and Europe took much longer to put forward far less extensive stimuli. In 2020, however, China has come out the miser, thus far injecting less than a quarter of what the United States has, while also placing serious constraints on how stimulus is used by average consumers. This comparison is not entirely fair, as America's service-led economy was far more vulnerable to a public health crisis than China's. Yet, even when considering the method, rather than the amount, of stimulus, there are notable differences in response strategies. For instance, while the US Treasury delivered direct deposits, China offered spending vouchers with short expiration dates. Similar caution preceded Chinese corporate stimulus and lending programs, in a stark departure from 2008. CCP propagandists have contrasted the more recent stimulus strategy with 2008, framing it as more prudent, calibrated, and cost-effective.[41] This argument may prove effective in the long run, but from the perspective of an average Chinese citizen the state's spendthrift approach is unlikely to instill confidence or buoyancy about the future.

Similarly, in concentrating power and symbolism within his own office, Xi Jinping is not only threatening Party institutions, he is also blurring the boundary between Party and state, and with it the ability of the former to shift blame for policy failures and miscalculations onto the latter. True, a mix of smart governance, censorship, and propaganda will help Xi and the Party avoid,

---

[40] Jonathan Wheatley and James Kynge. "China Curtails Overseas Lending in Face of Geopolitical Backlash." *Financial Times*, December 7, 2020.
[41] Frank Tang. "Coronavirus: China Claims Stimulus '10 Times More Efficient' than US Fed, as New Loans Top US$1 Trillion." *South China Morning Post*, April 10, 2020.

downplay, and deflect from future shortcomings and blunders. But there are limits. Most recently, we saw Xi's profile take a hit after obvious missteps in the early response to the Covid epidemic. Even before Covid, it was apparent that Xi's public ambitions for economic nationalism had inadvertently provoked the United States. While the CCP has abandoned some of the rhetoric, such as the "Made in China 2025" campaign aimed to boost domestic manufacturing in key tech-intensive industries, the Party has doubled down on Xi worship and praise for "Xi Jinping Thought." Some ardent Xi supporters have even proposed renaming Tsinghua University, China's most prestigious academic institution, as "Xi Jinping University," in honor of its former alumnus.

It is likely that new, unanticipated challenges and policy failures will emerge, and centralizing authority around Xi Jinping will make it harder to shield him from criticism. Even so, we should not expect the risk of criticism to temper idolatry. Instead, rising insecurity within the top leader's office will, in turn, make it less likely that any criticism will emerge at all; this will only increase the risk of miscalculation. Given the importance of criticism within the inclusive control architecture, we can conclude that even if Xi's personally aggrandizing strategy were a hedge against a more revolutionary populist contender, it is nevertheless undercutting control by blurring the boundary between political leadership and administration.

A China Model

While it remains uncertain whether the CCP will lean toward technocracy, ideology, or both, it is clear that those who interpreted China's participatory reforms as precursors to democratization have been sorely disappointed. As I have stressed throughout this book, public participation in China serves to perpetuate and refine political control. Across the board, the organizational logic that underpins mass inclusion in today's PRC also insures mass compartmentalization, political demobilization, and, by extension, CCP control. To the extent that a complementarity between inclusion and control continues to deliver improvements in governance, it will strengthen the incumbent regime's security and weaken the prospects for future political reform. Indeed, China seems farther from democracy today than it did twenty, thirty, or even forty years ago. As such, it is perhaps time to declare the possibility of "peaceful evolution," or the idea that China will liberalize as it modernizes, as effectively dead.[42]

This diagnosis, however, does not come with a full autopsy. For many, the blame again lies with Xi Jinping and his supporters, who are seen as having

---

[42] Russell Ong. "'Peaceful Evolution', 'Regime Change' and China's Political Security." *Journal of Contemporary China* 16.53 (2007), pp. 717–727.

abandoned prior reforms.[43] Such critiques, though necessary, might be missing the point. First, and as noted earlier, they overlook the fact that Xi Jinping's concentration of power was initiated and endorsed by CCP leaders before he became General Party Secretary.[44] Moreover, a narrow criticism of China's incumbent leader implies that his "reform era" predecessors were more open to democracy, or at least less concerned with authoritarian control. This is an overly generous portrayal. The CCP never abandoned its pursuit of control, and the failure of "peaceful evolution" cannot be appreciated without taking into account the CCP's fear of precisely such a development and its relentless preemptive actions.[45]

Viewed in hindsight it is hard to ignore the possibility that liberalizing reforms, though expedient for addressing pressing governance challenges, were widely, and perhaps correctly, perceived as politically risky by China's leaders.[46] In other words, the failure of peaceful evolution theory to run its course is hardly evidence against the argument. Over time and with the help of technology the Party has come to realize that good governance can be pursued via more easily controlled means. Ironically, China's modernization and technological progress, by helping improve authoritarian administration, has brought the PRC even closer to the technocratic vision of its Leninist origins. While this arc may not be sustainable, it is nevertheless likely to attract interest from other control-oriented states.

Digital Authoritarianism

When the Soviet Union collapsed in 1991, China become the premier authoritarian regime in a world dominated by Western-style democracies. For some, it was only a matter of time before the CCP leadership opened or splintered as well.[47] Given the odds, there is understandable intrigue about how China might offer a counter-narrative to Western models of government. The proposition is tantalizing on multiple dimensions. For leftists, China's example serves as a powerful objection to the claim that state intervention and economic modernization are incompatible. Likewise, for those concerned with the rise of democratic populism, China's technocratic approach is understandably appealing. Most of all, the CCP's ability to contain and exploit social tensions through non-political participation and technology is poised to find favor among control-minded

---

[43] Minzner, *End of an Era: How China's Authoritarian Revival is Undermining Its Rise*; David Shambaugh. *The Coming Chinese Crackup*. 2015.
[44] Gueorguiev, "Dictator's Shadow: Chinese Elite Politics Under Xi Jinping."
[45] Dimitar D. Gueorguiev. "Beyond Peaceful Evolution: Chinese Domestic Politics and U.S. Foreign Policy." *United States Relations with China and Iran: Towards the Asian Century*. Ed. by Osamah F. Khalil. Bloomsbury Academic Press, 2019, pp. 39–58.
[46] Qiang Zhai. "1959: Preventing Peaceful Evolution." *China Heritage Quarterly* 18 (2009).
[47] Francis Fukuyama. "The End of History?" *The National Interest* (1989), pp. 3–18.

leaders around the world. This sentiment has only been amplified by the coronavirus pandemic and China's apparent efficiency in containing, controlling, and acclimating to the health challenge.

What are the implications for other control-minded countries? If there is any general takeaway from the case of China, it is that autocrats will increasingly try to capitalize on technological opportunities to engage and control their people, and we should not be surprised to see inclusion and repression go hand in hand.[48] Dictators in the Middle East and Central Asia, for example, have made substantial investments in consultative institutions and are eagerly buying up surveillance and e-government technology. According to data on e-government and e-participation compiled by the United Nations, China has done the most in this regard in recent years, but it is followed by a host of other nondemocracies.[49] In particular, Vietnam, Uzbekistan, Azerbaijan, Saudi Arabia, and Bahrain have all made progress in e-participation and seen simultaneous improvements in their governance effectiveness, yet each has also seen declines in their political freedom scores, as illustrated in the contrasting panels of Figure C.1.[50]

There are, however, limits to technical control. As I have discussed in previous chapters, the CCP invested big and early, allowing China to adopt technology gradually and become a major player in its development. Today, China has domestic companies designing and maintaining its e-governance architecture alongside domestic alternatives for Western social media platforms. These allow the government not only to censor online discourse but also shape the content and substance of public discourse. This is simply not the case for most other countries. The Saudis, for example, have had to import their surveillance technology from the Chinese, and to a lesser extent the Israelis.[51] Vietnam reluctantly depends on Google for nearly all of its search and indexing services.

Moreover, China's technological dividend cannot be fully appreciated without considering the CCP's longstanding inclination to govern from the grassroots and the Chinese public's willingness to partake in that process. Put differently, even if technology offers regimes around the world quick, non-electoral means for reaching out to their citizens, it is unclear why citizens would participate or how their governments would make use of that information. As Rodan's comparative study of "participation without democracy" in Southeast Asia shows, inclusive institutions are rarely robust; only under the People's Action Party

[48] Kalathil and Boas, *Open Networks, Closed Regimes*.

[49] UN e-Government data can be accessed here: https://bit.ly/2VvPMbA.

[50] Political Rights is based on indicators from Freedom House, while Governance Effectiveness comes from the World Bank's *Worldwide Governance Indicators*.

[51] While there are no direct statistics on the sourcing of surveillance technology, media reports suggest that Chinese companies like ZTE and Israeli companies like NSO have sold surveillance hardware and software to the Saudi government. See: https://bit.ly/2TYOLIJ and https://bit.ly/2L5pbOO.

Figure C.1. E-Participation, Governance, and Democracy

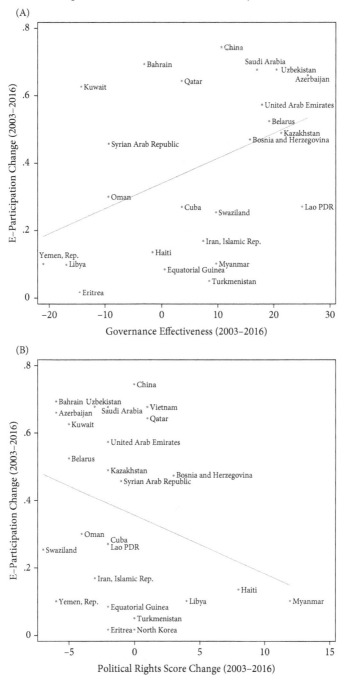

Notes: Data on *E-Participation* comes from the UN's *E-Government Knowledge Database*. Political Rights is taken from Freedom House. Data on *Governance Effectiveness* comes from the World Bank's *Worldwide Governance Indicators*. Only nondemocracies with a Polity Rating of less than (-.5) are included in the sample.

(PAP) in Singapore do we see an analogue to the Chinese version of controlled inclusion. As noted in Chapter 1, this is no surprise. The PAP, like the CCP and the GMD in China, was originally established as a Leninist organization and in a "united front" with the Malaysian Communist Party.[52] Although Lee Kuan Yew quickly turned on the communists, he did not abandon the Leninist organizational framework. Instead, like Mao, Lee attacked his critics in the open and supplanted exiting social organizations with PAP-organized substitutes.

As in the case of China, consultative methods in Singapore have facilitated the "atomization of citizens as political actors and the compartmentalization of their concerns."[53] That this has been possible alongside a considerably stronger base for rule of law—imparted by Singapore's colonial legacy and a staunch commitment to capitalism, albeit under state-led format—speaks to the resilience of a Leninist control architecture. This is, of course, why Deng Xiaoping and his colleagues were so fond of studying and emulating the Singaporean model in the 1980s.[54] In both cases, inclusion and now technology are instrumental to more effective regime control. Yet as the CCP pushes the frontiers of technology-driven control, it is also raising questions about the sustainability of inclusion. As social controls and methods for participation increasingly enter the virtual domain, there is reason to suspect the physical bond between the Party and the people is unlikely to hold.

Establishing inclusive control demands more than information control. Information needs to flow as well, both within the regime as well as between the public and the regime. At least on a qualitative level, a grip on debate, disagreement, and grievance-letting means there less information to control. Xi Jinping and his enablers have fundamentally undermined this flow and thus undercut the CCP's foundation for inclusive control, but Mr. Xi does not define the CCP. As now-exiled former Party School professor Cai Xia explains, it has become near impossible to criticize Xi;[55] but there is still room in China to criticize the Party and, even more so, the state.[56] The ability to differentiate between powerful individuals and powerful institutions is thus a prerequisite for inclusive control, and one that many authoritarian regimes lack. Xi Jinping's tenure risks taking China in that direction as well, and it would be a deep loss for the CCP. But perhaps this regression in China's inclusive authoritarianism reflects more on

---

[52] Lian, "The People's Action Party, 1954–1963."

[53] Rodan, *Participation Without Democracy: Containing Conflict in Southeast Asia*, p. 93.

[54] Ortmann and Thompson, "China's Obsession with Singapore: Learning Authoritarian Modernity."

[55] Pockets of criticism still exist. Most recently, and dramatically, the outspoken real estate tycoon, Ren Zhiqang, called Xi "a clown with no clothes" for his ruthless attacks on free speech and a botched early response to the Covid-19 outbreak. See Javier C. Hernández. "Ren Zhiqiang, a Chinese Tycoon, Denounced Xi Jinping. Now He Faces Prosecution." *New York Times*, July 24, 2020.

[56] RFA. *Interview: "You Can Criticize the CCP, But You Must Not Criticize Xi Jinping"*. 2020.

the insecurity of the man in charge than of the organization that placed him in power. More generally, however, the growing prominence of personalistic authoritarianism[57] represents what I see as a fundamental political barrier for the inclusive type of control explored in this book.

Final Thoughts

One of the things I have learned and internalized over the course of researching this book is that China's leaders are profoundly fortunate to have such willing and critical citizens, and they would do well to engage them further. By all accounts, China's authorities appear intent on tapping into the public pulse, for they recognize the gains from inclusive authoritarianism. In order for these methods to continue bearing fruit, however, Chinese citizens must continue playing an active role. Such active engagement is far from assured unless citizens believe their comments and complaints are taken seriously. How this belief can be nurtured if citizens are reminded on a daily basis, whether it be the surveillance camera at their doorway or the cell phone in their pockets, that they too are subjects and accomplices to state control? Even if such a state control delivers more optimal economic and administrative performance, it is unlikely that the masses will be moved to volunteer their time, attention, and engagement the way they have in the past.

Given the importance the CCP places on understanding and interfacing with the masses, it is unfortunate how little outsiders know about Chinese public opinion—all the more so when juxtaposed with how much information Chinese strategists have about their foreign counterparts' domestic political environments. In the United States, for instance, open networks combined with frequent polling offer a granular and almost instantaneous reading of the American public mood, and with it a gauge of the political atmosphere. This is simply not the case with China, where scholars and casual observers alike are often forced to draw inferences from stories and statements in the tightly controlled press. To be sure, the Chinese media does at times reference the public mood, and careful analysis can be highly productive.[58] Yet, relying on a curated version of public discourse and opinion has its obvious downsides. Unfortunately, barriers to access are difficult to circumvent and unlikely to change.

---

[57] Erica Frantz et al. "Personalization of Power and Repression in Dictatorships." *The Journal of Politics* 82.1 (2020), pp. 372–377.

[58] Richard Baum. *China Watcher: Confessions of a Peking Tom*. University of Washington Press, 2011.

There are other factors, however. In particular, a state-centric approach to studying Chinese politics has, for decades, dominated over societal approaches.[59] Again, this division reflects the difficulty scholars face in accessing and studying the Chinese public. It also underscores how effective the elite-centric approach has been in shedding light on areas such as reform strategy, political competition, and even mass protest.[60] That said, a preoccupation with the state and the elite over that of the public comes with its own limitations. Consider, for instance, our understanding of elite politics in China. While we have some grasp of factions and internal rules for promotion and succession,[61] the public profile of elite politicians is almost missing from the scholarly discussion. As a result, when the Party leader eliminates a constitutional provision on term limits, China watchers rightly see it as a power play that tramples on elite norms for power sharing. Few, however, consider whether such a move enjoys public support.

Again, this is understandable. China is not a democracy, and so perhaps what the public thinks about elite politics is neither here nor there. Focusing solely on elites, however, overlooks important context. Xi Jinping's long-running and broad-reaching anticorruption campaign, for instance, is hard to explain through elite politics alone.[62] Yes, the campaign offered Xi an opportunity to purge rivals, but even critical observers concede that the campaign also acknowledged a paramount public grievance.[63] Another example concerns the 2019 protest movement in Hong Kong. While there were numerous rounds of speculation in the press over when or how Beijing might use military force to quell dissent in the autonomous region, no such move took place. Most observers focused in on the logic behind Beijing's wait-it-out strategy.[64] On the few occasions when public opinion was considered, it focused on Hong Kong residents.[65] But what about the mainland audience? While there is abundant

[59] Marie-Eve Reny. "Authoritarianism as a Research Constraint: Political Scientists in China." *Social Science Quarterly* 97.4 (2016), pp. 909–922.

[60] Susan L. Shirk. *The Political Logic of Economic Reform in China*. University of California Press, 1993, Victor Shih, Christopher Adolph, and Mingxing Liu. "Getting Ahead in the Communist Party: Explaining the Advancement of Central Committee Members in China." *American Political Science Review* 106.1 (2012), pp. 166–187; Weiss, *Powerful Patriots: Nationalist Protest in China's Foreign Relations*.

[61] Victor Shih, Christopher Adolph, and Mingxing Liu. "Getting Ahead in the Communist Party." *American Political Science Review* 106.1 (2012), pp. 166–187; Zhengxu Wang and Anastas Vangeli. "The Rules and Norms of Leadership Succession in China: From Deng Xiaoping to Xi Jinping and Beyond." *The China Journal* 76 (2016), pp. 24–40.

[62] Melanie Manion. "Taking China's Anticorruption Campaign Seriously." *Economic and Political Studies* 4.1 (2016), pp. 3–18.

[63] Pei, *China's Crony Capitalism*.

[64] Robyn Dixon, "What if China Sends Paramilitary Forces to Crush the Hong Kong Protests?" *Los Angeles Times*, August 16, 2019. See: https://lat.ms/2qgWtV2.

[65] Francis L. F. Lee, "Our Research in Hong Kong Reveals What People Really Think." *Independent*, October 16, 2019. See: https://bit.ly/338FAtZ.

speculation that the protests hardened mainland public support *for* the regime and *against* Hong Kong, the matter has received little scholarly attention.

I suspect very few would go as far as to say that public opinion in China does not matter. On the contrary, it is becoming increasingly common to see references to public opinion in discussions of Chinese politics. The problem is that in the absence of reliable and specific metrics on public opinion, it is easy to disregard some aspects of public opinon while overstating others. An incomplete accounting of Chinese public opinion can also be counterproductive. For example, when the US Congressional Executive Commission on China put out its annual report in 2014, stating that the United States "should increase support for Hong Kong's [ongoing "Umbrella"] democracy movement," it simply played into Beijing's narrative that the movement was orchestrated from abroad.[66] A similar concern applies to human rights critiques generally. Public condemnation of China for jailing dissidents is incredibly important, but it also reinforces the CCP's fiction and thus the public perception, that critics are foreign agents. Given China's tight restrictions on information and debate, the official narrative is unfortunately hard to challenge. More broadly, it is unclear how much influence human rights critiques have on the Chinese public, since the CCP has never based its legitimacy on individual rights. Instead, China's leaders carry the soft-authoritarian mantle of good growth and governance.[67] It is therefore on these dimensions where public attention is greatest.

The point here is not to compromise values or principles, but rather to better understand the Chinese domestic audience. Again, we are confronted with the issue of access; and it is only getting worse. Yet while the window on research in China is tightening, it is not closed. Chinese social media platforms harvest tremendous amounts of information, and many have been handing it over quite readily to private polling firms and Chinese academics.[68] The Chinese government is also supporting Chinese social scientists with funding and data access.[69] For US-based researchers, this may mean more small-scale

---

[66] See Congressional-Executive Commission on China, 2014, p.9, available at: https://goo.gl/1HtvWQ.

[67] Zhao, "The Mandate of Heaven and Performance Legitimation in Historical and Contemporary China."

[68] Recent estimates suggest that there are over 800 public opinion monitoring companies in China (public and private), employing over two million analysts, charged with dissecting and reporting public sentiment data to government departments. See Michelle Fong, "China Monitors the Internet and the Public Pays the Bill." *Global Voices*, July 29, 2014, https://goo.gl/N8zZNU.

[69] For examples of Chinese researchers working with social media data, see Xueqi Cheng et al. *Social Media Processing 6th National Conference, SMP 2017, Beijing, China, September 14-17, 2017, Proceedings.* 2017, p. 356.

collaboration with China-based colleagues, but we know that the fruits of such labor are rewarding.[70]

Those who run surveys may need to start asking different questions. Questions concerning trust in government are frequent favorites in Chinese public opinion research for good reason, but the intellectual potential of such broad-reaching concepts is dwindling. Other pressing issues, like nationalism, are less often pursued but rife with disagreement.[71] Perhaps even nationalism is too abstract a concept to study carefully? It may be time to start asking smaller questions, on issues such as immigration, retirement age, childcare, and foreign aid Such questions may not help us predict whether or when the Party could collapse, but they do bring us closer to the Chinese citizens and the issues that animate them. Taking smaller steps will also push researchers to take a more intimate look at Chinese citizens. Shi Tianjian's pioneering work demonstrated as much nearly thirty years ago. Budding research on the attitudes and preferences of Chinese consumers, business leaders, lawyers, and police officers underscores the immense potential of this focus. In short, public opinion research on China is on the rise. That is a good thing.

The surveys and analyses presented in this book are intended collectively to shade in our understanding of why and how the Chinese Communist Party leadership coopts input and opinion from the public, both for practical utility in policymaking and for the credibility and legitimacy of one-party control. It is also my hope that this book will help further the argument for multi-method and multi-perspective research. The surveys, interviews, field experiments, and econometric solutions, when considered independently, have notable short-comings and limitations. Triangulating across different approaches, however, allowed me to build confidence around some core features of the argument, even as the analysis introduced new questions and concerns. The overall empirical picture has led me to conclude that governments can leverage public input and technology in the service of both good governance and authoritarian control. In exploring some of the psychology behind public participation, however, I have also grown pessimistic about the sustainability of inclusive control in the PRC. It may very well end up that, in its quest for control and optimization, the CCP will further distance the people of China from one another and from their government.

---

[70] Consider for instance all the invaluable survey research programs that relied on collaborations with China-based scholars like Shen Mingming.

[71] Alastair Iain Johnston. "Is Chinese Nationalism Rising? Evidence from Beijing." *International Security* 41.3 (2017), pp. 7–43.

Bibliography

"Abolish Petitions Ranking and Let Petitions Go Towards the Rule of Law." (取消信排名，信走向法治). *Beijing News*, 2013.

Alon, Ilan, Matthew Farrell, and Shaomin Li. "Regime Type and COVID-19 Response." *FIIB Business Review* (2020), pp. 152–160.

Ang, Yuen Yuen. *How China Escaped the Poverty Trap*. Cornell University Press, 2016.

Ashforth, Blake E., and Barrie W. Gibbs. "The Double-Edge of Organizational Legitimation." *Organization Science* 1.2 (1990), pp. 177–194.

Austen-Smith, David, and William H. Riker. "Asymmetric Information and the Coherence of Legislation." *American Political Science Review* 81.3 (1987), pp. 897–918.

Backer, Larry Catá, Flora Sapio, and James Korman. "Popular Participation in the Constitution of the Illiberal State—An Empirical Study of Popular Engagement and Constitutional Reform in Cuba and the Contours of Cuban Socialist Democracy 2.0." *Emory International Law Review* 34 (2020), 101–196.

Bai, Jingli. 2012. "Network Supervision and the Power of the Public." Xinhua News Agency, September 22, 2012.

Bak, Joan Lamaysou. *Militants and Citizens: The Politics of Participatory Democracy in Porto Alegre (review)*. Vol. 42. 2. Stanford University Press, 2006, pp. 166–169.

Baker, Scott R., Nicholas Bloom, and Steven J. Davis. "Measuring Economic Policy Uncertainty." *NBER Working Paper* No. w21633. May (2015), pp. 1–75.

Barber, Benjamin. *Strong Democracy: Participatory Politics for a New Age*. University of California Press, 1984.

Baum, Richard. *Burying Mao: Chinese Politics in the Age of Deng Xiaoping*. Princeton University Press, 1996.

Baum, Richard. *China Watcher: Confessions of a Peking Tom*. University of Washington Press, 2011.

Baum, Richard D. "'Red and Expert': The Politico-Ideological Foundations of China's Great Leap Forward." *Asian Survey* (1964), pp. 1048–1057.

Becker, Gary, and George Stigler. "Law Enforcement, Malfeasance, and Compensation of Enforcers." *The Journal of Legal Studies* 3.1 (1974), pp. 1–18.

Bellin, Eva. "Contingent Democrats: Industrialists, Labor, and Democratization in Late-Developing Countries." *World Politics* 52.2 (2000), pp. 175–205.

Bennett, Gordon A. *Yundong: Mass Campaigns in Chinese Communist Leadership*. Center for Chinese Studies, University of California Berkeley, 1976.

Berinsky, Adam J., Gregory A. Huber, and Gabriel S. Lenz. "Evaluating Online Labor Markets for Experimental Research: Amazon.com's Mechanical Turk." *Political Analysis* 20.3 (2012), pp. 351–368.

Berkman, Alexander. *Die Kronstadt Rebellion*. 3. Der Syndikalist Berlin, 1922.

Blaydes, Lisa. *State of Repression: Iraq under Saddam Hussein*. Princeton University Press, 2018.

Blecher, Marc. "Consensual Politics in Rural Chinese Communities: The Mass Line in Theory and Practice." *Modern China* 5.1 (1979), pp. 105–126.

Boix, Carles, and Milan W. Svolik. "The Foundations of Limited Authoritarian Government." *The Journal of Politics* 75.02 (2013), pp. 300–316.

Brandeis, Louis D. "What Publicity Can Do." *Harper's Weekly*, December 20, (1913).

Bristow, Michael. 2010. "China's Democratic 'Window Dressing.'" BBC News, March 5, 2010.

Brodsgaard, Kjeld Erik. "The Democracy Movement in China, 1978–1979: Opposition Movements, Wall Poster Campaigns, and Underground Journals." *Asian Survey* 21.7 (1981), pp. 747–774.

Brown, Archie. *The Gorbachev Factor.* Oxford University Press, 1997.

Brumberg, Daniel. "The Trap of Liberalized Autocracy." *Journal of Democracy* 13.4 (2002), pp. 56–68.

Buchanan, James M., and Gordon Tullock. *The Calculus of Consent: Logical Foundations of Constitutional Democracy.* University of Michigan Press, 1965.

Buck, J. Lossing. "Fact and Theory about China's Land." *Foreign Affairs* 28 (1949), p. 92.

Buckley, Tim, and Simon Nicholas. *China's Global Renewable Energy Expansion.* Tech. rep. Institute for Energy Economy and Financial Analysis, 2017, p. 45.

Burgess, John Stewart. *The Guilds of Peking.* Beijing (China): Columbia University Press, 1928.

Burns, John P. "China's Governance: Political Reform in a Turbulent Environment." *The China Quarterly* 119 (1989), pp. 481–518.

Burns, John P. *The Chinese Communist Party's Nomenklatura System: A Documentary Study of Party Control of Leadership Selection, 1979–1984.* M.E. Sharpe, 1989.

Cabannes, Y., and Z. Ming. "Participatory Budgeting at Scale and Bridging the Rural-Urban Divide in Chengdu." *Environment and Urbanization* 26.1 (2014), pp. 257–275.

Cai, Hongbin, Hanming Fang, and Lixin Colin Xu. "Eat, Drink, Firms, Government: An Investigation of Corruption from the Entertainment and Travel Costs of Chinese Firms." *Journal of Law and Economics* 54. February (2011), pp. 55–78.

Cai, Hongbin, and Daniel Treisman. "Did Government Decentralization Cause China's Economic Miracle?" *World Politics* 58.04 (2006), pp. 505–535.

Cai, Yongshun. "Managed Participation in China." *Political Science Quarterly* 119.3 (2004), pp. 425–451.

Campbell, Donald T. "Assessing the Impact of Planned Social Change." *Evaluation and Program Planning* 2.1 (1979), pp. 67–90.

Campbell, James E. "Cosponsoring Legislation in the U. S. Congress." *Legislative Studies Quarterly* 7.3 (1982), pp. 415–422.

Cao, Yuanzheng, Yingyi Qian, and Barry R. Weingast. "From Federalism, Chinese Style to Privatization, Chinese Style." *The Economics of Transition* 7.1 (1999), pp. 103–131.

Cell, Charles P. *Revolution at Work: Mobilization Campaigns in China.* Academic Press New York, 1977.

C.E. Shannon. "Two-way Communications Channels." *4th Berkeley Symposium on Math. Statistics and Probability*, Chicago, IL (1961), pp. 611–644.

Chang, C.M. "Mao's Stratagem of Land Reform." *Foreign Affairs* 29.4 (1951), pp. 550–563.

Chen, Dan. "Local Distrust and Regime Support." *Political Research Quarterly* 70.2 (2017), pp. 314–326.

Chen, Feng. "Between the State and Labour: The Conflict of Chinese Trade Unions. Double Identity in Market Reform." *The China Quarterly* 176 (2003), pp. 1006–1028.

Chen, Jidong, Jennifer Pan, and Yiqing Xu. "Sources of Authoritarian Responsiveness: A Field Experiment in China." *American Journal of Political Science* 60.2 (2015), pp. 383–400.

Chen, Jidong, and Yiqing Xu. "Why Do Authoritarian Regimes Allow Citizens to Voice Opinions Publicly?" *The Journal of Politics* 79.3 (2017), pp. 792–803.

Chen, Jing. *Useful Complaints: How Petitions Assist Decentralized Authoritarianism in China*. Rowman & Littlefield, 2016.

Chen, Y., et al. "Evidence on the Impact of Sustained Exposure to Air Pollution on Life Expectancy from China's Huai River Policy." *Proceedings of the National Academy of Sciences* 110.32 (2013), pp. 12936–12941.

Chen, Zhi. "Xinhua Insight: Real-Name Whistleblowing Fuels China's Online Anticorruption Efforts." Xinhua News Agency, May 15, 2013.

Cheng, Xueqi, et al. *Social Media Processing 6th National Conference, SMP 2017, Beijing, China, September 14–17, 2017, Proceedings*. Springer, 2017, p. 356.

China Internet Network Information Center (CNNIC), Annual Statistical Survey Report on Internet Development in China (Various Years).

Chiu, Joanna. "Chinese Censors Silence Corruption Blogger." *Committee to Protect Journalists* (2013).

Cho, Young Nam. "Public Supervisors and Reflectors: Role Fulfillment of the Chinese People's Congress Deputies in the Market Socialist Era." *Development and Society* 32.2 (2003), pp. 197–227.

Ch'o-Hsüan, Jen. "The Introduction of Marxism-Leninism into China." *Studies in East European Thought* 10.2 (1970), pp. 138–166.

Cliff, Thomas. "The Partnership of Stability in Xinjiang: State–Society Interactions Following the July 2009 Unrest." *The China Journal* 68 (2012), pp. 79–105.

Clifford, S., R.M. Jewell, and P.D. Waggoner. "Are Samples Drawn from Mechanical Turk Valid for Research on Political Ideology?" *Research & Politics* 2.4 (2015), p. 2053168015622072.

Collier, Ruth Berins, and Stephen Handlin. "Popular Representation in the Interest Arena." *In Reorganizing Popular Politics: Participation and the New Interest Regime in Latin America*. Penn State Press, 2009, pp. 3–31.

Cox, Gary W., and Mathew D. McCubbins. "Political Structure and Economic Policy: The Institutional Determinants of Policy Outcomes." *Presidents, Parliaments and Policy*. Ed. by Stephen Haggard and Mathew D. McCubbins. Cambridge University Press, 2001, pp. 21–63.

Creemers, Rogier. "Cyber China: Upgrading Propaganda, Public Opinion Work and Social Management for the Twenty-First Century." *Journal of Contemporary China* 26.103 (2017), pp. 85–100.

Crisp, Brian F., Kristin Kanthak, and Jenny Leijonhufvud. "The Reputations Legislators Build: With Whom Should Representatives Collaborate?" *American Political Science Review* 98.04 (2004), pp. 703–716.

Dahl, Robert A. *Polyarchy: Participation and Opposition*. Vol. 54. Yale University Press, 1971.

Dahl, Robert Alan. *Polyarchy: Participation and Opposition*. Yale University Press, 1973.

De Mesquita, Bruce Bueno, and Alastair Smith. *The Dictator's Handbook: Why Bad Behavior is Almost Always Good Politics*. PublicAffairs, 2011.

Deibert, Ronald, and Rafal Rohozinski. "Liberation vs. Control: The Future of Cyberspace." *Journal of Democracy* 21.4 (2010), pp. 43–57.

Deng, Xiaoping. "On the Reform of the System of Party and State Leadership." *Selected Works of Deng Xiaoping (1975–1982)*. University Press of the Pacific, 1980, pp. 302–325.

Deng, Yanhua, and Guobin Yang. "Pollution and Protest in China: Environmental Mobilization in Context." *The China Quarterly* 214 (2013), pp. 321–336.

Desposato, Scott W. "Legislative Politics in Authoritarian Brazil." *Legislative Studies Quarterly* 26.2 (2001), pp. 287–317.

Deutscher, Isaac. *Stalin: A Political Biography*. Oxford University Press, 1967.

Diamond, Larry. "The Rule of Law as Transition to Democracy in China." *Journal of Contemporary China* 12.35 (2003), pp. 319–331.

Diamond, Larry. "Liberation Technology." *Journal of Democracy* 21.3 (2010), pp. 69–83.

Diamond, Larry. "The Illusion of Liberal Autocracy." *Journal of Democracy* 14.4 (2003), pp. 167–171.

Dickson, Bruce J. *The Dictator's Dilemma: The Chinese Communist Party's Strategy for Survival*. Oxford University Press, 2016.

Dikotter, Frank. *The Tragedy of Liberation: A History of the Chinese Revolution 1945–1957*. Bloomsbury Publishing USA, 2015.

Dimitrov, Martin K. "The Functions of Letters to the Editor in Reform-Era Cuba." *Latin American Research Review* 54.1 (2019).

Dimitrov, Martin K. "Understanding Communist Collapse and Resilience." *Why Communism Did Not Collapse: Understanding Authoritarian Regime Resilience in Asia and Europe*. Ed. by Martin K. Dimitrov. Cambridge University Press, 2013. Chap. 1.

Dimitrov, Martin K. "Vertical Accountability in Communist Regimes: The Role of Citizen Complaints in Bulgaria." *Why Communism Did Not Collapse: Understanding Authoritarian Regime Resilience in Asia and Europe*. Ed. by Martin K. Dimitrov. Cambridge University Press, 2013, pp. 276–302.

Ding, Iza. "Performative Governance." *World Politics* 72.4 (2020), pp. 525–556.

Dong, Lisheng. "In Search of Direction After Two Decades of Local Democratic Experiments in China." *China Perspectives*, December 2008 (2009).

Dou, Ding. "China's Ambitious Path to Poverty Eradication." *Global Asia* 11.2 (2016), pp. 22–26.

Dryzek, John S. "Legitimacy and Economy in Deliberative Democracy." *Political Theory* 29.5 (2001), pp. 651–669.

Economy, Elizabeth. *The Third Revolution: Xi Jinping and the New Chinese State*. Oxford University Press, 2018.

Enlai, Zhou. "Continue To Exercise Dictatorship and at the Same Time to Broaden Democracy." *Selected Works of Zhou Enlai*. Vol. I. Peking: Foreign Languages Press, 1981, pp. 210–216.

Fearon, James D. "Deliberation as Discussion." *Deliberative Democracy*. Ed. by Jon Elster. Cambridge University Press, 1998. Chap. 3, pp. 44–68.

Fewsmith, Joseph. "Exercising the Power of the Purse? Zeguo Reform." *China Leadership Monitor* 19 (2006).

Fewsmith, Joseph. *Party, State, and Local Elites in Republican China: Merchant Organizations and Politics in Shanghai, 1890–1930*. University of Hawaii Press, 1985.

Fewsmith, Joseph. *The Logic and Limits of Political Reform in China*. Cambridge University Press, 2013.

Fischer, Bill, Umberto Lago, and Fang Liu. *Reinventing Giants: How Chinese Global Competitor Haier Has Changed the Way Big Companies Transform*. John Wiley & Sons, 2013.

Fishkin, James S. *Democracy and Deliberation: New Directions for Democratic Reform.* 1991.

Fishkin, James S. *When the People Speak: Deliberative Democracy and Public Consultation.* Oxford University Press, 2009.

Fishkin, James S., et al. "Deliberative Democracy in an Unlikely Place: Deliberative Polling in China." *British Journal of Political Science* 40.02 (2010), pp. 435–448.

Fitzpatrick, Sheila. "Supplicants and Citizens: Public Letter-Writing in Soviet Russia in the 1930s." *Slavic Review* 55.01 (1996), pp. 78–105.

Frakt, Phyllis M. "Mao's Concept of Representation." *American Journal of Political Science* (1979), pp. 684–704.

Frantz, Erica. *Authoritarianism: What Everyone Needs to Know.* Oxford University Press, 2018.

Frantz, Erica, et al. "Personalization of Power and Repression in Dictatorships." *The Journal of Politics* 82.1 (2020), pp. 372–377.

Fravel, M. Taylor. "Regime Insecurity and International Cooperation: Explaining China's Compromises in Territorial Disputes." *International Security* 30.2 (2005), pp. 46–83.

French, Howard W. "China's New Frontiers: Tests of Democracy and Dissent." *New York Times,* June 19, 2005.

Frynas, Jedrzej George, Michael J. Mol, and Kamel Mellahi. "Management Innovation Made in China: Haier's Rendanheyi." *California Management Review* 61.1 (2018), pp. 71–93.

Fu, Diana, and Greg Distelhorst. "Grassroots Participation and Repression under Hu Jintao and Xi Jinping." *The China Journal* 79 (2018), pp. 100–122.

Fukuyama, Francis. "Asia's Soft-Authoritarian Alternative." *New Perspectives Quarterly* 9.2 (1992), pp. 60–61.

Fukuyama, Francis. "The End of History?" *The National Interest* (1989), pp. 3–18.

Gaines, Brian J., and James H. Kuklinski. "Treatment Effects." *Cambridge Handbook of Experimental Political Science* (2011), pp. 445–458.

Gallagher, Mary E., "Industrial Relations in the World's Workshop: Participatory Legislation, Bottom-Up Law Enforcement, and Firm Behavior." *APSA 2010 Annual Meeting Paper.* 2010.

Gallagher, Mary E., and Baohua Dong. "Legislating Harmony: Labor Law Reform in Contemporary China." *From Iron Rice Bowl to Informalization: Markets, State and Workers in a Changing China.* Ed. by Mary E. Gallagher, Sarosh Kuruvilla, and Ching Kwan Lee. Cornell University Press, 2011, pp. 36–60.

Gallagher, Mary E., and Blake Miller. "Can the Chinese Government Really Control the Internet? We Found Cracks in the Great Firewall." *Washington Post,* February 21, 2017.

Gandhi, Jennifer. *Political Institutions under Dictatorship.* Cambridge University Press, 2008.

Gandhi, Jennifer, and Adam Przeworski. "Authoritarian Institutions and the Survival of Autocrats." *Comparative Political Studies* 40.11 (2007), pp. 1279–1301.

Garland, David. *The Culture of Control: Crime and Social Order in Contemporary Society.* University of Chicago Press, 2012.

Geddes, Barbara. "What Do We Know About Democratization After Twenty Years?" *Annual Review of Political Science* 2.1 (1999), pp. 115–144.

Geddes, Barbara, Joseph Wright, and Erica Frantz. "Autocratic Breakdown and Regime Transitions: A New Data Set." *Perspectives on Politics* 12.2 (2014), pp. 313–331.

Geddes, Barbara, et al. *How Dictatorships Work: Power, Personalization, and Collapse.* Cambridge University Press, 2018.

Gerovitch, Slava. *From Newspeak to Cyberspeak: A History of Soviet Cybernetics.* MIT Press, 2004.

Gerovitch, Slava. "InterNyet: Why the Soviet Union Did Not Build a Nationwide Computer Network." *History and Technology* 24.4 (2008), pp. 335–350.

Getty, J. Arch. "Pragmatists and Puritans. The Rise and Fall of the Party Control Commission." *The Carl Beck Papers in Russian and East European Studies* 1208 (1997), p. 47.

Gilens, Martin, and Benjamin I. Page. "Testing Theories of American Politics: Elites, Interest Groups, and Average Citizens." *Perspectives on Politics* 12.03 (2014), pp. 564–581.

Gilley, Bruce. *China's Democratic Future: How It Will Happen and Where It Will Lead.* Columbia University Press, 2004.

Gong, Ting. "Dangerous Collusion: Corruption as a Collective Venture in Contemporary China." *Communist and Post-Communist Studies* 35.1 (2002), pp. 85–103.

Granick, David. *The Red Executive.* MacMillan & Co., 1960.

Greitens, Sheena Chestnut. *Dictators and Their Secret Police: Coercive Institutions and State Violence.* Cambridge University Press, 2016.

Groot, Gerry. "Managing Transitions: The Chinese Communist Party's United Front Work, Minor Parties and Groups, Hegemony and Corporatism." PhD thesis. 1997.

Gruning, James E., and Todd T. Hunt. *Managing Public Relations.* Holt, Rinehart and Winston, 1984.

Gueorguiev, Dimitar D. "Beyond Peaceful Evolution: Chinese Domestic Politics and U.S. Foreign Policy." *United States Relations with China and Iran: Towards the Asian Century.* Ed. by Osamah F. Khalil. Bloomsbury Academic Press, 2019, pp. 39–58.

Gueorguiev, Dimitar D. "Dictator's Shadow: Chinese Elite Politics Under Xi Jinping." *China Perspectives* 1.2 (2018), pp. 17–26.

Gueorguiev, Dimitar D., and Edmund J. Malesky. "Consultation and Selective Censorship in China." *Journal of Politics* (2019).

Gueorguiev, Dimitar D., and Paul J. Schuler. "Collective Charisma: Elite–Mass Relations in China and Vietnam." *Problems of Post-Communism* (2020), pp. 1–12.

Gueorguiev, Dimitar D., and Paul J. Schuler. "Keeping Your Head Down: Public Profiles and Promotion Under Autocracy." *Journal of East Asian Studies* 16.01 (2016), pp. 87–116.

Guo, Gang "China's Local Political Budget Cycles." *American Journal of Political Science* 53.3 (2009), pp. 621–32.

Hamel, Gary, and Michele Zanini. "The End of Bureaucracy." *Harvard Buisness Review* (2018), pp. 3–11.

Hannah, Gayle Durham. *Soviet Information Networks.* Center for Strategic and International Studies, Georgetown University, 1977.

Hanson, Lisa. "The Chinese Internet Gets A Stronger Backbone." *Forbes* (2015).

Hao, Yazhou, and Yong Hu. *Haier Purpose: The Real Story of China's First Global Super-Company.* 2017.

Harding, Harry. "Maoist Theories of Policy-Making and Organization." In *The Cultural Revolution in China* (1971), pp. 130–134.

Harding, Harry. *Organizing China: The Problem of Bureaucracy, 1949-1976.* Stanford University Press, 1981.

He, Baogang. "Civic Engagement through Participatory Budgeting in China: Three Different Logics at Work." *Public Administration and Development* 31.2 (2011), pp. 122–133.

He, Baogang. "Deliberative Culture and Politics: The Persistence of Authoritarian Deliberation in China." *Political Theory* 42.1 (2014), pp. 58–81.

He, Baogang, and Mark E. Warren. "Authoritarian Deliberation: The Deliberative Turn in Chinese Political Development." *Perspectives on Politics* 9.02 (2011), pp. 269–289.

He, Junzhi. "Independent Candidates in China's Local People's Congresses: A Typology." *Journal of Contemporary China* 19.64 (2010), pp. 311–333.

Heilmann, Sebastian. "Maximum Tinkering under Uncertainty: Unorthodox Lessons from China." *Modern China* 35.4 (2009), pp. 450–462.

Heilmann, Sebastian. "Policy Experimentation in China's Economic Rise." *Studies in Comparative International Development* 43.1 (2008), pp. 1–26.

Hellman, Joel S. "Winners Take All: The Politics of Partial Reform in Postcommunist Transitions." *World Politics* 50.2 (1998), pp. 203–234.

Hernández, Javier C. "Ren Zhiqiang, a Chinese Tycoon, Denounced Xi Jinping. Now He Faces Prosecution." *New York Times*, July 24, 2020.

Heurlin, Christopher. *Responsive Authoritarianism in China*. Cambridge University Press, 2016.

Hill, Robert G. Jr., Lynn Marie Sears, and Scott W. Melanson. "4000 Clicks: A Productivity Analysis of Electronic Medical Records in a Community Hospital ED." *The American Journal of Emergency Medicine* 31.11 (2013), pp. 1591–1594.

Hinnebusch, Raymond. "Syria: From 'Authoritarian Upgrading' to Revolution?" *International Affairs* 88.1 (2012), pp. 95–113.

Hirschman, Albert O. *Exit, Voice, and Loyalty: Responses to Decline in Firms, Organizations, and States*. Vol. 25. Harvard University Press, 1970.

Hobson, L.T. "Preface." In *Village and Town Life in China*. Ed. by Y.K. Leong and L.K. Tao. London: George Allen & Unwin, 1915, p. 14.

Hoffman, Samantha. "Programming China." *China Monitor* (2017).

Hornby, Lucy. "China Blocks $4bn Xiaonanhai Dam Development." *Financial Times*, April 8, 2015.

Hornsby, Robert. *Protest, Reform and Repression in Khrushchev's Soviet Union*. Cambridge University Press, 2013.

Horsley, Jamie P. "China Adopts First Nationwide Open Government Information Regulations." *Freedominfo.org* (Online) (2007), pp. 1–13.

Horsley, Jamie P. "Public Participation in the People's Republic: Developing a More Participatory Governance Model in China." *Yale China Law Center* September (2009), pp. 1–19.

Hough, Jerry F., and Merle Fainsod. *How the Soviet Union is Governed*. Harvard University Press, 1979.

Hu, Yong, and Hao Yazhou. *Haier Purpose: The Real Story of China's First Global Super Company*. Infinite Ideas, 2017.

Hu, Baohua. *A Study of the Supervising System under the Tang Dynasty* (唐代监察制度研究). Beijing: Shangwu Publishers, 2005.

Hua, Gao. *Hong taiyang shi zenyang shengqi de—Yan'an zhengfeng yundong de lailong qumai* (How the Red Sun Rose: The History of the Yan'an Rectification Campaign). Chinese University of Hong Kong Press, 2000.

Huang, Yasheng. "Central-Local Relations in China during the Reform Era: The Economic and Institutional Dimensions." *World Development* 24.4 (1996), pp. 655–672.

Huntington, Samuel. *Political Order in Changing Societies*. Vol. 76. 5. Yale University Press, 1968.

Huntington, Samuel P. *The Third Wave: Democratization in the Late Twentieth Century*. University of Oklahoma Press, 1991.

Hurst, William. *Ruling Before the Law*. Cambridge University Press, 2018.

Hurst, William. *The Chinese Worker after Socialism*. Cambridge University Press, 2009.

Jensen, Michael C., and William H. Meckling. "Theory of the Firm: Managerial Behavior, Agency Costs and Ownership Structure." *Journal of Financial Economics* 3.4 (1976), pp. 305–360.

Johnston, Alastair Iain. "Is Chinese Nationalism Rising? Evidence from Beijing." *International Security* 41.3 (2017), pp. 7–43.

Jones, Bryan D., and Michelle C. Whyman. "Lawmaking and Agenda Setting in the United States, 1948–2010." *Agenda Setting, Policies, and Political Systems. A Comparative Approach* (2014), pp. 36–52.

Kalathil, Shanthi, and Taylor C. Boas. *Open Networks, Closed Regimes: The Impact of the Internet on Authoritarian Rule*. Carnegie Endowment, 2003.

Kalyvas, Stathis N. "The Decay and Breakdown of Communist One-Party Systems." *Annual Review of Political Science* 2.1 (1999), pp. 323–343.

Kamo, Tomoki, and Hiroki Takeuchi. "Representation and Local People's Congresses in China: A Case Study of the Yangzhou Municipal People's Congress." *Journal of Chinese Political Science* 18.1 (2013), pp. 41–60.

Karatnycky, Adrian. "Ukraine's Orange Revolution." *Foreign Affairs*, March/April (2005).

Kennedy, John James. "From the Tax-for-Fee Reform to the Abolition of Agricultural Taxes: The Impact on Township Governments in North-west China." *The China Quarterly* 189.1 (2007), pp. 43–59.

Kessler, Daniel, and Keith Krehbiel. "Dynamics of Cosponsorship." *The American Political Science Review* 90.3 (1996), pp. 555–566.

Khan, Sulmaan Wasif. *Haunted by Chaos: China's Grand Strategy from Mao Zedong to Xi Jinping*. Harvard University Press, 2018.

Kim, Ilpyong J., et al. *The Politics of Chinese Communism: Kiangsi under the Soviets*. Vol. 12. University of California Press, 1973.

Kim, W. Chan, and Renee Mauborgne. "Parables of Leadership." *Harvard Business Review* (1992).

King, Cheryl Simrell, Kathryn M. Feltey, and Bridget O'Neill Susel. "The Question of Participation: Toward Authentic Public Participation in Public Administration." *Public Administration Review* 58.4 (1998), pp. 317–326.

King, Gary, Jennifer Pan, and Margaret E. Roberts. "How Censorship in China Allows Government Criticism but Silences Collective Expression." *American Political Science Review* 107.02 (2013), pp. 326–343.

Kittur, Aniket, Ed H. Chi, and Bongwon Suh. "Crowdsourcing User Studies with Mechanical Turk." *Proceedings of the 2008 SIGCHI Conference on Human Factors in Computing Systems* (2008), pp. 453–456.

Kizzier-Carnahan, Vanessa et al. "Frequency of Passive EHR Alerts in the ICU: Another form of Alert Fatigue?" *Journal of Patient Safety* 15.3 (2019), p. 246.

Klitgaard, Robert. *Controlling Corruption*. Berkeley: University of California Press, 1988.

Knutsen, Carl Henrik, Håvard Mokleiv Nygård, and Tore Wig. "Autocratic Elections: Stabilizing Tool or Force for Change?" *World Politics* 69.1 (2017), pp. 98–143.

Koss, Daniel. *Where the Party Rules: The Rank and File of China's Communist State.* Cambridge University Press, 2018.

Kostka, Genia. "China's social credit systems and public opinion: Explaining high levels of approval." *New Media & Society* 21.7 (2019): 1565–1593.

Kotkin, Stephen. *Stalin: Paradoxes of Power 1878–1928.* Penguin Books, 2014.

Kraus, Richard Curt. "Class Conflict and the Vocabulary of Social Analysis in China." *The China Quarterly* 69 (1977), pp. 54–74.

Kung, James, and Shuo Chen. "The Tragedy of the Nomenklatura: Career Incentives and Political Radicalism During China's Great Leap Famine." *American Political Science Review* 105.01 (2011), pp. 27–45.

Kuran, Timur. "Now Out of Never: The Element of Surprise in the East European Revolution of 1989." *World Politics* 44.01 (1991), pp. 7–48.

Lai, Hairong. "Semi-Competitive Elections at Township Level in Sichuan Province." *China Perspectives* 51.51 (2004), pp. 1–21.

Lam, Willy. "The Maoist Revival and the Conservative Turn in Chinese Politics." *China Perspectives* 2012.2012/2 (2012), pp. 5–15.

Landry, Pierre F., Deborah Davis, and Shiru Wang. "Elections in Rural China: Competition Without Parties." *Comparative Political Studies* 43.6 (2010), pp. 763–790.

Lankov, Andrei. *The Real North Korea: Life and Politics in the Failed Stalinist Utopia.* Oxford University Press, 2013.

Hairong, Lai. "Semi-Competitive Elections at Township Level in Sichuan Province." *China Perspectives* 51.51 (2004), pp. 1–21.

Lau, Lawrence J., Yingyi Qian, and Gerard Roland. "Reform Without Losers: An Interpretation of China's Dual-Track Approach to Transition." *Journal of Political Economy* 108.1 (2000), p. 120.

Lax, Jeffrey R., and Justin H. Phillips. "The Democratic Deficit in the States." *American Journal of Political Science* 56.1 (2012), pp. 148–166.

Lee, Ching Kwan. *Against the Law: Labor Protests in China's Rustbelt and Sunbelt.* University of California Press, 2007.

Lee, Ching Kwan, and Yonghong Zhang. "The Power of Instability: Unraveling the Microfoundations of Bargained Authoritarianism in China." *American Journal of Sociology* 118.6 (2013), pp. 1475–1508.

Lelkes, Yphtach. "Mass Polarization: Manifestations and Measurements." *Public Opinion Quarterly* 80.S1 (2016), pp. 392–410.

Lenin, Vladimir Ilyich. *"Left-wing" Communism: An Infantile Disorder.* The Marxian Educational Society, 1921.

Lenz, Gabriel S. *Follow the Leader?: How Voters Respond to Politicians' Policies and Performance.* Chicago: University of Chicago Press, 2012.

Leung, Parry, and Alvin YC So. "The New Labor Contract Law in 2008: China's Legal Absorption of Labor Unrest." *Journal of Studies in Social Sciences* 4.1 (2013): 131–161.

Levitsky, Steven and Lucan Way. "The Rise of Competitive Authoritarianism." *Journal of Democracy* 13.2 (2002), pp. 51–65.

Li, He. "The Chinese Discourse on Good Governance: Content and Implications." *Journal of Contemporary China* (2020), pp. 1–14.

Li, Lianjiang. "Reassessing Trust in the Central Government: Evidence from Five National Surveys." *The China Quarterly* 225 (2016), pp. 100–121.

Li, Shenming. *Preparing for Danger in Times of Safety: Recollections on the 20-Year Anniversary of the Collapse of the Russian Communist Party* (居安思危:苏共亡党二

十年的思考, *Ju an siwei: Sulian wang dang ershi nian de sikao*). Chinese Academy of Social Sciences Press, 2011.

Li, Shi, Terry Sicular, and Hiroshi Sato. *Rising Inequality in China: Challenges to a Harmonious Society*. Cambridge University Press, 2013.

Li, Shi, Terry Sicular, Finn Tarp, et al. *Inequality in China: Development, Transition, and Policy*. Tech. rep. World Institute for Development Economic Research (UNUWIDER), 2018.

Li Shi-nung, "The Bourgeoisie and Peasantry as Reserves of the Chinese Communist Party," 1950. Cited in CM Chang. "Mao's Stratagem of Land Reform." *Foreign Affairs* 29.4 [1951], pp. 550–563.

Li, Terry H.Y., S. Thomas Ng, and Martin Skitmore. "Public Participation in Infrastructure and Construction Projects in China: From an EIA-based to a Whole-Cycle Process." *Habitat International* 36.1 (2012), pp. 47–56.

Li, Xiaoying, and Richard B. Freeman. "How Does China's New Labour Contract Law Affect Floating Workers?" *British Journal of Industrial Relations* (2014), pp. 1–25.

Lian, Pang Cheng. "The People's Action Party, 1954–1963." *Journal of Southeast Asian History* 10.1 (1969), pp. 142–154.

Liao, Xingmiu, Wen-Hsuan Tsai, and Zheng-Wei Lin. "Penetrating the Grassroots: First-Secretaries-in-Residence and Rural Politics in Contemporary China." *Problems of Post-Communism* 67.2 (2020), pp. 169–179.

Lindblom, Charles E. "The Science of 'Muddling Through.'" *Public Administration Review* 19.2 (1959), pp. 79–88.

Linebarger, Paul Myron Anthony. *The China of Chiang K'ai-shek*. Boston: World Peace Foundation, 1943.

Link, Perry. "China: The Anaconda in the Chandelier." *The New York Review of Books*, April, 2002.

Linz, Juan J., and Alfred C. Stepan. "Toward Consolidated Democracies." *Journal of Democracy* 7.2 (1996), pp. 14–33.

Liu, Hin-Yan. "Mercenaries in Libya: Ramifications of the Treatment of 'Armed Mercenary Personnel' under the Arms Embargo for Private Military Company Contractors." *Journal of Conflict & Security Law* 16.2 (2011), pp. 293–319.

Liu, Ling. *China's Industrial Policies and the Global Business Revolution: The Case of the Domestic Appliance Industry*. Routledge, 2005.

Liu, Xuming. "网络监督在反腐败中的作用研究 (Research on the Role of Network Supervision in Anticorruption)." PhD thesis. The Central Party School, 2012.

Lorentzen, Peter. "Designing Contentious Politics in Post-1989 China." *Modern China* 43.5 (2017), pp. 459–493.

Lorentzen, Peter L. "Regularizing Rioting: Permitting Public Protest in an Authoritarian Regime." *Quarterly Journal of Political Science* 8.2 (2013), pp. 127–158.

Lorentzen, Peter L., Pierre Landry, and John Yasuda. "Undermining Authoritarian Innovation: The Power of China's Industrial Giants." *The Journal of Politics* 76.01 (2013), pp. 182–194.

Lu, Xiaobo. "Booty Socialism, Bureau-Preneurs, and the State in Transition: Organizational Corruption in China." *Comparative Politics* 32.3 (2000), pp. 273–294.

Lu, Xiaobo. *Cadres and Corruption: The Organizational Involution of the Chinese Communist Party*. Stanford University Press, 2000.

Lubbers, Jeffrey S. "Notice-and-Comment Rulemaking Comes to China." *Administrative and Regulatory Law News* 32.1 (2006), pp. 5–6.

Luehrmann, Laura M. "Facing Citizen Complaints in China, 1951–1996." *Asian Survey* 43.5 (2003), pp. 845–866.

Ma, Damien. "Beijing's "Culture War Isn't About the US—It's About China's Future." *The Atlantic* 5, January 5, 2012.

Ma, Jun. "The Dilemma of Developing Financial Accountability without Election—A Study of China's Recent Budget Reforms." *Australian Journal of Public Administration* 68 (2009), S62–S72.

Maccoby, Eleanor E., and Nathan Maccoby. "The Interview: A Tool of Social Science." *Handbook of Social Psychology: Vol. 1*. 1954, pp. 449–487.

MacFarquhar, Roderick. *The Hundred Flowers Campaign and the Chinese Intellectuals*. Praeger, 1966.

Magaloni, Beatriz. "The Game of Electoral Fraud and the Ousting of Authoritarian Rule." *American Journal of Political Science* 54.3 (2010), pp. 751–765.

Malesky, Edmund. "The Single-Party Dictator's Dilemma: Information in Elections Without Opposition." *Legislative Studies Quarterly* 36.4 (2011), pp. 491–530.

Malesky, Edmund. "Vietnam in 2013: Single-Party Politics in the Internet Age." *Asian Survey* 54.1 (2014), pp. 30–38.

Malesky, Edmund, and Paul Schuler. "Nodding or Needling: Analyzing Delegate Responsiveness in an Authoritarian Parliament." *American Political Science Review* 104.03 (2010), pp. 482–502.

Malinovsky, Boris, Anne Fitzpatrick, and Emmanuel Aronie. "Pioneers of Soviet Computing." Edited by Anne Fitzpatrick. Translated by Emmanuel Aronie. Np: published electronically (2010).

Mamdani, Mahmood. *Citizen and Subject: Contemporary Africa and the Legacy of Late Colonialism*. Princeton University Press, 1996.

Manin, Bernard, Adam Przeworski, and Susan C. Stokes. *Democracy, Accountability, and Representation*. Cambridge University Press, 1999.

Manion, Melanie. "Authoritarian Parochialism: Local Congressional Representation in China." *The China Quarterly* 218 (2014), pp. 311–338.

Manion, Melanie. *Information for Autocrats: Representation in Chinese Local Congresses*. Cambridge University Press, 2016.

Manion, Melanie. *Retirement of Revolutionaries in China: Public Policies, Social Norms, Private Interests*. Princeton University Press, 1993.

Manion, Melanie. "Taking China's Anticorruption Campaign Seriously." *Economic and Political Studies* 4.1 (2016), pp. 3–18.

Manion, Melanie. "When Communist Party Candidates Can Lose, Who Wins? Assessing the Role of Local People's Congresses in the Selection of Leaders in China." *The China Quarterly* 195 (2008), pp. 607–630.

Marquetti, A., C.E. Schonerwald da Silva, and A. Campbell. "Participatory Economic Democracy in Action: Participatory Budgeting in Porto Alegre, 1989–2004." *Review of Radical Political Economics* 44.1 (2012), pp. 62–81.

Marquis, Christopher, and Yanhua Bird. "The Paradox of Responsive Authoritarianism: How Civic Activism Spurs Environmental Penalties in China." *Organization Science* 29.5 (2018), pp. 948–968.

Mattingly, Daniel C. *The Art of Political Control in China*. Cambridge University Press, 2019.

McCrary, Justin. "Manipulation of the Running Variable in the Regression Discontinuity Design: A Density Test." *Journal of Econometrics* 142.2 (2008), pp. 698–714.

McCubbins, Mathew D., and Thomas Schwartz. "Congressional Oversight Overlooked: Police Patrols versus Fire Alarms." *American Journal of Political Science* 28.1 (1984), pp. 165–179.

McCulloch, Warren S. "A Heterarchy of Values Determined by the Topology of Nervous Nets." *The Bulletin of Mathematical Biophysics* 7.2 (1945), pp. 89–93.

Means, Gordon Paul. "Soft Authoritarianism in Malaysia and Singapore." *Journal of Democracy* 7.4 (1996), pp. 103–117.

Meisner, Mitch. "Dazhai: The Mass Line in Practice." *Modern China* 4.1 (1978), pp. 27–62.

Meng, Tianguang, Jennifer Pan, and Ping Yang. "Conditional Receptivity to Citizen Participation: Evidence from a Survey Experiment in China." *Comparative Political Studies* 50.4 (2014), pp. 399–433.

Mill, John Stuart. *Considerations on Representative Government* (1861). Henry Holt and Co., 1873.

Miller, Blake. "The Limits of Commercialized Censorship in China." SocArXiv, 2019. Web.

Minzner, Carl. F. *End of an Era: How China's Authoritarian Revival is Undermining Its Rise*. Oxford University Press, 2018.

Minzner, Carl F. "Xinfang: An Alternative to Formal Chinese Legal Institutions." *Stanford Journal of International Law* 42 (2006), p. 103.

Monas, Sidney. "The Political Police: The Dream of a Beautiful Autocracy." In *Transformation of Russian Society: Aspects of Social Change Since 1861*. Ed. by Cyril Black. Harvard University Press, pp. 164–190.

Mu, Xuequan. 2008. "China's State Council to Use Internet for Public Opinion." *China Daily*, February 22, 2008.

Mu, Yifei, and Yimin Chen. *Democratic Consultation: Creation of the People of Wenling (Minzhu Kentan: Wenling Ren de Chuangzao)*. Beijing: Central Translation and Compilation Press, 2005.

Murthy, Viren. "The Democratic Potential of Confucian Minben Thought." *Asian Philosophy* 10.1 (2000), pp. 33–47.

Nathan, Andrew J. "China's Changing of the Guard: Authoritarian Resilience." *Journal of Democracy* 14.1 (2003), pp. 6–17.

Naughton, Barry. *Growing Out of the Plan: Chinese Economic Reform, 1978–1993*. Cambridge University Press, 1996.

Neuweld, Mark. "The Origin of the Communist Control Commission." *American Slavic and East European Review* 18.3 (1959), pp. 315–333.

Niou, Emerson. *Bean Voting: The History and Politics of Secret Ballot*. Beijing: People's University Press, 2014.

North, Douglass C. *Institutions, Institutional Change, and Economic Performance*. Cambridge University Press, 1990.

O'Brien, Kevin J. "Chinese People's Congresses and Legislative Embeddedness: Understanding Early Organizational Development." *Comparative Political Studies* 27.1 (1994), pp. 80–107.

O'Brien, Kevin J., and Lianjiang Li. "Accommodating 'Democracy' in a One-Party State: Introducing Village Elections in China." *The China Quarterly* 162.162 (2000), pp. 465–489.

O'Brien, Kevin J., and Laura M. Luehrmann. "Institutionalizing Chinese Legislatures: Trade-Offs Between Autonomy and Capacity." *Legislative Studies Quarterly* 23.1 (1998), pp. 91–108.

O'Donnell, Guillermo and Phillipe Schmitter. "Tentative Conclusions About Uncertain Democracies." *Transitions from Authoritarian Rule: Prospects for Democracy.* Johns Hopkins University Press, 1986.

Oksenberg, Michel, and James Tong. "The Evolution of Central–Provincial Fiscal Relations in China, 1971–1984: The Formal System." *The China Quarterly* 125 (1991), pp. 1–32.

Oldendick, Robert, et al. "A Comparison of the Kish and Last Birthday Methods of Respondent Selection in Telephone Surveys." *Journal of Official Statistics* 4.4 (1988), pp. 307–318.

Ong, Russell. "'Peaceful Evolution', 'Regime Change' and China's Political Security." *Journal of Contemporary China* 16.53 (2007), pp. 717–727.

Ortmann, Stephan, and Mark R. Thompson. "China's Obsession with Singapore: Learning Authoritarian Modernity." *The Pacific Review* 27.3 (2014), pp. 433–455.

Osnos, Evan. *Age of Ambition: Chasing Fortune, Truth, and Faith in the New China.* Macmillan, 2014.

Page, Benjamin I., and Robert Y. Shapiro. "Effects of Public Opinion on Policy." *American Political Science Review* 77.1 (1983), pp. 175–190.

Pan, Wei. "Toward a Consultative Rule of Law Regime in China." *Journal of Contemporary China* 12.34 (2003), pp. 3–43.

Park, Albert, et al. "Distributional Consequences of Reforming Local Public Finance in China." *The China Quarterly* 147 (1996), pp. 751–778.

Pei, Minxin. "China's Coming Upheaval: Competition, the Coronavirus, and the Weakness of Xi Jinping." *Foreign Affairs* 99 (2020), pp. 82–95.

Pei, Minxin. *China's Crony Capitalism: The Dynamics of Regime Decay.* Harvard University Press, 2016.

Pei, Minxin. *China's Trapped Transition: The Limits of Developmental Autocracy.* Harvard University Press, 2006.

Pei, Minxin. "Citizens vs. Mandarins: Administrative Litigation in China." *The China Quarterly* 152.152 (1997), pp. 832–862.

Pepinsky, Thomas. "The Institutional Turn in Comparative Authoritarianism." *British Journal of Political Science* (2014), pp. 631–653.

Perry, Elizabeth J. "Challenging the Mandate of Heaven: Popular Protest in Modern China." *Critical Asian Studies* 33.2 (2001), pp. 163–180.

Perry, Elizabeth J. "From Mass Campaigns to Managed Campaigns." *Mao's Invisible Hand: The Political Foundations of Adaptive Governance in China.* Ed. by Elizabeth J. Perry and Sebastian Heilmann. Harvard University Press, 2011, Chap. 2, pp. 30–61.

Peters, Benjamin. *How Not to Network a Nation: The Uneasy History of the Soviet Internet.* MIT Press, 2016.

Peters, Philip. "A Viewer's Guide to Cuba's Economic Reform." Lexington Institute, Washington DC, May (2012).

Piao, Vanessa. 2015. "China Lets Citizens' Fingers Do the Talking to Report Graft." *New York Times*, June 19, 2015.

Pieke, Frank N. "Party Spirit: Producing a Communist Civil Religion in Contemporary China." *Journal of the Royal Anthropological Institute* 24.4 (2018), pp. 709–729.

Png, Poh-seng. "The Kuomintang in Malaya, 1912–1941." *Journal of Southeast Asian History* 2.1 (1961), pp. 1–32.

Pringle, Tim. "Industrial Relations in the People's Republic of China." *Trade Unions in China: The Challenge of Labour Unrest.* Taylor & Francis, 2011, pp. 11–56.

Prior, Markus. *Hooked: How Politics Captures People's Interest.* Cambridge University Press, 2018.

Przeworski, Adam. *Democracy and the Market: Political and Economic Reforms in Eastern Europe and Latin America.* Cambridge University Press, 1991.

Putnam, Robert. "Bowling Alone: America's Declining Social Capital." *Journal of Democracy* 6.1 (1995), pp. 65–78.

Quade, Elizabeth A. "The Logic of Anticorruption Enforcement Campaigns in Contemporary China." *Journal of Contemporary China* 16.50 (2007), pp. 65–77.

Quinlivan, James T. "Coup-Proofing: Its Practice and Consequences in the Middle East." *International Security* 24.2 (1999), pp. 131–165.

Radio Free Asia. "You Can Criticize the CCP, But You Must Not Criticize Xi Jinping.'" Interview, August 18, 2020.

Reilly, James. *Strong Society, Smart State: The Rise of Public Opinion in China's Japan Policy.* Columbia University Press, 2011.

Reny, Marie-Eve. *Authoritarian Containment: Public Security Bureaus and Protestant House Churches in Urban China.* Oxford University Press, 2018.

Reny, Marie-Eve. "Authoritarianism as a Research Constraint: Political Scientists in China." *Social Science Quarterly* 97.4 (2016), pp. 909–922.

Riker, William H., and Peter C. Ordeshook. "A General Theory of the Calculus of Voting." *American Political Science Review* 62.1 (1972), pp. 32–78.

Roberts, Margaret E. *Censored: Distraction and Diversion Inside China's Great Firewall.* Princeton University Press, 2018.

Rodan, Garry. *Participation Without Democracy: Containing Conflict in Southeast Asia.* Cornell University Press, 2018.

Roeder, Philip G. "Modernization and Participation in the Leninist Developmental Strategy." *American Political Science Review* 83.3 (1989), pp. 859–884.

Roessler, Philip. "The Enemy Within: Personal Rule, Coups, and Civil War in Africa." *World Politics* 63.2 (2011), pp. 300–346.

Rose-Ackerman, Susan. *Corruption: A Study in Political Economy.* Academic Press, 1978.

Rourke, Francis Edward. *Bureaucracy, Politics, and Public Policy.* Little, Brown, 1969, p. 173.

Roy, Denny. "Singapore, China, and the 'Soft Authoritarian' Challenge." *Asian Survey* 34.3 (1994), pp. 231–242.

Ruscio, Kenneth P. "Trust, Democracy, and Public Management: A Theoretical Argument." *Journal of Public Administration Research and Theory* 6.3 (1996), pp. 461–477.

Saich, Tony. *Governance and Politics of China.* Macmillan International Higher Education, 2010.

Schaberg, David. "Playing at Critique: Indirect Remonstrance and the Formation of Shi Identity." In *Text and Ritual in Early China.* Ed. by Martin Kern. University of Washington Press, 2005, pp. 194–218.

Schapiro, Leonard. "'Putting the Lid on Leninism': Opposition and Dissent in the Communist One-party States." *Government and Opposition* 2.2 (1967), pp. 181–203.

Scharpf, Fritz. *Governing in Europe: Effective and Democratic?* Oxford University Press, 1999.

Schatz, Edward. "The Soft Authoritarian Tool Kit: Agenda-Setting Power in Kazakhstan and Kyrgyzstan." *Comparative Politics* 41.2 (2009), pp. 203–222.

Schedler, Andreas. "The Logic of Electoral Authoritarianism." *In Electoral Authoritarianism: The Dynamics of Unfree Competition*. Ed. by Andreas Schedler. Lynne Rienner, 2006. Chap. 1, pp. 1–23.

Schmidt, Vivien A. "Democracy and Legitimacy in the European Union Revisited: Input, Output and 'Throughput.'" *Political Studies* 61.1 (2013), pp. 2 22.

Schoenhals, Michael. *Spying for the People: Mao's Secret Agents, 1949–1967*. Cambridge University Press, 2013.

Schram, Stuart R. *The Political Thought of Mao Tse-tung*. Praeger, 1969.

Schuler, Paul J., Dimitar D. Gueorguiev, and Francisco Cantu. "Risk and Reward: The Differential Impact of Authoritarian Elections on Regime Decay and Breakdown." *SSRN Electronic Journal* (2013), pp. 1–46.

Schulte, Fred and Erika Fry. "Death by 1,000 Clicks: Where Electronic Health Records Went Wrong." *Kaiser Health News* 18 (2019).

Schurmann, Franz. *Ideology and Organization in Communist China*. University of California Press, 1966.

Schwartz, Thomas. "Vote Trading and Pareto Efficiency." *Public Choice* 24.1 (1975), pp. 101–109.

Scott, James C. *Seeing Like a State: How Certain Schemes to Improve the Human Condition Have Failed*. Yale University Press, 1998.

Selden, Mark. *China in Revolution: Yenan Way Revisited*. Routledge, 2016.

Sen, Amartya Kumar. "Democracy as a Universal Value." *Journal of Democracy* 10.3 (1999), pp. 3–17.

Shambaugh, David L., "The Coming Chinese Crackup." *Wall Street Journal*, March 6, 2015, p. 382.

Shambaugh, David L. "Training China's Political Elite: The Party School System." *The China Quarterly* 196 (2008), pp. 827–844.

Shambaugh, David L. *China's Communist Party: Atrophy and Adaptation*. University of California Press, 2008.

Shearer, David R. *Policing Stalin's Socialism: Repression and Social Order in the Soviet Union, 1924–1953*. Yale University Press, 2014.

Sheng, Huaren, "县乡人大换届面临问题,须坚持三大原" (The Term Change of the County and Township People's Congresses Faces New Problems and Three Major Principles Must Be Adhered To). *Seeking Truth*. August 30, 2006.

Sheng, Yap Kioe. "Good Urban Governance in Southeast Asia." *Environment and Urbanization ASIA* 1(2), 2000, pp. 131–147. Bangkok, 2010.

Shi, Tianjian. *Political Participation in Beijing*. Harvard University Press. 1997.

Shi, Tianjian, and Jie Lu. "The Meanings of Democracy: The Shadow of Confucianism." *Journal of Democracy* 21.4 (2010), pp. 123–130.

Shi, Weimin. "The Development of Grassroots Democratic Elections in China." *Social Sciences in China* 25.1 (2004), pp. 113–125.

Shi, Weimin and Liu Zhi. 2004. "*Jianjie xuanju* (Indirect Elections)," Vol. 2 (Beijing: Zhongguo shehui kexue chubanshe, 2004).

Shih, Victor. *Financial Instability in China*. Tech. rep. MERICS Mercator Institute for China Studies, Klosterstraße 64, 2017.

Shih, Victor, Christopher Adolph, and Mingxing Liu. "Getting Ahead in the Communist Party." *American Political Science Review* 106.1 (2012), pp. 166–187.

Shirk, Susan L. *China: Fragile Superpower*. Oxford University Press, 2008.

Shirk, Susan L. "China in Xi's 'New Era': The Return to Personalistic Rule." *Journal of Democracy* 29.2 (2018), pp. 22–36.

Shirk, Susan L. "The Delayed Institutionalization of Leadership Politics." *The Nature of Chinese Politics: From Mao to Jiang*. Ed. by Jonathan Unger. 2002, pp. 297–312.

Shirk, Susan L. *The Political Logic of Economic Reform in China*. University of California Press, 1993.

Silver, Laura, Kat Devlin, and Christine Huang. *Unfavorable Views of China Reach Historic Highs in Many Countries*. Tech. rep. Pew Research Center, 2020.

Simon, Herbert A. *Administrative Behavior. A Study of Decison-Making Processes in Administrative Organizations*. Macmillan, 1946.

Sintomer, Yves, et al. "Learning from the South: Participatory Budgeting Worldwide–An Invitation to Global Cooperation." *Dialog Global* 25.25 (2010), p. 86.

Slater, Dan, and Sofia Fenner. "State Power and Staying Power: Infrastructural Mechanisms and Authoritarian Durability." *Journal of International Affairs* (2011), pp. 15–29.

Smith, Graham. "Political Machinations in a Rural County." *China Journal* 31.62 (2009), pp. 29–59.

Smyth, Russell. "Asset Stripping in Chinese State-Owned Enterprises." *Journal of Contemporary Asia* 30.1 (2000), pp. 3–16.

So, Alvin Y. "The Changing Pattern of Classes and Class Conflict in China." *Journal of Contemporary Asia* 33.3 (2003), pp. 363–376.

Sobolev, Sergei, Alexey Lyapunov, and Anatoly Kitov. "The Main Features of Cybernetics (Основные черты кибернетики)." *Problems of Philosophy (Voprosy filosofii)* 4 (1955), pp. 136–148.

Spence, Jonathan D. *The Search for Modern China*. W.W. Norton, 1990.

Steiner, H. Arthur. "Current 'Mass line' Tactics in Communist China." *American Political Science Review* 45.2 (1951), pp. 422–436.

Stockmann, Daniela, and Ting Luo. "Which Social Media Facilitate Online Public Opinion in China?" *Problems of Post-communism* 64.3-4 (2017), pp. 189–202.

Stromseth, Jonathan R., Edmund J. Malesky, and Dimitar D. Gueorguiev. *China's Governance Puzzle: Enabling Transparency and Participation in a Single-Party State*. Cambridge University Press, 2017.

Sullivan, Lawrence R. "The Role of the Control Organs in the Chinese Communist Party, 1977–83." *Asian Survey* 24.6 (1984), pp. 597–617.

Sun, Yan. *Corruption and Market in Contemporary China*. Cornell University Press, 2004.

Sun, Ying. "Municipal People's Congress Elections in the PRC: A Process of Co-option." *Journal of Contemporary China* 23.85 (2014), pp. 183–195.

Svolik, Milan W. *The Politics of Authoritarian Rule*. Cambridge University Press, 2012.

Swearer, Howard R. "Popular Participation: Myths and Realities." *Problems of Communism* September (1960), pp. 42–51.

Tan, Zixiang, William Foster, and Seymour Goodman. "China's State-Coordinated Internet Infrastructure." *Communications of the ACM* 42.6 (1999), pp. 44–52.

Tang, Frank. "Coronavirus: China Claims Stimulus '10 Times More Efficient' than US Fed, as New Loans Top US$1 Trillion." *South China Morning Post*, April 10, 2020.

Tang, Wenfang. *Populist Authoritarianism: Chinese Political Culture and Regime Sustainability*. Oxford University Press, 2016.

Tanner, Murray Scot. "The Erosion of Communist Party Control over Lawmaking in China." *The China Quarterly* 138 (1994), pp. 381–403.

Tanner, Murray Scot. "The National People's Congress." *The Paradox of China's post- Mao Reforms*. Ed. by Merle Goldman and Roderick MacFarquhar. Harvard University Press, 1999, pp. 100–129.

Tata, Sam, and Ian McLachlan. *Shanghai 1949: The End of an Era*. Deneau Publishers, 1990.

Tatlow, Kirsten D. 2014. "Rights Group Details Abuse in 'Black Jails.'" *New York Times*, October 14, 2014.

Taylor, Adam. 2014. "Are the Men of North Korea Really Being Forced to Get Kim Jong Un Haircuts?" *Washington Post*, March 26, 2014.

Teets, Jessica C. *Civil Society under Authoritarianism: The China Model*. Cambridge University Press, 2014.

Teets, Jessica C., and William Hurst. *Local Governance Innovation in China: Experimentation, Diffusion, and Defiance*. Routledge, 2014.

Teng, Ssu-yu, and John King Fairbank. *China's Response to the West: A Documentary Survey, 1839–1923*. Harvard University Press, 1954.

Thomas, Craig W. "Maintaining and Restoring Public Trust in Government Agencies and their Employees." *Administration & Society* 30.2 (1998), pp. 166–193.

Thornton, Patricia. "Retrofitting the Steel Frame: From Mobilizing the Masses to Surveying the Public." *Mao's Invisible Hand: The Political Foundations of Adaptive Governance in China*. Harvard University Council on Asian Studies, 2011. Chap. 8, pp. 237–268.

Thurston, Robert W. *Life and Terror in Stalin's Russia, 1934–1941*. Yale University Press, 1998.

Tian, Huaiyu, et al. "An Investigation of Transmission Control Measures During the First 50 Days of the COVID-19 Epidemic in China." *Science* 368.6491 (2020), pp. 638–642.

Townsend, Roger James. *Political Participation in Communist China*. University of California Press, 1969.

Truex, Rory. "Consultative Authoritarianism and Its Limits." *Comparative Political Studies (2014), pp. 1–33*.

Truex, Rory. "Focal Points, Dissident Calendars, and Preemptive Repression." *Journal of Conflict Resolution*. 64.4 (2019), pp. 1032–1052.

Truex, Rory. *Making Autocracy Work: Representation and Responsiveness in Modern China*. New York: Cambridge University Press, 2016.

Tsai, Lily L. *Accountability Without Democracy: Solidary Groups and Public Goods Provision in Rural China*. Cambridge University Press, 2007.

Tsai, Lily L., and Yiqing Xu. "Outspoken Insiders: Political Connections and Citizen Participation in Authoritarian China." *Political Behavior* 40.3 (2018), pp. 629–657.

Tsang, Steve. "Consultative Leninism: China's New Political Framework." *Journal of Contemporary China* 18.62 (2009), pp. 865–880.

Tsui, Kai-yuen. "Local Tax System, Intergovernmental Transfers and China's Local Fiscal Disparities." *Journal of Comparative Economics* 33.1 (2005), pp. 173–196.

Tucker, Joshua A. "Enough! Electoral Fraud, Collective Action Problems, and Post-Communist Colored Revolutions." *Perspectives on Politics* 5.03 (2007), p. 535.

Turner, Anthony G. *Sampling Strategies*. Tech. rep. November. Geneva: United Nations Statistics Division, 2003, pp. 2.6–2.8.

Twitchett, Denis Crispin. "Provincial Autonomy and Central Finance in Late T'ang." *Asia Major* 11.2 (1965), pp. 211–232.

Tyler, Tom R. *Why People Obey the Law*. Princeton University Press, 2006.

Unger, Jonathan. "The Class System in Rural China: A Case Study." *Class and Social Stratification in Post-revolution China* (1984), pp. 121–141.

Van Slyke, Lyman P. *Enemies and Friends: The United Front in Chinese Communist History.* Stanford University Press, 1967.

Vaughan, Liwen, and Yue Chen. "Data Mining from Web Search Queries: A Comparison of Google Trends and Baidu Index." *Journal of the Association for Information Science and Technology* 66.1 (2015), pp. 13–22.

Verba, Sidney. *Participation and Political Equality: A Seven-Nation Comparison.* Chicago: University of Chicago Press, 1978.

Walder, Andrew G. *China Under Mao.* Harvard University Press, 2015.

Walder, Andrew G. *Communist Neo-traditionalism: Work and Authority in Chinese Industry.* University of California Press, 1986.

Wallechinsky, David. *Tyrants: The World's Worst Dictators.* HarperCollins, 2009, p. 368.

Wampler, Brian. *Participatory Budgeting in Brazil—Contestation, Cooperation, and Accountability.* Vol. 54. 5. Penn State Press, 2010, pp. 294–294.

Wang, Fei-Ling. *Organizing through Division and Exclusion: China's Hukou System.* Stanford University Press, 2005.

Wang, Hairong. "New Platform for Whistleblowers." *Beijing Review* 44 (2013), pp. 22–23.

Wang, Luyao. "The Impacts of Anti-corruption on Economic Growth in China." *Modern Economy* 7.02 (2016), p. 109.

Wang, Xixin. "The Public, Expert, and Government in the Public Decision-Making Process: A Study of China's Price-Setting Hearing System and Its Practice." *Peking University Journal of Legal Studies* 1(2008), pp. 71–117.

Wang, Yuhua, and Bruce Dickson. "How Corruption Investigations Undermine Regime Support: Evidence from China." Available at *SSRN 3086286* (2018).

Wang, Zhengxu, and Anastas Vangeli. "The Rules and Norms of Leadership Succession in China: From Deng Xiaoping to Xi Jinping and Beyond." *The China Journal* 76 (2016), pp. 24–40.

Wanless, P.T. *Taxation in Centrally Planned Economies.* Routledge, 2018.

Warren, Mark. "Democratic Theory and Self-transformation." *American Political Science Review* 86.1 (1992), pp. 8–23.

Weber, Max. *Economy and Society: An Outline of Interpretive Sociology.* Vol. 1. University of California Press, 1978.

Weingast, Barry R. "The Economic Role of Political Institutions." *The Journal of Law, Economics and Organization* 7.1 (1995), pp. 1–31.

Weingast, Barry R. "Political Foundations of Democracy and the Rule of Law." *American Political Science Review* 91.2 (1997), pp. 245–263.

Weiss, Jessica Chen. *Powerful Patriots: Nationalist Protest in China's Foreign Relations.* Oxford University Press, 2014.

Wheatley, Jonathan, and James Kynge. "China Curtails Overseas Lending in Face of Geopolitical Backlash." *Financial Times*, December 7, 2020.

Wheeler, David. "Racing to the Bottom? Foreign Investment and Air Pollution in Developing Countries." *The Journal of Environment & Development* 10.03 (2001), pp. 225–245.

White, Stephen. "Economic Performance and Communist Legitimacy." *World Politics* 38.3 (1986), pp. 462–482.

White, Tyrene. *China's Longest Campaign: Birth Planning in the People's Republic, 1949–2005.* Cornell University Press, 2006.

Whiting, Susan H. "The Cadre Evaluation System at the Grass Roots: The Paradox of Party Rule." In B. Naughton & D. Yang (Eds.), *Holding China Together: Diversity and National Integration in the Post-Deng Era*. Cambridge University Press, 2004, pp. 101–120.

Whyte, Martin King. "Inequality and Stratification in China." *The China Quarterly* 64 (1975), pp. 684–711.

Whyte, Martin King. *Small Groups and Political Rituals in China*. University of California Press, 1975.

Wiener, Norbert. *Cybernetics or Control and Communication in the Animal and the Machine*. Technology Press, 1948.

Wilbur, C. Martin. *The Nationalist Revolution in China, 1923–1928*. Cambridge University Press, 1984.

Winckler, Edwin A. "Institutionalization and Participation on Taiwan: From Hard to Soft Authoritarianism?" *The China Quarterly* 99 (1984), pp. 481–499.

Wintrobe, Ronald. *The Political Economy of Dictatorship*. Vol. 94. Penguin 2006. Cambridge University Press, 1998.

Wintrobe, Ronald. "The Tinpot and the Totalitarian: An Economic Theory of Dictatorship." *American Political Science Review* 84.3 (1990), pp. 849–872.

Wong, Christine. "Paying for the Harmonious Society." *China Economic Quarterly* 14.2 (2010), pp. 20–25.

Wong, Christine. "Central–Local Relations in an Era of Fiscal Decline: The Paradox of Fiscal Decentralization in Post-Mao China." *The China Quarterly* 128 (1991), pp. 691–715.

World Bank. *Toward a More Inclusive and Effective Participatory Budget in Porto Alegre*. Tech. rep. 40144. Public Expenditure Review (PER), 2008, pp. 1–106.

Wright, Joseph. "Do Authoritarian Institutions Constrain? How Legislatures Affect Economic Growth and Investment." *American Journal of Political Science* 52.2 (2008), pp. 322–343.

Xi, Jinping, "China's Victory over Poverty." Speech at the National Poverty Alleviation Conference (习近平：在全国脱贫攻坚总结表彰大会上的讲话), Feb. 25, 2021.

Xia, Ming. *The People's Congresses and Governance in China: Toward a Network Mode of Governance*. Routledge, 2008.

Xu, Xu. "To Repress or to Co-opt? Authoritarian Control in the Age of Digital Surveillance." *American Journal of Political Science* 65.2 (2021), pp. 309–325.

Yang, Dali L. *Remaking the Chinese Leviathan: Market Transition and the Politics of Governance in China*. Stanford University Press, 2004.

Yang, Dali L., Huayu Xu, and Ran Tao. "A Tragedy of the Nomenklatura? Career Incentives, Political Loyalty and Political Radicalism during China's Great Leap Forward." *Journal of Contemporary China* 23.89 (2014), pp. 1–20.

Young, Graham. "Control and Style: Discipline Inspection Commissions Since the 11th Congress." *The China Quarterly* 97 (1984), pp. 24–52.

Young, Graham. "On the Mass Line." *Modern China* 6.2 (1980), pp. 225–240.

Young, Jock. *The Exclusive Society: Social Exclusion, Crime and Difference in Late Modernity*. Sage, 1999.

Yu, Keping. "Civil Society in China: Concepts, Classification and Institutional Environment (World Scientific)." *State and Civil Society* 1 (2010), pp. 63–96.

Yu, Keping. *Democracy Is a Good Thing: Essays on Politics, Society, and Culture in Contemporary China*. Vol. 1. Brookings Institution Press, 2009.

Zeng, Jin. *State-Led Privatization in China: The Politics of Economic Reform*. Taylor & Francis, 2013.

Zhai, Qiang. "1959: Preventing Peaceful Evolution." *China Heritage Quarterly* 18 (2009).

Zhang, Jianjun. "State Power, Elite Relations, and the Politics of Privatization in China's Rural Industry—Different Approaches in Two Regions." *Asian Survey* 48.2 (2008), pp. 215–238.

Zhang, Ruimin. *Haier is the Sea: Zhang Ruimin's Selected Essays (海尔是海：张瑞敏随笔选录)*. Mechanical Industry Press, 2015.

Zhang, Wei, et al. "Open Source Information, Investor Attention, and Asset Pricing." *Economic Modelling* 33 (2013), pp. 613–619.

Zhao, Dingxin. "The Mandate of Heaven and Performance Legitimation in Historical and Contemporary China." *American Behavioral Scientist* 53.3 (2009), pp. 416–433.

Zhao, Dingxin. *The Power of Tiananmen: State–Society Relations and the 1989 Beijing Student Movement*. University of Chicago Press, 2004.

Zhao, Yuhong. "Assessing the Environmental Impact of Projects: A Critique of the EIA Legal Regime in China." *Natural Resources Journal* 49.2 (2009), pp. 485–524.

Zhu, Jiangnan. "Why are Offices for Sale in China? A Case Study of the Office-Selling Chain in Heilongjiang Province." *Asian Survey* 48.4 (2008), pp. 558–579.

Index

petition reporting, 111
government blunt costs approach to,
110–112
risks for petitioners, 75–76
Petropavlovsk and *Sevastopol*, 87. *See also*
Kronstadt mutiny
polarization, of public opinion on policy topics,
102–105
policies, legislative, effect of consultation on
policy adoption delay, 139–141
policy lifespan, 138–139, 143
policy stability, repeal, and amendment rates,
133, 135, 137–139, 141, 143–146
Policy Uncertainty Index for China, 139
political competition, 12, 113, 174, 206
political freedom scores, 202
political indoctrination, 180
pollution, 4, 131, 149, 155, 195. *See also*
environment
populism, 195, 197, 201
Porto Alegre, Brazil, 151
poverty and inequality, 4, 195
poverty reduction and eradication, 192, 196,
199
pre-treatment bias, 186
Price Law, 1996, 62
price reform, 58, 135
Price Law, 1996, 62
Prior, Markus, 179
private property rights, 101
public support for, 184, 207
procedural performance, by government, 74
propaganda, 4, 12, 46, 59, 98, 102, 106, 192, 199
protests, 33,
in China, 110, 113, 147–148, 153, 206–207
NIMBY (Not in my Backyard) protests,
149
over government land expropriation,
147–148, 153
public complaint bureaus, 49
public criticism meetings, in early communist
era in China, 53–54
public hearings, 13, 62–63, 113, 134, 136, 155
public interest
as criteria for policy consultation, 97, 134,
136
in politics, 162, 180
public opinion, of Chinese citizens, 183, 194,
205, 207–208
measuring public opinion, 95–105
surveys on, 31, 96 *see also* China Policy
Barometer

public satisfaction with government, 94, 150,
159, 162–164
public security
expenditures in China, 176
expenditures by province in China, 29–31
as a measure of control, 29
public support for, 184, 207

Q-Zone. *See* social media
Qingdao, 171, 173
Qingdao municipal government, 171
Qingdao Refrigerator Corporation, 171, 173
quasi-democratic institutions, 9–10, 22
qunzhong luxian, mass line, 172. *See also* mass
line

Rabkrin (Soviet Workers' and Peasants'
Inspectorate), 48
Rajapksa, Mahinda, 132
randomization, selection, 157, 160. *See also*
Zeguo
Reform and Opening Up period (1979–1989)
in China, 56, 195, 198
rendan heyi (zero distance to customers),
171–173. *See also* Haier
renkou kapian (population cards), 55
repression, 7, 24–25, 28–29, 33, 196, 202
Republic of Korea. *See* North Korea
Republican China, system of governance, 44–45
resilience, of regimes, 6–8, 85
responsiveness, government, 5–6, 24, 32,
149–150, 165–166
on anticorruption, 32, 77–78, 80
retirement rules, reforms to, 60, 192
retrofitting Leninism, conceptual, 13, 37
Rodan, Garry, 9, 202
Roeder, Philip, 13, 150
rule of law, 7, 23, 31, 72, 76, 94, 151, 204
Rumsfeld, Donald, 109
rural development residencies, 196

San-Min Chu Youth Corps, 45
Sanmin Zhuyi (Three Principles of the People),
45
Saudi Arabia, 202
Schurmann, Franz, 36–37, 42, 45, 50, 55
scientific supervision, 73
screening and sorting information, 109, 111,
112, 116, 127, 128
heuristics of, 14, 116, 127
screening "logic", 115
screening of protests, 33
secret societies, 44

CPSIA information can be obtained
at www.ICGtesting.com
Printed in the USA
BVHW050342100622
639364BV00001B/3